D0713065

The Children's Song Index

The Children's Song Index, 1978-1993

Compiled by

Kay Laughlin
Pollyanne Frantz
Ann Branton

1996
LIBRARIES UNLIMITED, INC.
Englewood, Colorado

LIBRARIES UNLIMITED, INC.
P.O. Box 6633
Englewood, CO 80155-6633
1-800-237-6124

Production Editor: Stephen Haenel
Design: Michael Florman
Layout: Kay Minnis
Database Support: Suzanne Hawkins Burke

Library of Congress Cataloging-in-Publication Data

The children's song index, 1978-1993 / compiled by Kay Laughlin, Pollyanne Frantz, Ann Branton.
  xii, 153 p. 17x25 cm.
  ISBN 1-56308-332-9
  1. Children's songs--Indexes. I. Laughlin, Kay. II. Frantz, Pollyanne. III. Branton, Ann.
ML128.S3C55   1995
016.78242'026'8--dc20   95-40236
                                                         CIP
                                                         MN

Contents

The Children's Song Index, 1978-1993 is a compilation of 2,654 songs derived from 77 books as indexed by *Cumulative Book Index*, 1977-1994, under the subject heading "Children's Songs." All the song books were selected based upon their availability to the authors. Their inclusion in this index was dependent upon the copyright dates falling within the specified range of years.

Intended Audience

The song books selected are intended for a juvenile audience. The index is designed for use as a reference tool by classroom teachers and music instructors, as well as public, school, church, and academic libraries.

Scope

The songs included reflect Western culture and are primarily in the English language, although other languages are represented. Many songs are familiar songs from childhood. The newer songs reflect current issues and concerns regarding secular and religious education and acculturation of all children.

Criteria for Inclusion

The song books selected were American works published between the years of 1977 and 1994. All are in English. Most books selected were made available to the authors by direct solicitation from the publishers. Books not available from publishers were requested and received through interlibrary loan from libraries in the United States. The song books contain both lyrics and scores, and consist of several songs within a single book. The one-song book, such as an illustrated version of a single song, has been excluded. While all songs included are appropriate for children, no other attempt has been made to be selective in the choice of songs to be indexed from each song book. Therefore, songs are not excluded that may be judged politically incorrect by current standards.

Arrangement

The index is arranged in the following manner: 1) "Song Title Index," a list of songs by title; 2) "First Line Index," a list of each song's first line; 3) "Subject Guide," a thesaurus of subject headings arranged by

broadest term; and 4) "Subject Index." All subject headings are alphabetically listed in uppercase letters. *Index to Children's Songs*, compiled by Carolyn Sue Peterson and Ann D. Fenton (H. W. Wilson, 1979), was used as a guide for arrangement and format. Some subject headings were selected and implemented from this publication. These subject headings are terms and phrases universally used and understood by educators of children. However, new terms were created and included in the subject thesaurus of this publication that reflect contemporary usage.

In order to ensure a true alphabetical arrangement, initial articles, regardless of language, have been relocated to the end of the title or deleted in the song title index. "See also" references have been established for variant forms and wording of the same or similar song titles. In the first line index, entries are filed without regard to initial articles (e.g., "The little bells of Christmas say" follows "Little barefoot boy, running through the sand").

Each title or first line entry is followed by a numeric book code and page number, separated by a colon. For example:

> **There's a Cow in My Bedroom! 55:13**
>
> The title and full bibliographic citation for the book can be found
> by number in "Books Indexed," beginning on page ix.

A final word. Music enhances the learning experience, but without access to the vast number of songs published, educators and librarians have difficulty identifying, selecting, and using materials as they are needed for musical activities. The authors hope that this index will fill the need for information access.

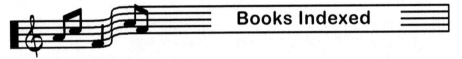

1. Aronoff, Frances Webber. *Move With the Music.* New York: Turning Wheel Press, 1982.

2. Beall, Pamela Conn and Susan H. Nipp. *Wee Sing for Christmas.* Los Angeles, CA: Price Stern Sloan, 1984.

3. Brady, Janeen. *I Have a Song for You About Animals.* Salt Lake City, UT: Brite Music, 1988.

4. Brady, Janeen. *I Have a Song for You About People and Nature.* Salt Lake City, UT: Brite Music, 1986.

5. Brady, Janeen. *I Have a Song for You About Seasons and Holidays.* Salt Lake City, UT: Brite Music, 1979.

6. Brady, Janeen. *My Body Machine.* Salt Lake City, UT: Brite Music, 1989.

7. Brady, Janeen. *Safety Kids, Vol. 1: Personal Safety Songbook.* Salt Lake City, UT: Brite Music, 1984.

8. Brady, Janeen. *Safety Kids, Vol. 2: Play It Smart.* Salt Lake City, UT: Brite Music, 1985.

9. Brady, Janeen. *Show a Little Love.* Salt Lake City, UT: Brite Music, 1981.

10. Brady, Janeen. *Standin' Tall, Vol. 1.* Salt Lake City, UT: Brite Music, 1987.

11. Brady, Janeen. *Standin' Tall, Vol. 2.* Salt Lake City, UT: Brite Music, 1988.

12. Brady, Janeen. *Standin' Tall, Vol. 3.* Salt Lake City, UT: Brite Music, 1989.

13. Brady, Janeen. *Take Your Hat Off When the Flag Goes By!* Salt Lake City, UT: Brite Music, 1987.

14. Brady, Janeen. *Watch Me Sing, Vol. 2.* Salt Lake City, UT: Brite Music, 1986.

15. Brown, Marc. *Party Rhymes.* New York: Dutton Children's Books, 1994.

16. Brown, Marc. *Play Rhymes.* New York: Dutton Children's Books, 1993.

17. Caggiano, Rosemary. *Circus Songbook for Children, The.* New York: Clarus Music, 1978.

18. Caggiano, Rosemary and Bernie Fass. *Power Is You, The.* New York: Clarus Music, 1979.

19. Cassidy, Nancy and John Cassidy. *Kids Songs, A Holler-Along Handbook.* Staunten, CT: Klutz Press, 1986.

20. Cassidy, Nancy and John Cassidy. *Kids Songs Two, Another Holler-Along Handbook.* Staunten, CT: Klutz Press, 1989.

21. Clarkson, Ginger. *Stop, Look & Listen.* San Diego, CA: Neil A. Kjos Music, 1986.

22. Cohn, Amy L. *From Sea to Shining Sea.* New York: Scholastic, 1993.

23. Cosgrove, Shaerie Grames. *Sing & Read a Christmas Song.* Nashville, TN: Ideals Children's Books, 1989.

24. Cosgrove, Shaerie Grames. *Sing & Read a Country Song.* Nashville, TN: Ideals Children's Books, 1988.

25. Cosgrove, Shaerie Grames. *Sing & Read a Sleepy Song.* Nashville, TN: Ideals Children's Books, 1988.

26. Cosgrove, Shaerie Grames. *Sing & Read a Sunday Song.* Nashville, TN: Ideals Children's Books, 1988.

27. Cosgrove, Shaerie Grames. *Sing & Read More Sunday Songs.* Nashville, TN: Ideals Children's Books, 1989.

28. dePaola, Tomie. *Tomie dePaola's Book of Christmas Carols.* New York: G. P. Putnam's Sons, 1987.

29. Di Silvestro, Frank. *Americans Are Singing About Lady Liberty.* Bronx, NY: Songs and Stories Children Love, 1986.

30. Di Silvestro, Frank. *Sing Along with Me.* Bronx, NY: Songs and Stories Children Love, 1985.

31. Edison, Roger. *Family Album of Favorite Nursery Songs, A.* Van Nuys, CA: Alfred Publishing, 1992.

32. *For Our Children.* New York: Disney Press, 1991.

33. Fox, Dan, ed. *Go In and Out the Window.* New York: Metropolitan Museum of Art, 1987.

34. Gill, Madelaine. *Praise for the Singing.* New York: Little, Brown, 1993.

35. Glazer, Tom. *Music for Ones and Twos.* New York: Doubleday, 1983.

36. Glazer, Tom. *Tom Glazer's Treasury of Songs for Children.* New York: Doubleday, 1988.

37. Goode, Diane. *Diane Goode's Book of Silly Stories & Songs.* New York: Dutton Children's Books, 1992.

38. Hart, Jane. *Singing Bee!* New York: Lothrop, Lee & Shepard Books, 1989.

39. Kolosick, Timothy and Helga Kolosick. *Canons Austrian Children Sing, The.* Tucson: Arizona University Music Press, 1987.

40. Krull, Kathleen. *Gonna Sing My Head Off!* New York: Alfred A. Knopf, 1992.

41. Lamont, Priscilla. *Ring-a-Round-a-Rosy.* New York: Little, Brown, 1990.

42. Lancaster, Reid. *Children's Songs of Joy.* Ft. Worth, TX: Sweet Publishing, 1983.

43. Langstaff, John. *Climbing Jacob's Ladder.* New York: Macmillan Publishing, 1991.

44. Larrick, Nancy. *Songs from Mother Goose.* New York: Harper & Row, 1989.

45. *Little Mermaid: An Under the Sea Christmas, The.* New York: Disney Press, 1993.

46. Mitchell, Donald and Roderick Biss. *Children's Songbook, The.* Ithaca, NY: Faber & Faber, 1987.

47. Mochnick, Beth R. *New Holiday Songs for Children: A Creative Approach.* Champaign, IL: Mark Foster Music, 1988.

48. *More Songs to Play.* Nashville, TN: Broadman Press, 1988.

49. Nelson, Esther L. *Fun-to-Sing Songbook, The.* Fallbrook, CA: Sterling Publishing, 1986.

50. Nelson, Esther L. *Funny Songbook, The.* Fallbrook, CA: Sterling Publishing, 1984.

51. Nelson, Esther L. *World's Best Funny Songs.* Fallbrook, CA: Sterling Publishing, 1989.

52. Olliver, Jane. *Doubleday Christmas Treasury, The.* New York: Doubleday, 1986.

53. Oram, Hiawyn. *Creepy Crawly Song Book, A.* New York: Farrar, Straus and Giroux, 1993.

54. Perry, Frances Burk. *Let's Sing Together.* Orem, UT: Perry Enterprises, 1984.

55. Phipps, Bonnie. *Singing with Young Children.* Herndon, VA: Alfred Publishing, 1991.

56. Polisar, Barry Louis. *Noises from Under the Rug.* Rainbow Morning, 1985.

57. Raffi. *Raffi Christmas Treasury, The.* New York: Crown Publishers, 1988.

58. Raffi. *Raffi Everything Grows Songbook, The.* New York: Crown Publishers, 1989.

59. Raffi. *Raffi Singable Songbook, The.* New York: Crown Publishers, 1988.

60. Raffi. *2nd Raffi Songbook, The.* New York: Crown Publishers, 1986.

61. Rosenkrans, B. *My Book of Christmas Carols.* New York: Platt & Munk, 1986.

62. Scott, Anne. *Laughing Baby, The.* Westport, CT: Bergin & Garvey, 1988.

63. Seeger, Ruth Crawford. *Animal Folk Songs for Children.* Hamden, CT: Linnet Books, 1992.

64. *Sharon, Lois and Bram the All New Elephant Jam.* New York: Crown Publishers, 1989.

65. *Sharon, Lois and Bram's Mother Goose.* New York: Little, Brown, 1985.

66. Simon, William L., ed. *Reader's Digest Children's Songbook, The.* New York: Reader's Digest, 1988.

67. *Songs for Children of the World.* Secaucus, NJ: Suzuki Method International, 1984.

68. *Songs for the Joy of Living.* Loveland, CO: Eden Valley Press, 1985.

69. Watson, Clyde. *Father Fox's Feast of Songs.* Honesdale, PA: Wordsong, 1992.

70. Weiss, Nicki. *If You're Happy and You Know It.* New York: Greenwillow Books, 1987.

71. Weissman, "Miss Jackie." *Sniggles, Squirrels, and Chicken Pox.* Mt. Rainer, MD: Miss Jackie Music, 1984.

72. Weissman, "Miss Jackie." *Songs to Sing with Babies.* Mt. Rainer, MD: Miss Jackie Music, 1983.

73. Wolfson, Mack and Bernie Fass. *Halloween Machine, The.* Yonkers, NY: Clarus Music, 1984.

74. Wood, Jenny. *First Songs & Action Rhymes.* New York: Aladdin Books, 1991.

75. Yolen, Jane. *Jane Yolen's Mother Goose Songbook.* Honesdale, PA: Caroline House, 1992.

76. Yolen, Jane. *Jane Yolen's Songs of Summer.* Honesdale, PA: Caroline House, 1993.

77. Yolen, Jane. *Lullaby Songbook, The.* San Diego, CA: Harcourt Brace Jovanovich, 1986.

A Cheval 62:77
A-Driving We Will Go 72:36
A-Hunting We Will Go 36:19, 38:88, 55:40
A Paris 62:73
A-Roving 46:18
A-Tisket, A-Tasket 15:41, 24:6, 31:63, 38:100, 66:110, 70:12. *See also* Itiskit, Itaskit
ABC Song 65:17
Abe Lincoln 47:40
About Water 4:29
Ach! Du Lieber Augustin 36:16
Acres of Clams 22:192, 40:2
Acrobats, The 17:33
Afton Water 46:24
Ah Si Mon Moine 64:66
Ah, Mama Mier 55:18
Aiken Drum 25:20, 51:12, 75:16. *See also* Aikendrum; There Was a Man Lived in the Moon
Aikendrum 59:30. *See also* Aiken Drum; There Was a Man Lived in the Moon
Ain't Gonna Rain 31:77
Al Citron 64:110
Alfabet Song 56:119
Alfie the Elf 2:56
Alison's Camel 64:93
All by Myself 42:43
All Hid 64:19
All I Really Need 60:23
All I Want Is You 56:61
All of Me 42:104
All That Has Life and Breath, Sing to the Lord 39:20
All the Fish 72:42
All the Little Fishies Do a Hoochie Koochie Dance 55:23
All the Pretty Little Horses 22:268, 33:7, 35:72, 38:11, 77:18. *See also* Go to Sleepy; Hush A Bye; Hush'n Bye; Hush-You-Bye; Rock-a-Bye Baby; Rockabye, Baby
All Things Bright and Beautiful 42:91, 48:2
All Through the Night 77:8
All You Gotta Say Is No 8:15

Allee, Allee-O 65:65
Alleluia 34:17
Alley Cat Song 66:206
Aloha 71:9
Alouette 66:194
Alphabet Song 31:72, 50:63, 66:212
Always Remember You Were Born in America 29:56
Amazing Grace 33:11, 34:39
Amen 1:60
America 33:13
America at Last! 29:30
America, I Love You 5:43, 13:58
America the Beautiful 33:14, 36:20
Americans Are Singing About Lady Liberty 29:6
Anansi 59:72
And We Hunted and We Hunted 63:36
Angel Band 2:26
Angels We Have Heard on High 23:2, 28:22, 61:28
Animal Fair 36:22, 66:87, 70:18
Animal Song 63:80
Animals Are My Friends 71:19
Ants Go Marching 24:10, 50:6, 64:78
Apple of My Eye 56:74
Apples and Bananas 19:32, 55:19, 60:70
Arabella Miller 50:43, 64:37. *See also* Little Arabella Miller
Are You Sleeping 39:26, 72:25. *See also* Frere Jacques
Arkansas Traveler 36:24, 40:4
Around the Corner 50:74, 51:8
As He Walks on High 17:36
As I Have Loved You 54:83
Aserrin, Aserran 62:75
Ash Grove 67:13
Astronauts and Airplane Pilots 42:31
Au Clair de la Lune 36:27
Auld Lang Syne 36:28, 45:46
Aunt Anna Came to Our House 56:130
Autumn Day 54:55
Autumn Leaves Are Now Falling 48:9
Away in a Manger 2:19, 28:32, 36:30, 45:24, 52:78, 61:10

1

Baa, Baa, Black Sheep 31:3, 33:17, 33:32, 36:31, 38:47, 44:7, 59:14, 66:223, 75:32
Babies 5:28
Baby Bear's Chicken Pox 71:52
Baby Beluga 19:18, 60:7
Baby Bumble Bee 50:8, 51:112
Baby Bunting 31:17
Baby Bye 65:81
Baby Cakewalk 69:16
Baby Doll 35:24
Baby Moses 71:51
Baby's Face 72:50
Baby's Going Bye-Bye 35:22
Back of a Crocodile 64:49. *See also* Crocodile, The; Smile on the Crocodile
Baiu-Baiushki-Baiu 62:42
Balloon, The 35:44
Baloo Baleerie 77:20
Baptism 54:69
Barney Google 66:135
Barnyard Song 24:12, 40:6, 67:5
Barnyard Stomp 56:68
Bassez Down 64:92
Bath, The 35:32
Bathtime 58:4
Battle Hymn of the Republic 36:32
Battle of the Stags 53:29
Be a Friend 9:26
Be Glad! 42:69
Be Kind to Your Web-Footed Friends 51:124, 66:190
Be Thankful unto Him 42:21
Be Ye Kind 42:39
Beans in My Ears 40:8
Bear Song 50:56
Bear Went over the Mountain 36:34, 38:112, 70:22
Bear, Bear, Bear 3:32
Beautiful Autumn 5:8
Beauty Everywhere 54:45
Because I Love Him 11:62
Because It's Spring 54:43
Because She Shines 6:12
Bells Are Ringing 2:36
Belly and Tubs 69:19
Benjy Met a Bear 51:48
Bennington Rifles 36:35
Better Obey 10:12
Betty Wants to Be an Astronaut 30:42
Beware 73:18
B-I-B-L-E, The 26:14
Bible Is a Special Book, The 42:13

Bible Is a Wonderful Book, The 42:76
Bible Thought Song 42:16
Big Beautiful Planet 60:50
Big Brother 42:72
Big Moon, Bright Moon 4:38
Big Rock Candy Mountain 22:354, 36:37
Big Sheep, The 63:58
Big Wheels 10:50
Big Words 13:40
Bike Song 68:15
Bile Them Cabbage Down 49:81
Billboard Song 50:78
Billy Barlow 36:40
Billy Boy 33:18, 36:42, 38:111, 66:220
Bim Bom 1:56
Bimbo Bombo 69:20
Bingo 31:36, 33:21, 35:57, 36:44, 38:82, 66:124. *See also* Bingo Was His Name
Bingo Was His Name 51:26. *See also* Bingo
Birds in the Wilderness 50:35
Birthday of a King 2:22
Biscuits in the Oven 60:9
Black Cat, The 71:14
Black Sheep, Black Sheep 63:57
Black Socks 51:54
Black Widow's Waltz, The 53:39
Blanket for a Sail 32:36
Bless This Meal 39:20
Blessing the Earth 68:48
Blocks 35:26
Blow the Man Down 46:66
Blow, Boys, Blow 22:110
Blow, Ye Winds, in the Morning 22:103
Blowin' in the Wind 22:360
Blue-Tail Fly 36:45
Bluebird 38:83, 65:9
Bobby Shafto 44:51, 65:39, 75:13. *See also* Bobby Shaftoe
Bobby Shaftoe 74:15. *See also* Bobby Shafto
Boci Tarka 1:88
Bona Nox 39:30
Book of Mormon Stories 14:61
Boom Boom 51:68, 59:70. *See also* Boom, Boom Ain't It Great to Be Crazy
Boom, Boom Ain't It Great to Be Crazy 20:30. *See also* Boom Boom
Boom da li-da 1:84

Born This Night 2:31
Botany Bay 46:78
Bought Me a Cat 22:264
Bow Belinda 38:102
Boys and Girls Come Out to Play
    44:12
Brahms' Lullaby 77:31. *See also*
    Cradle Song; Cradlesong; Lulla-
    by; Lullaby, and Good Night
Bring a Torch, Jeannette, Isabella!
    28:60
Bring Back My Neighbors to Me 51:96
Bringing in the Sheaves 33:22
Brite Bites 6:38
Bronx Zoo Is for Me and You 30:10
Brown Eyes, Black Eyes 13:62
Brown Girl in the Ring 58:9, 64:104
Brush Your Teeth 19:26, 59:8
Bubble Toes 12:29
Buffalo Gals 36:47, 40:9
Bumblebee Song 56:112
Bumping Up and Down 59:5
Bunny Hop 66:211
Bus Song 20:16, 36:49, 38:130. *See
    also* Wheels on the Bus
Busy Bee 53:33
But I Still Don't Like Asparagus
    56:170
But I'm Just Thirteen 56:70
Butterprint 69:7
By the Barnyard Gate 55:61
By'm Bye 77:14. *See also* Bye 'n' Bye;
    Bye'm Bye
Bye'm Bye 22:196, 72:58. *See also*
    By'm Bye; Bye 'n' Bye
Bye 'n' Bye 49:66, 64:25. *See also*
    By'm Bye; Bye'm Bye
Bye, Baby Bunting 35:68, 38:14,
    41:67, 77:15
Bye, Bye, Baby 72:61
Bye-Low, My Baby 48:8

Cabin in the Wood 64:39
Caissons, The 36:51
Called to Serve 54:75
Calling All Junk Foods 6:28
Camptown Races 66:150
Can of Worms 53:21
Candy Man, Salty Dog 64:26
Canoe Round 76:12
Canticle of the Sun, The 34:9
Captain Dependable 12:60
Car Car 72:38

Carol of the Bells 28:72
Casey Jones 40:11, 46:52
Casper the Friendly Ghost 66:80
Cat Came Back 40:14, 49:52, 51:114
Catch a Wiffer Woffer 50:76
Caterpillar 38:22, 56:186
Cement Mixer 66:121
Chapel Doors 54:71
Charades 14:13
Charlie Is My Darling 46:20
Charlie over the Ocean 64:95
Che Che Koolay 64:105
Checks and Balances 13:27
Cheerio 64:84
Cherry Blossoms 67:8
Cherry Tree Carol 28:69
Chester 64:53
Chevaliers de la Table Ronde 46:62
Chick, Chick, Chicken 65:69
Chicken Lips and Lizard Hips 19:34,
    32:39
Chickens in the Barnyard 3:12
Chickery Chick 66:113
Children All over the World 54:77
Children Who Love Jesus 42:37
Children, Go Where I Send Thee 2:34
Children, Obey Your Parents 42:97
Chivalrous Shark 46:46
Choose the Animal 14:19
Christian Families 42:98
Christmas Bells 2:50, 54:27
Christmas Cradle Song 54:29
Christmas Day 2:53
Christmas Decorations 47:21
Christmas Eve 47:24
Christmas Is Coming 2:48, 36:54,
    45:14, 47:26
Christmas Joybells 68:42
Christmas Time's a Coming 57:75
Christmastime Is Here 47:25
Christopher Columbus 47:1
Christopher McCracken 50:48
Cindy 46:44
Cinnamon Ship, The 55:8
Circle Games 21:26
Circus Is Coming 17:3
Circus, The 17:45
City Cowboy 30:14
City of New Orleans 40:16
Clap, Clap, Clap 4:34
Clap Your Hands 21:14, 38:86
Clementine 33:26, 36:55, 40:20,
    50:40, 51:87, 66:164, 67:6. *See
    also* My Darling Clementine

Clever Amphibian 3:21
Clever Cow 3:15
Climb, Climb Up Sunshine Mountain 27:24
Climbing Up the Tower 72:54
Clipety Clop 72:12
Clock Without a "C" Is Still a Lock 56:116
Clothes Clothes 72:32
Clowns, The 17:11
Cluck, Cluck, Red Hen 20:32, 59:84
Cock-a-Doodle-Doo! 38:68, 75:43
Cockles and Mussels 66:196
Cocky Doodle Doodle Doo 72:21
C-O-F-F-E-E 39:29
Colores, De 60:96
Columbus 5:9, 47:2
Come and Praise the Lord Our King 42:82
Come Dance and Sing 34:52
Come Here and Sing! 46:90
Come, Let Me Tell 42:3
Come Meet a Little Birdy Friend 39:12
Come Play with Me 5:39
Come, Ye Thankful People, Come 34:58, 36:57
Comin' Down the Chimney 59:34
Comin' Through the Rye 70:24. *See also* Comin' Thru the Rye
Comin' Thru the Rye 66:203. *See also* Comin' Through the Rye
Communication 18:39
Confession of a Praying Mantis 53:13
Conversation with a Tree 71:55
Cookie Jar 64:51
Corner Grocery Store, The 59:76
Cotton Candy 17:6
Coventry Carol 2:39, 28:35, 61:16
Covered Wagons 54:67
Cowboy's Lament 40:22
Cradle Is Warm 41:66
Cradle Song 35:70, 36:59. *See also* Brahms' Lullaby; Cradlesong; Lullaby; Lullaby, and Good Night; Schlaf, Kindlein, Schlaf; Sleep, Baby, Sleep
Cradlesong 31:11. *See also* Brahms' Lullaby; Cradle Song; Lullaby; Lullaby, and Good Night
Crawdad 36:60. *See also* Crawdad Song
Crawdad Song 40:24. *See also* Crawdad

Creepy Crawly Caterpillar 53:41
Crocodile, The 16:31. *See also* Back of a Crocodile; Smile on the Crocodile
Crocodile Song 63:72
Cross-Eyed Gopher 63:20
Cuanto Le Gusta 37:28
Cucanandy 1:52
Cuckoo in the Forest 39:10
Cum By Yah 77:22. *See also* Kum Ba Yah; Kumbaya
Cumberland Gap 22:82
Curly Locks 38:61, 65:38. *See also* Curly Locks, Curly Locks
Curly Locks, Curly Locks 44:50. *See also* Curly Locks
Cute, Cuddily Koala 30:32

Dad Says That I Look Like Him 56:100
Daddy Shot a Bear 63:78
Daddy's Homecoming 54:17
Dainty Little Snowflakes 4:35
Dance to Your Daddy 44:58, 65:80, 77:26
Dancing Horses 17:25
Daniel 60:45
Dare to Do Right 54:63
Dark Brown Is the River 35:87
Day-O 19:10, 60:15
Dayenu 34:26
Dear Old Daddy's Whiskers 25:16, 51:36
Dearest Names 54:23
December 54:27
Deck the Halls 2:7, 23:8, 28:58, 36:62, 45:12, 61:12
Deer Song, The 63:34
Designer Genes 8:19
Desperado, The 20:14
Devil's Questions, The 22:206
Did and Didn't 10:9
Did Jesus Really Live Again? 54:35
Did You Ever See a Lassie? 24:24, 33:28, 36:64, 38:96
Did You Feed My Cow? 64:50
Did You Say Your Prayers Last Night? 9:22
Diddle Diddle Dumpling 38:76, 71:48, 72:28
Didn't It Rain? 43:2
Didn't My Lord Deliver Daniel? 43:16
Die Musica 67:7

Dilly Dilly 69:12
Ding, Dong, Bell 31:14
Ding-Dong! The Witch Is Dead 66:28
Dinga Dinga Doodle 36:66
Dinosaur Song 56:147
Dirty Bill 50:39, 51:35
Dixie 33:31, 36:68
Do As I'm Doing 54:57
Do It Song 10:14
Do Lord 26:22
Do This, Do That 56:106
Do You Know That You're a Person?
    42:105
Do You Want to Feel Happy? 9:34
Do Your Ears Hang Low? 16:30,
    38:113, 50:66, 51:75, 70:6
Do-Re-Mi 66:44
Doctor, Doctor 35:88
Doctor Foster 38:41
Don't Forget the Family 12:14
Don't Leave Me in the House Alone
    56:114
Don't Put Your Finger up Your Nose
    56:84
Don't You Push Me Down 35:74
Dona Nobis Pacem 34:33, 46:91
Donkey Riding 36:71
Douglas Mountain 57:72, 59:54
Down at the Station 74:37
Down by the Bay 19:28, 24:22, 49:71,
    59:2
Down by the Creek Bank 42:133
Down by the River 65:66
Down by the Riverside 33:33, 40:26
Down by the Station 33:37, 36:73,
    38:129, 66:116
Down Derry Down 69:27
Down in the Valley 40:28, 67:5
Down on Grandpa's Farm 60:87
Dr. Knickerbocker 64:90
Dream Song 22:14
Drill, Ye Tarriers 22:158, 36:74
Dromedaries 3:34
Drunken Sailor 46:68
Dry Bones 22:326
Du, Du Liegst Mir im Herzen 67:16
Duchess at Tea 50:26
Ducks Like Rain 60:62
Dunderbeck 36:76. See also Dunder-
    beck's Machine
Dunderbeck's Machine 49:21, 51:39.
    See also Dunderbeck

Early in the Morning 42:109
Early One Morning 46:10
Early Sunday Morning 56:44
Easter Bunny 38:141, 71:46
Easter Eggs 47:44
Eency Weency Spider 36:78. See also
    Eensy Weensy Spider; Eentsy
    Weentsy Spider; Incey Wincey
    Spider
Eenie Meenie and a Miney Moe 55:14
Eensy Weensy Spider 31:60, 33:38,
    65:61, 66:231, 72:19, 74:22. See
    also Eency Weency Spider;
    Eentsy Weentsy Spider; Incey
    Wincey Spider
Eentsy Weentsy Spider 35:58. See
    also Eency Weency Spider;
    Eensy Weensy Spider; Incey
    Wincey Spider
Eight Piggies in a Row 58:23
El Coquito 38:136
Eletelephony 38:124
Eli, the Priest 42:18
En Passant par la Lorraine 46:64
Epigram on Singers 46:89
E-ri-e, The 36:79
Erie Canal 22:116, 36:81, 40:30
Ev'rybody Loves Saturday Night
    49:34
Every Little Wish 57:65
Every Night and Every Morn 34:38
Every Night When the Sun Goes In
    46:50
Everybody Happy 65:6
Everybody Needs a Friend 12:42
Everybody Needs to Be Someone
    42:106
Everybody Needs to Feel Love 8:22
Everybody Ought to Know 42:114
Everybody Says Sit Down 55:49
Everybody Stand Up 10:16
Everything Grows 58:28
Everything That's Beautiful 68:26
Ezekiel Saw the Wheel 43:14

Fairest Lord Jesus 48:4
Fais Do Do 64:64. See also Fais Dodo
Fais Dodo 60:77. See also Fais Do Do
Fall Apart 13:35
Falling Snow 54:59
Families Can Be Together Forever
    54:25

Family 54:19
Family Love 42:136
Family Night 54:19
Family Prayer 54:21
Farmer in the Dell 15:40, 31:26,
    33:41, 36:84, 38:79, 66:232. *See
    also* Farmer's in the Dell
Farmer's in the Dell 74:40, 75:20. *See
    also* Farmer in the Dell
Father Fell Off 72:15
Father's Old Grey Whiskers 19:16,
    66:152
Fathers Are Forever 5:35
Fiddle-De-De 75:22. *See also* Fiddle-
    dee-dee
Fiddle-dee-dee 31:29. *See also* Fiddle-
    De-De
Fiddlers 46:42
Fingernails 12:24
Fingers 14:22
Fire Drill 21:35
Fire! Fire! 39:6
First Noel 2:14, 23:18, 28:10, 36:86,
    45:32, 57:62, 61:22
First Song of Isaiah, The 34:36
First-Last 21:25
Fish and Chips 64:24
Fisherman Peter 26:6
Five Little Chickadees 38:77, 65:22
Five Little Ducks 60:47, 70:10
Five Little Fingers 72:51
Five Little Frogs 59:1
Five Little Monkeys 17:18, 50:52
Five Little Pumpkins 59:6
Five Little Pussycats 74:44
Five More Minutes 56:198
Five Speckled Frogs 65:54
Flat Foot Floogee 66:140
Flea Circus 53:26
Flea Fly Song 50:11
Fly Little Butterfly 3:23
Fly My Kite with Me 30:46
Follow the Drinkin' Gourd 22:140.
    See also Follow the Drinking
    Gourd
Follow the Drinking Gourd 40:32. *See
    also* Follow the Drinkin' Gourd
Follow the Rules! 42:36
Following the Leader 14:9
Fooba-Wooba John 20:12
Foot Traveler 76:18
For My Sister, Wherever I May Find
    Her 56:64
For Us All 42:94

Forgiveness 10:42
Fox in a Box 15:44
Fox, The 19:40, 33:42, 36:88, 40:34,
    66:88. *See also* Old Fox
Fred 56:35
Free Enterprise 13:49
Freedom 47:31
Freight Train 40:36
French Cathedrals 1:24
Frere Jacques 1:114, 25:24, 31:7,
    36:91, 38:134, 46:61, 59:79,
    62:109, 66:234. *See also* Are You
    Sleeping
Friend in Need 12:4
Friendly Beasts 2:41, 28:26, 36:92
Friendly Cow, The 68:24
Frog Went A-Courtin' 33:44, 36:94,
    66:182. *See also* Froggie Went
    A-Courting
Froggie Went A-Courting 75:18. *See
    also* Frog Went A-Courtin'
Frosty the Snow Man 66:240. *See
    also* Frosty the Snowman
Frosty the Snowman 57:50. *See also*
    Frosty the Snow Man
Frozen Logger 22:284, 40:38
Fruit 21:30
Fruit Song 68:19
Fum, Fum, Fum 2:23
Fun to Do 54:57
Furry Squirrel 71:12
Fuzzy Wuzzy 50:60

Gallant Ship 38:84
Gee, Mom, I Want to Go Home
    22:356
George Washington 13:22, 47:39
Georgie Porgie 31:67, 44:13. *See also*
    Georgy Porgy
Georgy Porgy 75:33. *See also* Georgie
    Porgie
Get Along, Little Dogies 36:96. *See
    also* Git Along, Little Dogies
Get Your Fingers Off My Leg And
    Your Hand Off of My Shoe
    56:150
Ghost of Tom, The 22:330
Ghost Riders in the Sky 20:24
Giggle and a Hug and a Tickle and a
    Kiss 56:99
Giggle Tickle Fiddle Little Wiggle
    Around 56:39
GIGO 12:38

Git Along, Little Dogies 22:290, 40:40. *See also* Get Along, Little Dogies
Give 71:22
Give a Little Love 32:24
Give a Little Whistle 66:72
Give Me a Heart of Love 42:141
Give Me That Old-Time Religion 27:2
Give, Said the Little Stream 54:39
Giving Song 21:10
Glory to God in the Highest 42:110
Glory to Thee 46:92
Glunk, Glunk, Glunk 50:14
Go and Hush the Baby 56:165
Go Down, Moses 22:128, 34:24, 36:98, 42:79, 43:8
Go for a Natural High 8:8
Go In and Out the Window 31:45, 33:47, 36:100
Go On, Old 'gator 63:74
Go Round and Round the Village 38:85
Go Tell Aunt Rhody 36:101, 38:116, 40:42, 67:4
Go Tell It on the Mountain 2:40, 28:79, 40:43
Go the Second Mile 54:49
Go to Sleep 63:65
Go to Sleep Now, My Pumpkin 65:92
Go to Sleepy 36:102. *See also* All the Pretty Little Horses; Hush A Bye; Hush'n Bye; Hush-You-Bye; Rock-a-Bye Baby; Rockabye, Baby
Gobble Strut, Strut 3:13
God Bless the Statue of Liberty 29:70
God Can 42:108
God Gave Us the Bible 42:17
God Is Like My Daddy 42:58
God Is Love 11:70
God Is Our Wonderful God 42:92
God Is So Good 42:62, 48:12
God Is Stronger Than the Devil 42:78
God Knows Everything 42:60
God Knows Everything About Me 42:59
God Knows Where You Are 42:4
God Loves Each Child 42:28
God Made Me! 42:45
God Made the World 42:88
God of Wisdom 42:112
God Rest You Merry, Gentlemen 23:24, 28:54

God Watches Over Me 42:111
God Who Made the Earth 42:139
God's Big World 42:29
God's Creation 42:89
God's Own People 42:117
God's Plan for Families 42:96
Gogo 38:93
Going on a Picnic 59:64
Going Out to Play 71:28
Going to Kentucky 64:82
Going to the Zoo 40:45, 59:24, 66:90
Golden Plates 14:61
Golden Slumbers 25:28, 31:8, 38:16, 41:69, 74:6
Good King Wenceslas 28:62
Good Morning, Lord! 68:29
Good Morning to You 38:115
Good Night 35:35
Good Night, Irene 59:88. *See also* Goodnight, Irene
Good Night, Ladies 31:73
Good Night Song 4:39
Good-Bye Winter, Hello Spring 71:42
Goodnight, Irene 40:48. *See also* Good Night, Irene
Goosey, Goosey, Gander 31:10, 38:57, 75:25
Grand Old Duke of York 65:29
Grandpa Gum 12:22
Grasshopper Song 50:10
Gratitude Attitude 11:46
Gray Goose 36:104, 63:38
Grease and Sweets 6:10
Greasy, Grimy Gopher Guts 51:30
Great Ape 3:38
Great Big Family 42:99
Great Tom Is Cast 46:84
Green 66:10
Green Grass Grew All Around 49:22. *See also* Green Grass Grows All Around, The
Green Grass Grows All Around, The 24:4. *See also* Green Grass Grew All Around
Green Grow the Rushes-O 33:48, 36:106
Greensleeves 33:53, 46:12
Grey Goose 66:170
Groundhog 22:92, 71:38
Growing Tall 42:46
Gum Song 50:34
Gust of Fall Wind, A 22:168

Ha, Ha, This-a-Way 66:168. *See also* Ha, Ha, Thisaway

Ha, Ha, Thisaway 58:33. *See also* Ha, Ha, This-a-Way

Had a Little Dog 55:39. *See also* I Had a Little Dog

Hail to Britannia 64:102

Haiye Kirumbe 1:70

Halloween 71:15

Halloween Capers 47:8

Halloween Fun 47:9

Halloween Is Here! 47:11

Halloween Machine 73:22

Halloween Night 5:12

Hambone 55:37

Handcart Song 22:176

Hands to the Sun 67:11

Hanukah 71:20

Hanukkah 47:20

Hanukkah Is Happiness 47:18

Hanukkah Song 36:110, 38:144

Happiness 42:144, 54:47

Happy Birthday 4:25

Happy Birthday Miss Liberty 29:14

Happy Birthday to You 31:7, 54:9, 66:252

Happy Family 54:11

Happy, Happy! 42:70

Happy, Happy Birthday 54:9

Happy New Year 5:20

Happy Wanderer 36:112

Hark, Hark! 38:54

Hark! The Herald Angels Sing 28:30, 36:114, 45:36, 52:96, 61:18

Haru Ga Kita 58:42

Have You Ever Wondered 10:43

He Always Carried His Picture of Lady Liberty 29:48

He Eats Asparagus, Why Can't You Be That Way? 56:18

He Is Lord 42:67

He Owns the Cattle on a Thousand Hills 42:132

He Plants Me Like a Seed 42:142

He's a Dog 3:10

He's Got the Whole World 20:48, 26:24, 36:118, 60:48

He's My Responsibility 11:58

Head and Shoulders 1:108, 20:40, 42:53, 65:12. *See also* Head and Shoulders, Baby; Head, Shoulders, Baby; Tete, Epaules

Head and Shoulders, Baby 64:54. *See also* Head and Shoulders; Head, Shoulders, Baby; Tete, Epaules

Head, Shoulders, Baby 49:33. *See also* Head and Shoulders; Head and Shoulders, Baby; Tete, Epaules

Hear the Jingle Bells 2:51

Hear the Wind Blow 4:30

Heart Song 73:31

Heavenly Sunshine 27:22

Heigh-Ho 66:66

Hello 21:6

Hello, Hello! How Are You? 42:86

Hello There, Farmer 55:60

Helping God 42:49

Helping Mother 42:42

Here Are My Lady's Knives and Forks 38:24

Here Comes Santa Claus 2:44

Here in America 13:15

Here Is the Church 35:53, 38:25

Here Sits a Monkey 59:68

Here Stands a Redbird 38:106

Here We Are 68:38

Here We Come A-Caroling 2:6, 23:26

Here We Go Looby Loo 31:12, 36:116. *See also* Looby Loo

Here We Go Round the Mulberry Bush 15:41, 44:29, 74:45, 75:26. *See also* Mulberry Bush

Here's a Song 69:6

Hevenu Shalom Alechem 34:23

Hey, Diddle, Diddle 31:54, 38:67, 44:35, 66:226, 71:63, 75:28

Hey Dum Diddeley Dum 64:12. *See also* Hey Dum Diddley Dum

Hey Dum Diddley Dum 20:34. *See also* Hey Dum Diddeley Dum

Hey, Ho, Nobody Home 36:119

Hey Ho, to the Greenwood 46:83

Hey Jack, What's in the Sack? 56:82

Hey, Won't Somebody Come and Play 9:13

Hi-Diddle-Dee-Dee 66:70

Hickety, Pickety, My Black Hen 44:8

Hickory, Dickory, Dock 31:23, 33:55, 35:61, 36:120, 38:51, 44:2, 66:232, 72:43, 74:24

Higglety, Pigglety, Pop! 44:34, 65:48

Hine Ma Tov 34:51

Hippity Hop 3:14

Hippity Hop to Bed 38:13

Hippity Hop to the Barber Shop 38:55

Hokey-Pokey 66:204
Holiday of Love 73:41
Holidays 35:90
Holly and the Ivy 28:57, 45:22
Holy Bible, Book Divine 48:6
Holy, Holy, Holy 34:10
Home on the Range 33:56, 36:121,
    40:50, 67:7
Home Sweet Home 33:60
Honor Your Parents 66:246
Honoring Mother and Father 42:134
Hooray for Mr. Lincoln 71:34
Hooray for the Hippo 3:40
Hooray, Professor Un 12:62
Hop Up and Jump Up 34:53
Hop Up, My Ladies 63:66
Horse Named Bill 49:18, 51:72
Horse Went Around, The 50:16
Hosanna! 42:64
Hot Cross Buns! 31:16, 36:124,
    38:140, 44:40, 66:224
How Do You Obey God's Word? 42:73
How Many Miles to Babylon? 44:27
How Many People Do You Love? 4:13
How to Be a Good Citizen 71:10
How Would You Like? 55:53
Huckleberry, Gooseberry 69:11
Huff and Puff 11:24
Human Spirit 18:25
Humpty Dumpty 31:41, 38:71, 44:35,
    66:225, 75:29
Hundred Feet Ahead 53:1
Hush! 42:19
Hush A Bye 72:59. See also All the
    Pretty Little Horses; Go to
    Sleepy; Hush'n Bye; Hush-You-
    Bye; Rock-a-Bye Baby; Rock-
    abye, Baby
Hush-a-Bye Baby 41:67, 44:60
Hush, Little Baby 22:98, 25:18,
    31:20, 33:62, 36:126, 38:12,
    65:91, 66:181, 70:38, 72:57, 74:9,
    77:10
Hush'n Bye 62:36. See also All the
    Pretty Little Horses; Go to
    Sleepy; Hush A Bye; Hush-You-
    Bye; Rock-a-Bye Baby; Rock-
    abye, Baby
Hush-You-Bye 46:56. See also All the
    Pretty Little Horses; Go to
    Sleepy; Hush A Bye; Hush'n Bye;
    Rock-a-Bye Baby
Hushabye 69:18
Hut-Sut Song 66:146

I Am a Child of God 14:7, 54:7
I Am Learning How to Spell 9:7
I Am Learning How to Work 10:52
I Am Quiet 42:25
I Am Slowly Going Crazy 50:69,
    51:77, 64:79
I Am So Glad 48:1
I Am with Thee and Will Keep Thee
    42:122
I Brush My Teeth 72:29
I Can't Tie My Shoe 56:133
I Didn't Mean To 56:126
I Don't Brush My Teeth and I Never
    Comb My Hair 56:22
I Don't Care for Underwear 51:53
I Don't Think My Teacher Likes Me
    56:160
I Don't Wanna Go to School 56:128
I Eat Kids 56:46
I Feel My Savior's Love 54:37
I Get a Hundred 12:68
I Get Angry at Myself 10:36
I Got a Camel for Christmas 35:84
I Got a Letter 1:12
I Got a Teacher, She's So Mean 56:36
I Got Shoes 22:132
I Had a Little Dog 49:9. See also Had
    a Little Dog
I Had a Little Nut Tree 33:65,
    36:127, 44:41
I Had a Little Rooster 35:82. See also
    I Had a Rooster
I Had a Rooster 50:22. See also I Had
    a Little Rooster
I Have a Friend 42:5
I Have a Garden 54:51
I Have a Little Shadow 68:12
I Have Two Little Hands 54:73
I Hear Thunder 65:56
I Heard the Bells on Christmas Day
    28:37
I Just Keep Trusting My Lord 42:61
I Know a Little Pussy 36:128, 65:50.
    See also I Love Little Kitty; I
    Love Little Pussy
I Know an Old Lady 66:125
I Know My Father Lives 14:7, 54:7
I Know Where I'm Goin' 46:55
I Like Me 10:39
I Like Spring 68:10
I Like to Play in the Snow 5:17
I Looked into the Mirror-What Did
    the Mirror Say? 56:182
I Lost My Pants 56:144

I Love America 13:9
I Love God 42:63
I Love Jesus 42:71
I Love Little Kitty 31:65. *See also* I Know a Little Pussy; I Love Little Pussy
I Love Little Pussy 33:66, 36:130, 38:46, 44:6, 66:101, 75:30. *See also* I Know a Little Pussy; I Love Little Kitty
I Love My Daddy 56:162
I Love My Family 54:25
I Love My Grandpa 4:20
I Love the Flowers 4:28
I Love to Hear My Father Play the Piano 30:22
I Love to See the Temple 14:25
I Love Trash 66:19
I Love You 5:21
I Love Your Eyes 56:140
I Miss Grandma 56:138
I Need You Like a Doughnut Needs a Hole 56:24
I Never Did Like You, Anyhow 56:28
I Often Go Walking 54:13
I Often Think of God 42:6
I Open My Bible Book and Read 42:10
I Played a Joke on You 5:30
I Remember Ellis Island 29:20
I Ride an Old Paint 36:131, 40:52
I Rock My Doll 35:25
I Roll the Ball 35:27
I Sat Next to the Duchess at Tea 64:74
I Saw Three Ships 28:44, 38:139, 44:43, 45:30
I Say Thank You 11:53
I Sing a New Song 42:119
I Sing a Song of the Saints of God 34:42
I Sit Down 42:52
I Sneaked into the Kitchen in the Middle of the Night 56:32
I Take My Little Hand 72:18
I Talk to God Wherever I May Be 42:80
I Thank God 42:41
I Thank Thee, Dear Father 54:21
I Thank You, God 42:9. *See also* Thank You, God
I Think I'm Happy Now 11:30
I Think the World Is Glorious 54:53
I Think When I Read That Sweet Story 54:33

I Thought It Was a Kitten 3:36
I Told the Truth 10:22
I Wanna Be a Dog 56:111
I Want a Chocolate Malted 50:36
I Want to Be Your Friend 47:32
I Want to Go Teach the Gospel 54:75
I Was Born About Ten Thousand Years Ago 40:54
I Was Only Foolin' 25:8
I Went to the Movies Tomorrow 55:30
I Whistle a Happy Tune 66:48
I Will Listen 42:11
I Will Only Have a Sweet 6:44
I Will Sing 42:27
I Will Sing of the Mercies of the Lord 42:127
I Will Sing Praise 42:84
I Wish I Was 50:62
I Wish I Were a Fish 3:19
I With I Were 49:10, 51:18
I Wonder How It Felt 42:120
I Wonder If I'm Growing 59:9
I Wondered If I Were Dreaming 29:66
I Would Be True 34:54
I'd Be Me 56:180
I'll Be a Sunbeam 27:28
I'm a 3-Toed, Triple-Eyed, Double-Jointed Dinosaur 56:20
I'm a Little Cookie 31:4, 55:32
I'm a Little Teapot 16:32, 35:52, 38:95, 66:109, 74:28
I'm a Nut 50:67, 51:78
I'm a Special Person 42:100
I'm a V.I.P. 4:7
I'm a Very Happy Person 39:7
I'm a Walkin 72:9
I'm Being Eaten by a Boa Constrictor 51:33
I'm Going Up, Up, Up 42:124
I'm Gonna Sing 26:28
I'm in Charge 7:21
I'm in the Lord's Army 26:4
I'm in the Mood 60:52
I'm Late 56:159
I'm My Friend 12:53
I'm Not One of the Crowd 42:143
I'm Not Small 55:25
I'm Peeling My Banana 55:50
I'm Popeye the Sailor Man 66:77. *See also* Popeye, the Sailor Man
I'm Standing Naked on the Kitchen Table 56:166
I'm the Phone Girl 30:38
I'm the Statue of Liberty 30:28

I'm Trying to Be Like Jesus 54:61
I've Been Working on the Railroad
    33:70, 36:135, 40:59, 66:158,
    67:12
I've Got a Cold in My Nose-Kerchoo!
    49:86
I've Got a Dog and My Dog's Name Is
    Cat 56:69
I've Got a Little Sister 56:72
I've Got One Head 49:8
I've Got Peace Like a River 27:8
Ice Cream 66:143
If All the Raindrops 65:57
If I Could Fly 35:40
If I Had a Dinosaur 59:36
If I Had a Hammer 40:56
If I Only Had a Brain 66:30
If I Were a Little Bird 74:46
If I Were the Hero 11:4
If You Believe in Me, I'll Never Die
    29:44
If You Take Care of Your Body 18:29
If You're Happy 74:38. *See also* If
    You're Happy and You Know It
If You're Happy and You Know It
    49:28, 66:176, 70:20. *See also* If
    You're Happy
If You've Got a Kid Who Complains
    All the Time 56:136
If Your Friend's in Trouble 8:2
In 1776 13:12
In a Cabin 70:4
In a Minute 12:64
In and Out the Window 15:42
In My Garden 60:79
In the Beginning 42:90
In the Ev'ning the Nightingale
    39:9
In the Leafy Tree Tops 54:45
Incey Wincey Spider 38:28. *See also*
    Eency Weency Spider; Eensy
    Weensy Spider; Eentsy Weentsy
    Spider
Inch Worm 66:40
Indian Boy 11:6
Indian Brothers 47:13
Inequality Makes the World Go
    'Round 56:152
Ingrate Song 11:41
Intermission Rag 17:21
Is This What It Means to Have
    Courage 11:14
It Ain't Gonna Rain No More 51:60,
    66:148

It Came upon a Midnight Clear 61:8.
    See also It Came upon the Mid-
    night Clear
It Came upon the Midnight Clear
    28:15, 45:44. *See also* It Came
    upon a Midnight Clear
It Isn't Any Trouble Just to Smile
    49:65
It Pays to Advertise! 49:68
It Takes Courage 11:9
It's a Rosebud in June 76:25
It's Autumn Time 54:55
It's Bad, Bad Stuff 8:12
It's Easter Time 5:29
It's Fun to Take the Ferry to the
    Statue of Liberty 29:10
It's Raining, It's Pouring 31:55,
    33:69, 36:134
It's Spring Again 5:27
Itchy Flea 49:77, 51:120
Itchy Scritchy 53:7
Itiskit, Itaskit 36:133. *See also*
    A-Tisket, A-Tasket

Jack and Jill 31:41, 33:75, 36:138,
    38:39, 44:14, 65:26, 66:223, 75:36
Jack, Be Nimble 38:104
Jack, Can I Ride? 63:76
Jack-O'-Lantern 47:4
Jack Was Every Inch a Sailor 64:116
Jamaica Farewell 19:30
Jamais on na Vu 64:62
Japanese Maple 67:8
Jaws 55:46
Jazzy Three Bears 55:26
Jennie Jenkins 33:76, 36:139. *See
    also* Jenny Jenkins
Jenny Jenkins 22:74, 64:14. *See also*
    Jennie Jenkins
Jeremiah 65:83
Jesse James 40:62
Jesus 26:16
Jesus and the Children 42:123
Jesus Has Risen 54:35
Jesus Is Living in Heaven Today 42:1
Jesus, Jesus 42:65
Jesus Loves Me 26:20
Jesus Loves Me, Jesus Loves Me
    42:66
Jesus Loves the Little Children 48:5
Jesus Once Was a Little Child 54:31
Jesus Said Love Everyone 54:49
Jesus Wants Me for a Sunbeam 54:39

Jesus Went About Doing Good 42:8
Jesus Worked 42:7
Jig Along Home 31:18, 59:60
Jim Along Josie 36:141. *See also*
Jim-a-long Josie
Jim-a-long Josie 1:66. *See also* Jim
Along Josie
Jingle Bells 2:10, 23:4, 31:78, 36:142,
38:150, 45:26, 57:60, 61:20
Joe Hill 40:64
John 3:16 42:74
John Brown's Baby 16:30, 51:22,
66:177
John Henry 22:152, 36:144, 40:67
John Jacob Jingleheimer Schmidt
50:90, 51:9, 64:75, 66:134
John Peel 38:69, 46:6
Johnny Has Gone for a Soldier 22:66
Jolly Old Saint Nicholas 23:12, 45:16.
See also Jolly Old St. Nicholas
Jolly Old St. Nicholas 2:60. *See also*
Jolly Old Saint Nicholas
Joseph Dearest, Joseph Mine 2:30
Joshua Fit the Battle of Jericho
43:10. *See also* Joshua Fought
the Battle of Jericho
Joshua Fought the Battle of Jericho
36:146. *See also* Joshua Fit the
Battle of Jericho
Joy 68:31
Joy to the World 2:15, 23:16, 28:53,
45:34, 61:6
Joyful, Joyful, We Adore Thee
34:14
Jungle Gym 35:43
Junk Food Junkie 6:19
Just Like the Sun 58:45
Just Walkin' Along 42:131

Kangaroo, Kangaroo 3:35
Keemo Kyemo 22:226
Keep the Commandments 54:63
Keep Your Body Strong 6:26, 6:41
Keeper, The 36:148, 46:8
Kicking Mule 63:62
Kindness Begins with Me 54:49
King of the Jungle 71:44
Kintaro's Ride 62:78
Kitten in the Sun 3:8
Knock at the Door 38:25
Knock, Knock, Knock 5:22
Kookaburra 36:150, 46:75, 70:32
Koom Bachur Atsel 1:118

Kum Ba Yah 26:26. *See also* Cum By
Yah; Kumbaya
Kumbaya 19:22, 60:31. *See also* Cum
By Yah; Kum Ba Yah

La Bamba 20:28
La Bastringue 64:67
Lady Bird, Lady Bird 75:31
Ladybug's Lullaby 53:53
Lament of the House Flies 53:49
Land of Obey 10:6
Landlord, Fill the Flowing Bowl 46:32
Last Supper 42:14
Later 56:199
Lavender's Blue 20:18, 33:79, 36:151,
38:66, 44:54, 75:38
Lazy Days 5:40
Lazy Fred 51:50
Lazy Mary 33:80, 35:56, 36:153,
38:62, 65:8, 72:24, 75:41. *See
also* Lazy Mary, Will You Get
Up?
Lazy Mary, Will You Get Up? 31:64,
66:228. *See also* Lazy Mary
Lazy Susan 55:10
Left Right 4:24
Lend a Helping Hand 12:8
Leroy Is a Late Bloomer 56:102
Let Us Break Bread Together 27:12
Let's All Sing 39:7
Let's Ban Halloween, Let's Save Hal-
loween 73:11
Let's Be Friends 47:35
Let's Clap Hands for ... 55:45
Let's Do the Numbers Rumba 60:60
Let's Go Bowling in Bowling Green
50:64
Let's Go Trick or Treatin' 73:26
Let's Hear the Rhythm 21:16
Let's Make Some Noise 58:26
Let's Watch 21:20
Lift Up Your Voice and Sing 54:41
Lightly Row 38:138, 67:4, 76:10
Like Me and You 60:84
Lincolnshire Poacher 46:30
Lions 17:29
Listen to the Horses 59:50
Listen to the Noises 35:28
Listen to the Plink, Plink, Plink 42:24
Little Arabella Miller 74:23. *See also*
Arabella Miller
Little Bells of Christmas 2:49
Little Betty Blue 71:24

Little Bitty Baby 36:154
Little Black Bull, The 63:54
Little Bo-Peep 31:74, 36:156, 38:65,
  44:16, 66:221, 75:34
Little Boxes 40:69
Little Boy Blue 31:15, 38:70, 44:15,
  66:226, 75:44
Little Brown Church, The 26:2
Little Brown Dog 63:28
Little Brown Jug 66:166
Little Bumble Bee 3:22
Little David, Play on Your Harp 43:12
Little Dog Named Right 63:26
Little Drops of Water 38:63
Little Drummer Boy, The 2:32
Little Echo Voice 14:4
Little Girl/Boy Went Walking 55:55
Little Green Frog 55:59
Little House, The 58:13
Little Jack Horner 31:54, 36:157,
  38:36, 44:18, 65:71, 66:225, 75:45
Little Lap-Dog Lullaby 63:27
Little Man 1:46
Little Miss Muffet 31:66, 38:40,
  44:18, 66:227, 71:61
Little Nut Tree 38:53, 75:64
Little Peter Possum 24:2
Little Peter Rabbit 35:76, 50:19, 64:36
Little Pig 63:50
Little Pioneer Children 54:67
Little Purple Pansies 54:51
Little Raindrops 4:33
Little Red Bird 46:40
Little Sally Saucer 64:86, 65:23. See
  also Little Sally Waters
Little Sally Waters 38:101. See also
  Little Sally Saucer
Little Seed 9:16
Little Skunk Hole 50:53, 51:42
Little Tommy Tinker 64:74. See also
  Little Tommy Tucker
Little Tommy Tucker 31:75, 38:35,
  44:17, 75:48. See also Little
  Tommy Tinker
Little White Duck 36:158, 58:40,
  66:92
Living a Day 53:37
Lo, How a Rose E'er Blooming 28:38,
  39:23
Lock Lomond 67:14
London Bridge 31:61, 33:83, 36:160,
  38:105, 44:30, 65:24, 66:230,
  75:58. See also London Bridge Is
  Falling Down

London Bridge Is Falling Down
  15:43. See also London Bridge
Lone Wild Bird 34:48
Long John 22:136
Long Time Ago 35:92
Long, Long Ago 67:9
Looby Loo 24:26, 38:92, 64:83. See
  also Here We Go Looby Loo
Look For a Grandma 7:28
Look Ma! No Cavities 71:36
Looking In a Mirror 14:21
Looking Out the Window 72:40
Lord, I Want to Be a Christian 42:140
Lord Is a Great God, The 42:107
Lord Is My Shepherd, The 68:40
Lord of the Dance 34:18
Lord's Prayer, The 34:37
Lorelei, Die 46:34
Lots of Fish in Bonavist' Harbor
  64:112
Louder 56:47
Lovely Lady of Liberty 29:40
Lowly Germ 12:18
Lucy Locket 31:51, 44:19
Lulabel 50:50
Lullaby 4:15, 38:17. See also Brahms'
  Lullaby; Cradle Song; Cradlesong
Lullaby, and Good Night 74:11. See
  also Brahms' Lullaby; Cradle
  Song; Cradlesong
Lullaby, My Jamie 46:60
Lullaby, My Pretty One 41:67
Lullabye 69:23, 72:60
Lulloo Lullay 77:12

Mail Myself to You 20:44, 31:52,
  66:130
Mairzy Doats 66:138
Make Channels 34:50
Make People Laugh 18:20
Mama Don't 'Low 49:59. See also
  Mama Don't Allow
Mama Don't Allow 40:71. See also
  Mama Don't 'Low
Mama Mosquito's Midnight Whine
  53:45
Man on the Trapeze 17:40. See also
  Possum on the Flying Trapeze
Many Ways to Travel 14:24
March of the Kings 2:28
March of the Worker Ants 53:17
Marching Shoulder to Shoulder
  56:104

Marching Song 42:51
Marianne 66:191
Marines' Hymn 36:161
Martin Luther King, Junior 47:30
Marvelous Toy 66:118
Marvin Doesn't Like the New Baby
   56:154
Mary Ann 67:16
Mary Had a Little Car 72:35
Mary Had a Little Lamb 31:58,
   32:32, 36:163, 38:58, 44:20,
   65:16, 75:60
Mary, Mary, Quite Contrary 44:21.
   See also Mistress Mary; Mistress
   Mary, Quite Contrary
Mary Wore Her Red Dress 31:24,
   58:22
Matthew, Mark, Luke and John 64:18
May Day 5:33
May Jesus Christ Be Praised 42:115
Maybe You Laughed 9:28
Me and My Horse 15:47
Me and My Teddy Bear 66:94
Me and You 56:38
Me Stone 64:111
Meat, Milk, and Grain 6:16
Meow, Meow 39:17
Merrily Caroling 2:48
Merrily We Roll Along 38:59
Merry-Go-Round 30:18, 35:45
Mexican Counting Song 38:137
Michael Finnegan 22:244, 37:59,
   51:79, 64:79. See also Michael
   Finnigin
Michael Finnigin 75:62. See also
   Michael Finnegan
Michael, Row the Boat Ashore 20:26,
   27:10, 34:30, 40:73, 67:14
Michaud 60:57, 64:63
Mighty Pretty Motion 1:2
Military Song 13:43
Miracle in Philadelphia 13:24
Miss Lucy 51:82. See also Miss Lucy
   Had a Baby
Miss Lucy Had a Baby 49:40. See
   also Miss Lucy
Miss Mary Mack 1:78
Miss Polly 55:41. See also Miss Polly
   Had a Dolly
Miss Polly Had a Dolly 49:39, 65:77.
   See also Miss Polly
Miss Quiss 69:26
M-I-S-S-I-S-S-I-P-P-I 66:157
Mister Lister 69:24

Mister Rabbit 63:16
Mister Stand-On-One-Leg 3:25
Mister Sun 19:14
Mister Sunshine 4:27
Mister Wind Is a Mischief 4:31
Mistress Mary 38:38. See also Mary,
   Mary, Quite Contrary; Mistress
   Mary, Quite Contrary
Mistress Mary, Quite Contrary 31:67.
   See also Mary, Mary, Quite Con-
   trary; Mistress Mary
Mockingbird Song 40:74
Mole in the Ground 63:25
Mom and Dad Are Always Right
   56:88
Mommy, Mommy, I Gotta Get a
   Record 56:120
Monkey in the Treetop 3:29
Monkey See and Monkey Do 55:51
Monkey's Wedding 31:44
Monte Sur un Elephant 64:58
Moonlight on the Ruined Castle 67:15
More We Get Together 31:28, 59:16
More We Serve 12:11
Morning Has Broken 34:8
Morningtown Ride 19:46, 60:33
Mother and Son 46:58
Mother Dear 54:13
Mother Dear, I Love You 9:39
Mother Goose Summer 76:6
Mother, I Love You 54:11
Mother Needs Me 5:36
Motorcycle Song 40:77
Move Over 21:11
Mr. Earth, I Love You 11:60
Mr. Sun 59:12
Mr. Tickles 68:21
Mrs. Murphy's Chowder 20:46,
   22:236, 49:82
Mud, Mud, Glorious Mud 50:79, 51:31
Muffin Man 15:42, 36:165, 38:34,
   64:98, 75:47
Mulberry Bush 31:6, 33:84, 36:166,
   38:80, 65:14, 66:216. See also
   Here We Go Round the Mulberry
   Bush
Multiply 42:121
Muppet Show Theme 66:4
Muskrat 63:21
Muss I Denn 46:36
Must Be Santa 2:54, 57:70, 59:26
My Bible 42:12
My Body Machine 6:6
My Bonnie Lies over the Ocean 33:87

My Brother and I 4:16
My Brother Thinks He's a Banana 56:57
My Brother Threw Up on My Stuffed Toy Bunny 56:62
My Dad 9:10, 54:17
My Dame Hath a Lame, Tame Crane 46:87, 75:73
My Darling Clementine 31:27. *See also* Clementine
My Dentist Is an Awfully Nice Man 56:24
My Dog Rags 20:38, 64:42
My Dog's Bigger Than Your Dog 66:84
My Dreydel 59:20
My Father Hunted a Kangaroo 51:32
My Friend Jake 56:42
My Goose 46:86
My Guiding Light Is Miss Liberty 29:60
My Happy Home 42:35
My Heavenly Father Loves Me 54:53
My Home 42:135
My Home's in Montana 67:7
My Jumping Song 14:6
My Little Pony 3:9
My Love's an Arbutus 46:28
My Mommy Drives a Dump Truck 56:66
My Mother Ran Away Today 56:95
My Old Hen's a Good Old Hen 63:44
My Pony Boy 65:32
My Responsibility 42:95
My Song of Praise 42:128
My Tall Silk Hat 70:28
My Tongue 42:103
My Way Home 59:58

Name the Days 21:31
Namo Ganesha 62:65
Nancy's Gone to the Hospital 21:34
Nanny Banny 69:21
Never Cook Your Sister in a Frying Pan 56:92
Never Tell a Lie 9:42
New River Train 59:38
Night with a Dim Moon 67:15
Nina Nana 1:74
Nina, the Pinta, the Santa Maria, The 66:248
Nine Little Reindeer 71:26
Ninety-nine Miles from Home 50:72
No No No 71:29

No One Else Can Smile My Smile 4:9
No One Like You 66:14
Noble Duke of York 16:31, 38:88
Nobody Knows the Trouble I've Seen 33:89
North Pole 47:29
North Wind Doth Blow 38:33, 44:10, 75:66
Nothing 56:158
Nothing but Sing 42:30
Now I Lay Me Down to Sleep 25:12, 31:80
Now Is the Close of Day 39:21
Now the Day Is Over 33:91, 34:32, 38:21, 77:29
Now unto the King 42:129
Now You May Think 49:92, 51:123
Now, Now, Now 36:168
Numi Nim 62:45
Nuts in May 38:81

O Christmas Tree 2:9, 23:6, 28:66, 45:18
O Come, All Ye Faithful 2:17, 28:41, 45:20, 52:64, 61:4. *See also* Oh Come, All Ye Faithful
O Come, Little Children 2:37, 45:40
O Come, O Come Emmanuel 28:9
O Hangman, O Hangman 46:38
O How Lovely Is the Evening 48:7
O Little Town of Bethlehem 2:18, 28:46, 36:177, 61:14
O Pioneers 5:45
Oats and Beans and Barley 60:13. *See also* Oats, Peas, and Beans; Oats, Peas, Beans; Oats, Peas, Beans and Barley Grow
Oats, Peas, and Beans 33:93. *See also* Oats and Beans and Barley; Oats, Peas, Beans; Oats, Peas, Beans and Barley Grow
Oats, Peas, Beans 24:8, 36:171, 38:89, 75:68. *See also* Oats and Beans and Barley; Oats, Peas, and Beans; Oats, Peas, Beans and Barley Grow
Oats, Peas, Beans and Barley Grow 66:228. *See also* Oats and Beans and Barley; Oats, Peas, and Beans; Oats, Peas, Beans
Obwisana 64:111
Octopus's Garden 60:75
Of All the Beast-es 63:75

Oh, Blue 63:30
Oh, Chester! 51:25
Oh Come, All Ye Faithful 36:172. *See also* O Come, All Ye Faithful
Oh, Come, Let Us Worship 42:23
Oh, Dear, What Can the Matter Be? 33:94, 36:174, 44:52, 65:34, 67:9, 70:30
Oh, Dreidel I Will Play 55:22
Oh Hear the Bells Ringing 39:25
Oh, How I Love Jesus 42:2
Oh, How Lovely Is the Evening 33:96, 36:176, 38:134
Oh, I'm Riding in the Car 72:37
Oh, I'm So Embarrassed 12:46
Oh, John the Rabbit 22:216, 49:55
Oh, Jolly Santa Claus 47:22
Oh Me, Oh My 59:44
Oh Mules We Find 51:52
Oh, My Goodness! 69:10
Oh No! I Like My Sister! 56:184
Oh, Pretty Polly 31:13
Oh, Susanna! 31:68, 33:98, 36:179, 38:126, 40:79
Oh, Susannah 22:180
Oh, We Can Play 74:36
Oh, What a Summer 76:8
Oh, What Do You Do in the Summertime? 54:47
Oh Where, Oh Where Has My Little Dog Gone? 44:9, 66:86. *See also* Where Has My Little Dog Gone?; Where, O Where; Where, Oh Where, Has My Little Dog Gone?
Oh, You Can't Get to Heaven 26:8. *See also* You Can't Get to Heaven
Ol' Dan Tucker 22:88
Ol' Texas 20:22
Old Bell'd Yoe 63:60
Old Chisholm Trail 20:36
Old Cow Died 63:56
Old Dan Tucker 66:184
Old Family Toothbrush 25:6, 50:87, 51:34
Old Fox 63:32. *See also* Fox, The
Old Ground Hog 63:22
Old Hen Cackled and the Rooster Laid the Egg 63:42
Old Hogan's Goat 51:117
Old Joe Clark 40:81. *See also* Old Joe Clarke
Old Joe Clarke 50:44. *See also* Old Joe Clark

Old King Cole 31:30, 36:182, 38:74, 44:42, 65:40, 66:229, 75:70
Old Lady Goose 63:40
Old MacDonald 31:48, 33:100, 36:184, 74:48. *See also* Old MacDonald Had a Farm
Old MacDonald Had a Car 72:34
Old MacDonald Had a Farm 38:118, 66:96. *See also* Old MacDonald
Old MacTavish Is Dead 51:15
Old McDonald Had a Band 59:22
Old Mother Hubbard 71:58
Old Mother Leary 50:38
Old Mrs. Lazibones 50:46
Old Roger 64:88
Old Rugged Cross 27:26
Old Sow 63:52
Old Tin Cup 69:15
Old Toy Trains 57:74
Oliver Cromwell 46:16
On a Sunday 55:29
On Christmas Morning 57:55
On Halloween 47:5
On the Good Ship Lollipop 66:42
On Top of My Pizza 50:31, 51:98
On Top of Old Smokey 33:103. *See also* On Top of Old Smoky; On Top of Spaghetti
On Top of Old Smoky 31:25, 40:83, 67:6. *See also* On Top of Old Smokey; On Top of Spaghetti
On Top of Spaghetti 36:186, 37:38, 66:128. *See also* On Top of Old Smokey; On Top of Old Smoky
Once an Austrian Went Yodeling 55:33
Once I Saw Three Goats 64:77
Once in Royal David's City 28:16
Once There Was a Snowman 54:59
Once Within a Lowly Stable 54:29
One Bottle Pop 50:80, 51:16
One Day My Best Friend Barbara Turned Into a Frog 56:54
One Elephant, Deux Elephants 37:58, 64:9
One Finger, One Thumb 35:64, 49:30, 64:46, 74:41
One Inch Taller 42:102
One Light, One Sun 60:100
One Little Girl 4:10
One Little Nose Like Mine 12:44
One Misty, Moisty Morning 65:58
One Song 66:64
One Sparkling Star 4:37

One, Two, Buckle My Shoe 74:42
1,2,3,4,5 64:33
Only a Boy Named David 27:20
Onward, Christian Soldiers 27:4
Ooey Gooey 55:15
Open My Eyes That I May See 34:40
Open, Shut Them 55:58, 72:55
Opposites 9:19
Oranges and Lemons 44:31, 75:74
Our Dog Bernard 56:58
Our Prayer 54:31
Over in the Meadow 38:44, 49:16, 60:27
Over the Rainbow 66:34
Over the River and Through the Wood 38:142
Ox Cart 54:65

Pair of Feet 14:14
Pat Works on the Railway 36:188
Pat-a-Cake 31:32, 35:50, 38:27, 72:20. *See also* Pat-a-Cake, Pat-a-Cake
Pat-a-Cake, Pat-a-Cake 44:59. *See also* Pat-a-Cake
Pat-a-Pan 2:38, 38:152
Pawpaw Patch 15:44, 64:96
Peace Is Flowing Like a River 34:34
Peanut Butter 64:48
Peanut Butter and Jelly 55:57. *See also* Peanut Butter Song
Peanut Butter Sandwich 59:4
Peanut Butter Song 50:30. *See also* Peanut Butter and Jelly
Pease Porridge Hot 31:14, 38:104, 44:28, 65:11, 75:77
Peek at a Peacock 3:24
Peek-a-Boo 72:7, 74:20
Peep Squirrel 63:18
Peter Cottontail 66:243
Peter Piper 71:60
Petit Papa Noel 57:57
Petites Marionettes 59:49. *See also* Petites Marionettes
Petites Marionnettes 62:112. *See also* Petites Marionettes
Phoebe in Her Petticoat 65:13
Pick a Bale o' Cotton 31:70, 59:57. *See also* Pick a Bale of Cotton
Pick a Bale of Cotton 36:190. *See also* Pick a Bale o' Cotton
Pig Song 69:8
Piggy Back Song 69:14

Pilgrims and the Indians 5:14
Pioneer Children 54:65
Pizza Round 51:49
Plant a Little Tree 5:32
Play Your Horn Right Now 21:12
Playful Little Jack Frost 5:18
Please Be Quiet 42:87
Please Sit Down 55:48
Polly 65:67. *See also* Polly, Put the Kettle On
Polly, Put the Kettle On 31:39, 33:105, 36:192, 38:60, 44:22, 75:14. *See also* Polly
Polly-Wolly-Doodle 19:36, 31:50, 66:174
Poor Roger Is Dead and Gone to His Grave 50:70
Pop! Goes the Weasel 31:46, 33:106, 36:194, 38:32, 50:58, 65:47, 66:187, 70:26, 75:50
Popcorn Popping 54:43
Popeye, the Sailor Man 49:26, 51:121. *See also* I'm Popeye the Sailor Man
Possum on the Flying Trapeze 24:28. *See also* Man on the Trapeze
Power Is You, The 18:44
Power of Thinking 18:16
Power to Love 18:34
Praise and Thanksgiving 42:126
Praise God from Whom All Blessings Flow 34:20, 48:3
Praise God with Songs of Joy 42:26
Praise Him 42:81. *See also* Praise Him, Praise Him
Praise Him, Praise Him 27:16. *See also* Praise Him
Pray, Pray, Pray 42:83
Prayer Song 42:77
Precious Friends 64:118
Presidents Are Famous Men 47:38
Pressed and Dressed 12:35
Pretty White Teeth 72:14
Prune Song 50:27
Psalm 8 26:18
Puff, the Magic Dragon 19:44, 66:161
Pufferbellies 64:47
Pumpkin Picking 47:12
Pumpkins 47:10
Punchinello 47 64:94
Pussy Cat, Pussy Cat 31:35, 38:50, 44:6, 66:108, 75:49
Put Our Best Selves Forward 6:34

Put Your Finger in the Air 36:196, 66:132
Put Your Little Foot Right Out 66:208

Quack, Quack, Quack 3:7
Quartermaster Corps 50:29, 51:43
Queen Caroline 1:6
Quickly I'll Obey 54:15

Rabbit Ain't Got No Tail at All 49:85
Raccoon and Possum 63:15
Rain 71:62
Rain Is Falling All Around 54:51
Rain, Rain 38:49. See also Rain, Rain, Go Away
Rain, Rain, Go Away 65:60. See also Rain, Rain
Rain Song 68:12
Rainbow 'Round Me 55:16
Rainbow Connection 66:22
Raisins and Almonds 77:16
Rattlin' Bog 64:44
Read Read Books Books 71:18
Red Dragonflies 67:11
Red River Valley 33:108, 40:85, 67:13
Reindeer Are Tapping 2:59
Rejoice in the Lord Always 27:14
Rejoice, Give Thanks! 42:130
Remember September 5:7
Remember Your Name and Address 66:213
Repentance 54:61
Reptile World 56:148
Return of the Baby Bumblebee 55:9
Reuben, Reuben 50:68
Reverently, Quietly 54:73
Revolutionary Tea 22:54
Riddle 3:42
Riddle Song 33:110, 40:87
Ride a Cock-Horse 38:52, 66:186. See also Ride a Cock-Horse to Banbury Cross; Ride a Cockhorse
Ride a Cock-Horse to Banbury Cross 44:26. See also Ride a Cock-Horse; Ride a Cockhorse
Ride a Cockhorse 31:9, 74:16. See also Ride a Cock-Horse; Ride a Cock-Horse to Banbury Cross
Ride on a Bus 14:11
Ride Sally Ride 71:32
Ride Your Red Horse 69:22
Riding Along 64:16

Riding in an Airplane 60:81
Riding in the Buggy 72:39
Riding on the New River Train 55:31
Riding Round the Cattle 63:70
Rig-A-Jig-Jig 20:10, 25:4, 38:94, 65:30
Right Foot, Left Foot 21:19
Ring Around a Rosy 31:59, 38:107, 75:52. See also Ring Around the Rosy; Ring-a-Ring o' Roses
Ring Around the Rosy 72:13. See also Ring Around a Rosy; Ring-a-Ring o' Roses
Ring, Ring, Ring the Bells 2:49
Ring the Bell 21:36
Ring Those Bells 2:58
Ring-a-Long Bells 47:27
Ring-a-Ring o' Roses 44:28, 65:21. See also Ring Around a Rosy; Ring Around the Rosy
Ringel Rosen 1:124
Rings on Her Fingers 65:33
Rio Grande 46:70
Rise and Shine 34:44, 50:91, 60:35
Rise Up, Shepherd, and Follow 28:24
Road to the Isles 76:13
Robin in the Rain 59:28
Rock Island Line 22:172, 40:89, 66:172
Rock-a-Bye Baby 25:22, 31:34, 33:112, 36:198, 41:66, 65:93, 66:221, 74:8, 77:28. See also All the Pretty Little Horses; Go to Sleepy; Hush A Bye; Hush'n Bye; Hush-You-Bye; Rockabye, Baby
Rockabye, Baby 38:20. See also All the Pretty Little Horses; Go to Sleepy; Hush A Bye; Hush'n Bye; Hush-You-Bye; Rock-a-Bye Baby
Rock-a My Soul 43:4
Rockin' Robin 20:42
Rocking 2:42
Roll Over 25:14, 38:121. See also Roll Over, Roll Over; Ten in the Bed
Roll Over, Roll Over 70:34. See also Roll Over; Ten in the Bed
Roly Poly 4:23
Rooster Came into Our Yard 49:74
Rooster's Dead 39:18
Roses Are Red 71:8
Row, Row, Row 60:64. See also Row, Row, Row Your Boat
Row, Row, Row Your Boat 31:26, 36:199, 38:135, 65:83, 66:234, 74:25, 75:53. See also Row, Row, Row

Ru-ruque 1:20
Rub-a-Dub-Dub 38:45, 72:46
Rubber Duckie 66:16
Rudolph the Red-Nosed Reindeer 57:68, 66:235
Run Along Home 49:62
Russian Lullaby 55:24

Safety Don'ts 7:10
Safety Kid Smart 8:6
Sailor Went to Sea 51:63
Sailor Went to Sea Sea Sea 50:65
Sally Eats Shoelaces, Straw and String 56:156
Sally, Go Round 38:87. *See also* Sally Go Round the Sun
Sally Go Round the Sun 65:23. *See also* Sally, Go Round
Salom Chaverim 67:9
Sanctus 34:16
Sandbox, The 35:42
Sandman Comes 25:26, 38:15, 74:7
Sandwiches 20:8
Santa Claus Is Comin' to Town 66:238
Santa Claus Is Coming 2:50
Santa's Chimney 38:146
Santa's Coming 47:28
Sarasponda 1:30, 22:40, 67:10
Saturday 54:15
Saturday Night 1:40
Savez-vous Planter des Choux? 58:20. *See also* Savez-vous Planter les Choux?
Savez-vous Planter les Choux? 64:68. *See also* Savez-vous Planter des Choux?
Scarborough Fair 33:114
Schlaf, Kindlein, Schlaf 62:38. *See also* Cradle Song; Sleep, Baby, Sleep
Scrubit Land of Clean 12:40
Seahorse Merry-Go-Round 3:20
Seal and a Walrus 3:26
Seasons 42:34, 42:93, 68:9
Secret of Happiness 11:32
See My Fingers 72:53
See Saw 69:25
See-Saw 35:47
See-saw, Margery Daw 31:75, 44:27. *See also* See-Saw, Marjorie Daw; Seesaw, Marjorie Daw

See-Saw, Marjorie Daw 38:37. *See also* See-saw, Margery Daw; See-saw, Marjorie Daw
See the Pony Galloping, Galloping 38:98
Seeds Are Planted Deep 55:12
Seesaw, Marjorie Daw 75:72. *See also* See-saw, Margery Daw; See-Saw, Marjorie Daw
Senses Song 21:18
Sereno, El 64:108
Service with a Smile 12:16
Shake My Sillies Out 19:24, 59:31
Shake That Little Foot, Dinah-O 63:47
Shall We Gather at the River? 40:92
Shamrocks and Leprechauns 47:41
Sharing 4:12
Sharing Song 59:18
She Went into the Water 24:20
She'll Be Comin' 'Round the Mountain 31:37, 33:116, 49:46, 64:22, 66:178, 67:6. *See also* She'll Be Coming 'Round the Mountain; She'll Be Coming Around the Mountain; She'll Be Coming Round the Mountain
She'll Be Coming 'Round the Mountain 36:201. *See also* She'll Be Comin' 'Round the Mountain; She'll Be Coming Around the Mountain; She'll Be Coming Round the Mountain
She'll Be Coming Around the Mountain 15:46. *See also* She'll Be Comin' 'Round the Mountain; She'll Be Coming 'Round the Mountain; She'll Be Coming Round the Mountain
She'll Be Coming Round the Mountain 20:6, 38:128, 40:94. *See also* She'll Be Comin' 'Round the Mountain; She'll Be Coming 'Round the Mountain; She'll Be Coming Around the Mountain
She's My Sister 4:18
Shearer's Dream 46:80
Shenandoah 22:125, 33:119, 40:96, 46:72
Shepherd's Song 42:116
Shiloh, Liza Jane 40:98
Shine On 54:79

Shining 68:46
Shining Day 34:56
Shiny Lullaby 6:4
Shiny Silver Moon 35:36
Shoe Shoe Patch 72:30
Shoo Fly 24:14, 35:54, 36:203
Shortnin' Bread 31:76
Show a Little Love 9:4
Show Me the Path, Lord 42:101
Showing Love 42:38
Shuckin' of the Corn 76:28
Shut Up in the Library 56:30
Si-si-si 1:36
Sidewalks of New York 36:204
Silent Night 2:20, 23:14, 28:18,
    36:206, 45:42, 61:30
Silly Song 66:68
Simon Says 14:28
Simple Gifts 22:38, 33:120, 46:48. *See
    also* Tis a Gift to Be Simple; Tis
    the Gift to Be Simple
Simple Simon 33:123, 38:48, 44:44,
    65:31
Sing a Song of September 71:6
Sing a Song of Sixpence 31:38,
    36:208, 38:30, 44:45, 66:222,
    75:55
Sing About Martin 71:30
Sing Along with Me 30:6
Sing Hosanna 34:12
Sing Noel, Noel 23:10
Sing! 66:7
Six Little Ducks 24:18, 50:18, 59:52
Six Little Mice Sat Down to Spin 44:3
Skatter-Brak-Flath Who Lives in My
    Bath 56:53
Skin and Bones 22:336, 59:43
Skinnamarink 64:122, 65:95
Skip to My Lou 15:45, 31:21, 33:124,
    36:210, 38:90
Skye Boat Song 33:127
Sleep, Baby, Sleep 38:18, 41:68, 74:8,
    77:7. *See also* Cradle Song;
    Schlaf, Kindlein, Schlaf
Sleep My Baby 41:69
Sleepers Wake 39:24
Sleeping Princess 25:10
Sleeping Time 35:34
Sleigh Bells Ring 47:23
Slide, The 35:46
Slithery D 50:94
Sloop John B. 40:100
Slow, Slow Snail 53:4
Small Recorder 9:44

Smile, Dear Princess 11:23
Smile on the Crocodile 50:54. *See
    also* Back of a Crocodile;
    Crocodile, The
Smiles 54:41
Snail 15:47
Snake Baked a Hoecake 63:24
Snakes 68:23
Sniggle Song 71:25
So Long, It's Been Good to Know You
    40:103
So Many Things 10:29
Sodeo 59:46
Soft Falls the Snow 69:30
Soldier and the Maid 65:36
Somebody Loves 4:8
Something in My Shoe 60:55
Sometimes I Get a Feeling Inside 9:32
Song of Happiness 22:25
Sourwood Mountain 36:212
Special Gift 54:49
Special Kind of Love 11:65
Spell Some Names 21:8
Spider on the Floor 59:21
Spin, Spider, Spin 68:20
Spin, Spin, Spin 47:19
Spirit of Christmas Is Here 68:44
Spring Inside 68:11
Squirrel, The 35:39
Squirrel Is a Pretty Thing 63:19
St. Patrick's Day 47:42
Standin' Tall 10:4
Stanley Stole My Shoelace and
    Rubbed It in His Armpit
    56:163
Stay Outside of My Line 7:24
Stewball 40:106, 63:68
Still Small Voice 54:69
Still, Still, Still 2:39
Still We Have Love 11:68
Stop . . . and Go! 42:118
Straight Home, Straight Aim,
    Straight Arrow 12:70
Street Song 38:117
Streets of Forbes 46:76
Stretch and Bend 21:23
Summer Breeze 76:21
Summer Is A-Coming In 46:26
Summer's End 76:30
Suo Gan 77:24
Sur le Pont d'Avignon 38:108, 59:80,
    64:60
Swan, The 1:102
Sweet and Low 62:40

Sweet Betsy from Pike 22:186,
    33:128, 36:214, 40:108, 67:10
Sweet Potatoes 65:74
Sweet Rosie O'Grady 50:42
Sweet Water Rolling 62:30
Sweetly Sings the Donkey 46:88
Swing, The 35:38, 68:16
Swing Low, Sweet Chariot 22:148,
    59:66
Swiss Cheese Song 50:32

Ta Ta Ta Li 62:63
Tailor and the Mouse 49:72
Take Me Out to the Ball Game
    22:296, 40:110, 60:72
Take the Blame 42:48
Take Time 68:34
Take Your Hat Off 13:4
Tall Silk Hat 64:72
Tamzara 1:128
Tape Tape Petites Mains 62:59
Tapping 2:61
Taps 36:216
Teach Me to Walk in the Light 54:79
Teddy Bear Hug 58:35
Teddy Bear, Teddy Bear 49:38
Teddy Bears' Picnic 66:98
Telephone Song 7:18
Tell Me, Dear Lord 54:77
Tell Me the Stories of Jesus 54:33
Tell Me Why 32:6, 40:113
Ten Fingers 35:60
Ten in the Bed 65:88. See also Roll
    Over; Roll Over, Roll Over
Ten Little Indians 36:217, 66:217
Ten Little Toesies 72:45
Tete, Epaules 60:59. See also Head
    and Shoulders; Head and Shoul-
    ders, Baby; Head, Shoulders,
    Baby
Than I'll Ever Have with You! 49:90
Thank You Dance 11:56
Thank You, God 42:22. See also I
    Thank You, God
Thank You, Lord 68:39
Thanking Song 68:30
Thanks a Lot 60:19
Thanks to God for His Love 39:22
Thanksgiving 47:15
Thanksgiving Day Is Coming 47:16
Thanksgiving Time 47:17
That Doggie in the Window 66:82
That's Dependability 12:58

That's My Flag 5:42
The Bowling Song 60:89
There Came a Girl from France 59:82
There Was a Bee-Eye-Ee-Eye-Ee
    50:12
There Was a Crooked Man 44:46,
    75:57
There Was a Lady Loved a Swine
    44:36
There Was a Little Baby 57:80
There Was a Man and He Was Mad
    75:81
There Was a Man Lived in the Moon
    44:38. See also Aiken Drum;
    Aikendrum
There Was an Old Frog 63:48
There Was an Old Lady 33:131,
    36:221
There Was an Old Woman 38:42,
    49:14, 75:82. See also There Was
    an Old Woman Tossed Up in a
    Basket
There Was an Old Woman Tossed Up
    in a Basket 44:47. See also
    There Was an Old Woman
There Was an Old Woman Who Lived
    in a Shoe 31:40, 66:227
There Were Three Jolly Fishermen
    50:86
There's a Cow in My Bedroom! 55:13
There's a Hole in My Bucket 36:218.
    See also There's a Hole in the
    Bucket
There's a Hole in the Bucket 40:114,
    50:88, 70:8. See also There's a
    Hole in My Bucket
There's a Little Wheel A-Turnin' in
    My Heart 55:38. See also
    There's a Little Wheel A-Turn-
    ing; There's a Little Wheel A-
    Turning in My Heart
There's a Little Wheel A-Turning
    38:120. See also There's a Little
    Wheel A-Turnin' in My Heart;
    There's a Little Wheel A-Turn-
    ing in My Heart
There's a Little Wheel A-Turning in
    My Heart 20:20. See also
    There's a Little Wheel A-Turnin'
    in My Heart; There's a Little
    Wheel A-Turning
There's Always a Song to Sing 30:50
There's Always Room for Change
    18:13

There's No One Exactly Like Me 42:50

There's No Substitute for a Cat 56:141

They Said, "Eat the Broccoli" 56:90

Things Unseen 47:3

Think About a Thank You 11:50

Think Positively 73:35

Thirty Purple Birds 51:51

This Is My Commandment 42:75

This Is the Day We Come to Church 42:20

This Is the Way 72:31

This Is the Way the Ladies Ride 74:12

This Land Is Your Land 22:370, 40:116, 66:188

This Little Light 34:46. *See also* This Little Light of Mine

This Little Light of Mine 19:48, 26:10, 40:119, 60:65. *See also* This Little Light

This Little Pig 35:62, 38:26, 74:19, 75:11. *See also* This Little Piggy

This Little Piggy 72:8. *See also* This Little Pig

This Little Toe 72:44

This Makes a Happier Home 42:40

This Old Man 19:38, 31:56, 36:223, 54:13, 60:29, 65:59, 66:218, 70:16, 72:17, 75:86

Three Blind Mice 31:43, 36:224, 44:2, 65:51, 66:233, 75:78

Three Crow 64:114

Three Geese in Straw 39:16

Three Green Speckled Frogs 50:21

Three Little Fishies 66:154

Three Little Kittens 31:22, 38:72, 44:4, 75:90

Three Little Piggies 49:12

Three Little Witches 50:75

Three Steps Forward 11:12

Three Ways to Get Peanut Butter Off the Roof of Your Mouth 50:33

Three White Gulls 38:97

Throw the Ball 10:17

Thumbelina 60:41

Thumbkins 55:52

Thump, Thump, Thump 56:79

Ticka-Tacka 64:75

Ticklely 72:52

Time to Sing 60:67

Ting-a-lay-o 19:12. *See also* Tinga Layo; Tingalayo

Tinga Layo 24:16. *See also* Ting-a-lay-o; Tingalayo

Tingalayo 37:39, 60:92, 64:106, 70:14. *See also* Ting-a-lay-o; Tinga Layo

Tiny Tim 65:78

Tippy-Tippy Toes 14:16

Tiptoe March 21:15

Tis a Gift to Be Simple 40:122. *See also* Simple Gifts; Tis the Gift to Be Simple

Tis the Gift to Be Simple 34:62. *See also* Simple Gifts; Tis a Gift to Be Simple

Tit Galop Pour Mamou 22:50

To a Distant Friend 67:12

To Everyone in All the World 60:21

To Market 65:44. *See also* To Market, to Market

To Market, to Market 31:33, 38:99, 74:16. *See also* To Market

To Mommy 56:29

To Portsmouth 46:74

Today Is May 71:54

Togetherness Kids 7:14

Tom, He Was a Piper's Son 44:24. *See also* Tom, Tom, the Piper's Son

Tom, Tom, the Piper's Son 31:49, 38:56, 44:23, 65:44, 75:85. *See also* Tom, He Was a Piper's Son

Tomorrow 55:34, 56:60, 66:25

Town of Round 56:176

Train Is A-Comin' 49:50

Tree in the Wood 33:134, 36:226

Trot, Trot, Trot 62:71, 74:16

Trunk to Tail 17:15

Truth About Lions 3:30

Try to Please a Princess 11:20

Turkey in the Straw 36:228, 40:124, 51:84

Turkey Run 47:14

Turkey Song 63:46

Turkey Talk 71:21

Turn Again Whittington 46:85

Turn, Turn, Turn 40:126

Turtles 21:29

Twas in the Moon of Wintertime 2:24, 28:70

Twelve Days of Christmas 2:12, 23:20, 36:231

Twinkle, Twinkle, Little Star 19:42, 25:2, 31:47, 33:137, 36:235, 38:64, 41:68, 44:32, 60:99, 65:85, 66:202, 67:4, 75:93

Two Sides to Forgiveness 10:34
Tzena, Tzena, Tzena 66:198

Un Elephante 64:115
Uncle Reuben 36:237
Under the Spreading Chestnut Tree
    36:239
Underwear 56:174
Une Poule Blanche 62:32
Unite and Unite 76:4
United 71:40
Up and Over and Down 4:32
Up Goes the Baby 72:23
Up in the Air 35:30
Up in the Air, Junior Bird Man 51:10
Up on the Housetop 2:46, 23:22, 57:53
Uptown, Downtown 69:28
Uurgh, Eeegh, Ugh, 53:44

Valentine 47:36
Valentine Friends 47:34
Valentine's Dance 47:37
Valentines Are Special Greetings
    47:33
Vegetable Rap 6:14
Very Best Band 64:20
Very Best Part of Christmas Time
    5:19
Veterans Day Salute 5:10
Vista 64:76

Wabash Cannonball 19:8
Waddaly Atcha 64:52
Wake, Snake 22:248
Wake Up! Jonah 43:18
Wake Up, Little Baby 72:26
Walk Forward and Backward 21:22
Walk Outside 60:94
Walk, Walk, Walk 60:37
Walking Song 14:26, 76:16
Walking Sticks 53:11
Walloping Windowblind 50:83
Waltz of the Witch 73:6
Waltzing Matilda 66:200
Wash the Stickies down the Drain
    12:32
Wash Your Hair 12:20
Wassail Song 28:76
Water 56:190
Water in the Rain Clouds 71:53

We Are Climbing Jacob's Ladder
    34:31, 43:6
We Are Going to Grandma's House
    4:19
We Are One 68:37
We Are Soldiers 74:29
We Don't Have to Share 56:122
We Don't Want to Go Home 50:73
We Gather Together 33:138, 34:60,
    36:240. *See also* We Gather To-
    gether to Ask the Lord's Blessing
We Gather Together to Ask the Lord's
    Blessing 66:251. *See also* We
    Gather Together
We Have a Friend 55:54
We Hold These Truths 13:18
We Praise Thy Name 42:125
We Shall Overcome 34:28, 40:128
We Thank Thee, Father, for Our
    Homes 42:138
We the People 13:32
We Three Kings 2:16, 36:242, 48:10,
    52:28. *See also* We Three Kings
    of Orient Are
We Three Kings of Orient Are 28:48,
    61:24. *See also* We Three Kings
We Volunteer 12:6
We Wish You a Merry Christmas 2:8,
    23:28, 28:80, 36:244, 38:153,
    45:10, 48:11, 54:27, 57:82
We're Different 12:50
We're Glad You're Here 42:55
We're Just Two Friends 11:37
We're Off to See the Wizard 66:37
We're the Children of America 29:24
We're the Safety Kids 7:6
We've Got to Get Back to Basics 18:4
Wearin' o' the Green 5:24
Wee Cooper of Fife 46:14
Wee Willie Winkie 38:19, 71:16
Welcome April Sunshine 39:27
Westward Ho over the Oregon Trail
    We Go 54:65
Wet Again 56:169
What Child Is This? 2:35, 28:29, 61:26
What Did Delaware, Boys? 49:48,
    51:64
What Do I Have? 42:113
What Do We Do? 35:12
What Do You Do When You're Happy
    11:34
What Do You Like? 21:7
What Does Baby Hear 35:20

What Does Baby See 35:16
What If a Zebra Had Spots? 56:197
What Is the Answer? 68:41
What Is the Number? 21:28
What Kind of Trees Are Found Out
    There? 39:13
What Shall We Do When We All Go
    Out? 65:20
What Shall We Do with the Baby-O?
    55:43. *See also* What Will We Do
    with the Baby-O?
What Will We Do with the Baby-O?
    35:51. *See also* What Shall We
    Do with the Baby-O?
Wheels on the Bus 16:32, 49:44,
    60:43. *See also* Bus Song
When Good King Arthur Ruled This
    Land 44:39
When Grandpa Comes 54:23
When He Comes Again 54:37
When I First Came to This Land
    22:272
When I Go to Church 54:71
When I See an Elephant Fly 66:56
When I'm Happy 42:85
When Is the Day? 42:56
When Johnny Comes Marching Home
    36:245
When Poppa Put the Paper on the
    Wall 49:76
When Suzie Sneezed 56:40
When the House Is Dark and Quiet
    56:50
When the Saints Go Marching In
    27:6
When We're Helping 54:15
When You Come to the End of a
    Lollipop 49:89
When You Tell One Lie 10:25
Where Are You Going to, My Pretty
    Maid? 44:55
Where Are Your Eyes? 35:14
Where Can Baby Be? 35:33
Where Do You Live? 21:32
Where Go the Boats? 35:87
Where Has My Little Dog Gone?
    31:42, 70:36. *See also* Oh Where,
    Oh Where Has My Little Dog
    Gone?; Where, O Where; Where,
    Oh Where, Has My Little Dog
    Gone?
Where Is John? 1:96
Where Is the Baby? 2:33

Where Is Thumbkin? 31:62, 35:66,
    36:247, 38:29, 42:57, 64:30,
    65:19, 72:49
Where Is Your Goose? 50:15
Where Love Is 54:81
Where, O Where 74:21. *See also* Oh
    Where, Oh Where Has My Little
    Dog Gone?; Where Has My Little
    Dog Gone?; Where, Oh Where,
    Has My Little Dog Gone?
Where, Oh Where, Has My Little Dog
    Gone? 36:248, 38:114. *See also*
    Oh Where, Oh Where Has My
    Little Dog Gone?; Where Has My
    Little Dog Gone?; Where, O
    Where
Where's My Pajamas? 65:87
Where's the Justice 13:38
While Shepherds Watched Their
    Flocks by Night 28:12
Whiney Child 11:28
Whisper a Prayer 27:18
Whistle While You Work 66:62
Whistler and His Dog 66:102
Whistling Cowhand 71:50
White Coral Bells 36:249
White Covered Wagons 5:44
Who Broke My Window 10:19
Who Built the Ark? 59:32
Who Killed Cock Robin? 75:88
Who Made the Animals? 42:32
Who Made the Rainbow? 42:33
Who Stole My Chickens? 1:16
Who's Afraid of the Big Bad Wolf?
    66:52
Who's Complaining? 55:20
Whoa, Mule! Can't Get the Saddle
    On 63:64
Whoever Shall Have Peanuts 49:56
Whose Tail Is Curly? 3:16
Wiggle Song 4:22, 42:54
Wiggle Wiggle 72:48
Wild Mountain Thyme 76:22
Will the Circle Be Unbroken 40:133
Will Ye No Come Back Again? 46:22
Willie the Whistling Giraffe 66:105
Willie the Worm 55:44
Willoughby Wallaby Woo 19:20, 59:7
Wind Through the Olive Trees 2:30
Windmill 65:62
Wise Man and the Foolish Man, The
    26:12
Witch, The 47:7

Witches, Ghosts, and Goblins 47:6
With a Smile and a Song 66:59
With My Little Broom 74:35
Wolves A-Howling 63:79
Wonderful Things to Know 42:68
Word of God 42:15
Words 42:47
Words You Speak 9:36
Work Work Work 10:46
Workin' on the Railroad 59:40. *See also* Working on the Railroad
Working on the Railroad 38:132. *See also* Workin' on the Railroad
World in Harmony 29:36
Worms 71:56
Wriggledy Jiggledy Song 49:36

Y'a Un Rat 59:86
Yankee Doodle 22:62, 31:57, 33:140, 36:251, 38:122, 40:135, 44:48, 66:250
Yell and Scream 7:27
Yellow Submarine 66:74
You Are Special 42:44
You Better Not Giggle, Now Don't You Laugh, But I'm in Love with a Giraffe 56:188

You Can Be Anything 9:26
You Can't Build a Body on Junk 6:30
You Can't Get to Heaven 51:90. *See also* Oh, You Can't Get to Heaven
You Can't Make a Turtle Come Out 49:63
You Can't Say PSBPSBPSB on the Radio 56:81
You Gotta Sing 19:6, 59:56
You Sing a Song and I'll Sing a Song 59:63
You're a Hero at Last 11:16
You're as Sweet as Sugar on a Stick 56:103
You're Not Gonna Get Rich on Me 8:26
You're Something Special 42:137
Young Folks, Old Folks 51:56
Your Easter Basket 47:43
Your Neck's So Long 3:37
Your Power to Dream 18:9

Zebra, The 3:33
Zombis et les Loups-Garous, Les 59:81
Zoo, The 35:78
Zum Gali Gali 34:22

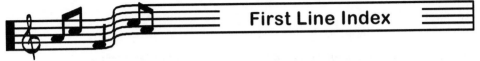

Songs that use a child's name are entered under Name.

A B C D E F G 31:72, 66:212
A, B, C, D, E, F, G 65:17
A-hunting we will go 15:44, 55:40
A is for armpit 56:119
A Paris, a Paris 62:73
A-tisket, a-tasket, a green and yellow
    basket 15:41, 31:63, 66:110,
    70:12
Abraham was a friend of God 42:83
Ah si mon moine voulait danser 64:66
Ainsi font, font, font 59:49, 62:112
Akinoyu hini Teruyamamomiji 67:8
Al Citron de un fandango 64:110
Alas, my love, you do me wrong
    33:53, 46:12
Alfie the elf was Santa's helper 2:56
Alison's camel has ten humps 64:93
All a-round the kitchen, Cocky doodle
    doodle doo 72:21
All around the cobbler's bench 31:46,
    36:194, 38:32, 50:58, 65:47,
    66:187, 70:26, 75:50
All around the mulberry bush 33:106
All by myself I can put on my coat
    42:43
All creatures of the earth and sky
    34:9
All hid, all hid 64:19
All I really need is a song in my
    heart 60:23
All in a wood there grew a tree
    33:134, 36:226
All night, all day 25:12
All night, all day, Mary Ann 67:16
All over the world at the end of day
    54:77
All that has life and breath, sing to
    the Lord 39:20
All the fish are swimming in the
    water 72:42
All things bright and beautiful 42:91,
    48:2
All together bend down 21:26
All you gotta say is no-woah 8:15
Allelu, allelu, allelu, allelu 34:17

Alligator, hedgehog, anteater, bear
    63:80
Aloha, aloha 71:9
Amazing grace! How sweet the sound
    33:11
Amazing grace, how sweet the sound
    34:39
Amen 1:60
America, I love you, believe me I do
    13:58
Americans are singing about Lady
    Liberty 29:6
Anansi, he is a spider 59:72
And so they called the little baby
    Shiny 6:4
And we hunted and we hunted and we
    hunted 63:36
Angels we have heard on high 23:2,
    28:22, 61:28
The animals are my friends 71:19
The ants go marching one by one
    24:10, 50:6, 64:78
Are you going to Scarborough Fair?
    33:114
Are you sleeping, are you sleeping
    39:26, 72:25
Around the corner 51:8
Around the corner, and under a tree
    50:74
As he walks on high, umbrella in his
    hands 17:36
As I came over yonders hill 63:46
As I get older I'm beginning to see
    56:170
As I have loved you, Love one
    another 54:83
As I help Mother dust 42:42
As I look outside my window 55:16
As I sat down one evening 22:284,
    40:38
As I walked out on the streets of
    Laredo 40:22
As I was a-going on down the road
    40:124
As I was a-gwine on down the road
    36:228

As I was a-walking one morning for pleasure 40:40
As I was going out for a walk 60:55
As I was going up the stair 1:46
As I was out walking one morning for pleasure 22:290, 36:96
As I was walking down the street 20:10, 36:47, 38:94, 50:78, 65:30
As I went to market 63:58
As soon as I finish the rest of this song 56:198
As we were playing with our toys, with our toys 25:4
Aserrin, aserran 62:75
The ash grove how graceful, how plainly 'tis speaking 67:13
Astronauts and airplane pilots see the world from far away 42:31
At home, whenever things go wrong 56:126
At Thanksgiving time when the winter has come 47:17
Au Clair de la Lune mon ami Pierrot 36:27
Aunt Anna came to our house to visit for a week 56:130
Autumn, autumn, gentle are the ways 5:8
Autumn day bright and gay 54:55
Autumn leaves are now falling 48:9
Away in a manger 61:10
Away in a manger, no crib for a bed 2:19, 28:32, 36:30, 45:24, 52:78

Baa, baa, black sheep 59:14, 59:84
Baa, baa, black sheep, have you any wool? 20:32, 31:3, 33:17, 33:32, 36:31, 38:47, 44:7, 66:223, 75:32
Baby, baby, wash your hands 35:32
Baby Beluga in the deep blue sea 19:18, 60:7
Baby bye, here's a fly 65:81
Baby Jaws, doot doot 55:46
Baby's going bye-bye 35:22
Back in the days when the world was flat 56:176
Baiu-baiushki-baiu 62:42
Baloo baleerie 77:20
Bamba bamba, bamba bamba 20:28
Barump, went the little green frog 50:14
Bassez mama, bassez down 64:92
Bats, cats, witches' hats 47:11

Bay bay, Bee bee 50:63
Be a friend, be a friend 9:26
Be glad! Be glad! 42:69
Be kind to your web-footed friends 51:124, 66:190
Be thankful unto him, for the Lord is good 42:21
Be ye kind to one another 42:39
The bear went over the mountain 38:112, 70:22
Because she shines, she shines 6:12
Bells are ringing 47:25
Bells are ringing, bells are ringing 2:36
Belly and Tubs went out in a boat 69:19
Benjy met a bear 51:48
Better obey your mother when she tells you what to do 10:12
Betty wants to be an astronaut 30:42
Beware of any stranger 73:18
The B-I-B-L-E, yes 26:14
The Bible is a special book 42:13
The Bible is a wonderful book 42:76
The Bible tells of Jesus 42:12
Big moon, bright moon, round and shiny white moon 4:38
Bim bom bi-ri bi-ri bom 1:56
Bimbo Bombo Tomkin Pie 69:20
Birds in the trees 76:30
Biscuits in the oven, gonna watch'em rise 60:9
Black cat, black cat 71:14
Black sheep, black sheep, where's your lamb? 63:57
Black socks, they never get dirty 51:54
Black widow's grieving 53:39
Bless this meal 39:20
Blow the man down, bullies 46:66
Bluebird, bluebird, through my window 38:83, 65:9
Bobby Shafto went to sea 75:13
Bobby Shafto's gone to sea 44:51, 65:39
Bobby Shaftoe's gone to sea 74:15
Boci boci tarka 1:88
Bokurawa minna ikiteiru 67:11
Bona nox, you're a silly ox 39:30
Bonnie Charlie's now awa' 46:22
Book of Mormon stories that my teacher tells to me 14:61
Boom Boom! ain't it great to be crazy 59:70

Boom, boom ain't it great to be crazy 20:30

Boom da li-da boom da li-da 1:84

Boomda, boomda, boomda 22:40

Boonda, boonda, boonda, Sarasponda 67:10

Born in the morning 53:37

Born this night in Bethlehem 2:31

Bought me a cat 22:264

Bow, bow, bow, Belinda 38:102

Boys and girls come out to play 44:12

Bring a torch, Jeannette, Isabella! 28:60

The Bronx Zoo is for me and you 30:10

Brown eyes, black eyes, blue eyes, green eyes 13:62

Brown girl in the ring 58:9

Bubble toes! Look at me I've got bubble toes 12:29

Buffalo gals, won't you come out tonight 40:9

Building sandy castles, look at me! 35:42

Bumping up and down in my little red wagon 59:5

Bun-da bun-da bun-da 1:30

The businessman is busy 53:33

Butterprint knocks at the milk-shop door 69:7

By yon bonnie banks and by yon bonnie braes 67:14

By'm bye, by'm bye 22:196, 77:14

Bye'm bye, bye'm bye 72:58

Bye 'n' bye, Bye 'n' bye 49:66

Bye, Baby Bunting 35:68, 38:14

Bye, Baby Bunting, Daddy's gone a hunting 41:67

Bye, Baby Bunting, your daddy's gone a hunting 77:15

Bye, bye, baby baby 72:61

Bye, bye, Baby Bunting 31:17

Bye-low, my baby 48:8

Call up your hounds and whistle up your dogs 22:92

Called to serve him, heav'nly King of glory 54:75

Calling all junk foods 6:28

Camptown ladies sing their song 66:150

A can of wriggling, wriggling worms 53:21

Can you clap, clap, clap, your hands 55:51

Candy man, candy man 64:26

A capital ship for an ocean trip 50:83

The car is big, the car is fast 35:16

Casper the friendly ghost 66:80

Cat fleas, rat fleas, hedgehog and bird 53:26

Cement mixer! putti, putti 66:121

C'est la belle nuit de Noel 57:57

The chapel doors seem to say to me 54:71

Charlie is my darling 46:20

Charlie over the ocean 64:95

Che che koolay 64:105

Chester, have you heard about Larry? 64:53

A cheval, gendarme 62:77

Chevaliers de la table ronde 46:62

Chick, chick, chick, chick, chicken 65:69

Chickens a crowin' on Sourwood Mountain 36:212

Chickens in the barnyard saying, saying 3:12

Children, bring your flute and drum 38:152

Children, go where I send thee 2:34

Children, go, I will send thee 36:154

Children, obey your parents 42:40, 42:97

Children who love Jesus watch for helpful tasks 42:37

Chomp, chomp, nibble nibble 50:34

Choose the animal you want to be 14:19

Christmas bells, ringing, singing 54:27

Christmas Day is coming, Santa will be here 47:22

Christmas Day will soon be here and I can hardly wait! 2:53

Christmas is coming 2:48, 45:14

Christmas is coming, it's almost here 47:26

Christmas is coming, the goose is getting fat 36:54

Christmas joys, Christmas toys 47:29

Christmas time's a coming 57:75

Christopher Columbus sailed the ocean blue 47:1

Christopher McCracken went a-fishing for some crabs 50:48

The circus has been here to visit our city 17:45

The circus is coming to visit our city 17:3

Clap! clap! clap! Hear the thunder when it rains 4:34

Clap, clap, clap your hands 38:86

Clap your hands up, up, up 21:14

Click your tongue 42:63

Climb, climb up sunshine mountain 27:24

Clipety, clipety, clipety clop 72:12

A clock without a "c" is still a lock 56:116

Clothes, clothes, where's my clothes 72:32

Cock-a-doodle-doo! My dame has lost her shoe 38:68, 75:43

C-O-F-F-E-E don't drink so much coffee! 39:29

Columbus discovered America in fourteen ninety two 47:2

Columbus sailed 'cross the Atlantic 5:9

Come all you Lacklan men 46:76

Come all you rounders if you want to hear 40:11

Come all you rounders listen here 46:52

Come along to the Land of Obey 10:6

Come and get your cotton candy 17:6

Come and praise the Lord our King 42:82

Come dance and sing around the ring 34:52

Come here and sing! 46:90

Come little child, it's sad but true 4:39

Come meet a little birdy friend of mine 39:12

Come play with me in the summertime 5:39

Come up, horsey, hey, hey 63:27

Come, let me tell great things the Lord has done 42:3

Come, let's be happy 36:168

Come, little children and sing Christmas carols 68:44

Come, they told me, pa-rum-pum-pum-pum 2:32

Come, ye shepherds, quickly gather 42:116

Come, ye thankful people, come 34:58, 36:57

Come, you little rascal, rock the baby's cradle 46:58

Computer people have a word 12:38

A cow can say "Moo," 42:47

A cow is the cleverest creature I've seen 3:15

The cradle is warm and there shall you sleep 41:66

A creepy crawly caterpillar lay upon a leaf 53:41

Creepy things on Halloween 47:3

Crystals in the window and stars in the sky 68:46

Cuanto le gusta 37:28

Cucanandy nandy cucanandy 1:52

The cuckoo in the forest, he sings his little song 39:10

Cum by yah, my Lord, cum by yah 77:22

Curly locks, curly locks 65:38

Curly locks, curly locks, will you be mine? 38:61

Curly locks, curly locks, wilt thou be mine? 44:50

Dad says that I've got his nose 56:100

Daddy, Daddy, Daddy 55:45

Daddy shot a bear 63:78

Daddy's taking us to the zoo tomorrow 40:45, 66:90

Dainty little snowflakes, soft and white 4:35

Dance to your daddy, my little baby 44:58, 77:26

Dance to your daddy, my little laddy 65:80

Dancing horses, dancing ladies 17:25

Daniel in the lion's den 60:45

Dare to do right! Dare to be true! 54:63

Dark brown is the river, golden is the sand 35:87

Dashing through the snow 36:142, 45:26, 57:60

Dashing through the snow in a one-horse open sleigh 2:10, 23:4, 31:78, 38:150, 61:20

Day after day the wagons are rolling 54:67

Day is done, gone the sun 36:216

Day-o missa day-o 60:15

Day-o, me say day-o 19:10

De colores, De colores se visten 60:96

Debbie got the radio 56:122
Deck the halls with boughs of holly 2:7, 23:8, 28:58, 36:62, 45:12, 61:12
Despite limitations, there's always room for change 18:13
Did Jesus really live again? 54:35
Did you ever go a-fishin' on a hot summer day 55:23
Did you ever go to meetin' Uncle Job 63:66
Did you ever hear of sweet Betsy from Pike 67:10
Did you ever see a cow in the sky? 36:66
Did you ever see a lassie 33:28, 36:64, 38:96
Did you ever see a lassie, a lassie, a lassie 24:24
Did you say your prayers last night 9:22
Diddle diddle dumpling, dumpling 71:48, 72:28
Diddle, diddle, dumping, my son John 38:76
Didn't my Lord deliver Daniel 43:16
Digging, digging, this is how we dig the ground 60:79
Dilly Dilly Pic-a-lil-li 69:12
Ding, dong, bell, Pussy's in the well 31:14
Ding-dong, the witch is dead! 66:28
Do as I'm doing, Follow, follow me! 54:57
Do the Baby Cakewalk 69:16
Do ye ken John Peel with his coat so gay 38:69
Do you know old Grandpa Gum? 12:22
Do you know that you're a person? 42:105
Do you want to feel happy? 9:34
Do your ears hang low? 16:30, 50:66, 51:75, 70:6
Do your ears hang low, do they wobble to and fro? 38:113
Doctor Foster went to Gloucester 38:41
Doctor Knickerbocker, Knickerbocker, number nine 64:90
Doctor, doctor, I feel sick 35:88
Doe, a deer, a female deer 66:44
Doing what you're taught to do, ought to do 12:58

Don't play in a vacant park 7:10
Don't put your finger up your nose 56:84
Don't send the children home 42:123
Dona nobis pacem 34:33
Dona nobis pacem, pacem 46:91
Down at the station, early in the morning 74:37
Down by the bay 59:2
Down by the bay (down by the bay) 24:22, 49:71
Down by the bay, where the water-melons grow 19:28
Down by the river where the green grass grows 65:66
Down by the station, early in the morning 33:37, 36:73, 38:129, 64:47
Down derry down, my Pippin, my Clown 69:27
Down in de meddy in a itty bitty poo 66:154
Down in the valley, the valley so low 40:28, 67:5
Down the way where the nights are gay 19:30
Driving in the car car car 72:38
Dromedaries have a hump 3:34
Du, du, liegst mir im Herzen 67:16
D'ye ken John Peel with his coat so gay 46:6

Each Halloween need not be mean 73:41
Early in the morning, Lord 42:109
Early one morning just as the sun was rising 46:10
Early Sunday morning when my parents were asleep 56:44
East side, West side 36:204
The eency weency spider went up the water spout 36:78
Eensy weensy spider went up the water spout 31:60, 33:38, 65:61, 66:231, 72:19, 74:22
Eentsy weentsy spider went up the water spout 35:58
Eight piggies in a row 58:23
El Coqui sings a sweet song at twilight 38:136
El sereno de mi calle 64:108
Eli, the priest met Samuel 42:18

Elves are dancing, reindeer prancing 47:24

En passant par la Lorraine 46:64

Every little tree, every little tree 5:32

Every little wish and every little dream 57:65

Every night and every morn 34:38

Everybody listen. Do what Simon says. 14:28

Everybody needs a friend, yes they do 12:42

Everybody stand up 10:16

Everyone tells me how to behave 7:21

Everyone was hoping we'd fall apart 13:35

Everything grows and grows 58:28

Ev're night when the sun goes in 46:50

Ev'ry body loves Saturday night 1:40

Ev'ry mornin' at seven o'clock 36:74

Ev'ry morning at seven o'clock 22:158

Ev'rybody loves Saturday night 49:34

Ev'rybody needs to be someone 42:106

Ev'rybody ought to know 42:114

Ev'rybody says, "Sit down" 55:49

Ev'rywhere you go there's stuff to waste your money on 56:120

Ezekiel cried, "Them dry bones!" 22:326

Ezekiel saw the wheel 43:14

Fairest Lord Jesus, ruler of all nature 48:4

Fais do do colas mon p'tit frere 64:64

Fais dodo Colin mon p'tit frere 60:77

Falling down, gently down 54:59

Farewell to old England forever 46:78

Farmer in the dell 15:40, 31:26, 33:41, 36:84, 38:79, 66:232

Farmer's in the dell 74:40, 75:20

Father and I went down to camp 36:251

Father, Mother, and Uncle John went to the doctor 72:15

Fathers are for lifting you 5:35

Feet, feet, feet, feet, what can you do with a pair of feet? 14:14

Feliz Cumple a nos 54:9

Fiddle-de-de, fiddle-de-de 75:22

Fiddle-dee-dee, fiddle-dee-dee 31:29

Fiddlers playing, dancers dancing 46:42

Fingernails can be so good looking, looking 12:24

Fingers, fingers, fingers, fingers 14:22

Fire! Fire! House on fire! 39:6

The first grasshopper jumped 50:10

First I am small, then I grow tall 42:46

The first noel the angel did say 23:18

The first Noel, the angels did say 2:14, 28:10, 36:86, 45:32, 61:22

The first Noel, the angels did sing 57:62

First you dig the peanuts 64:48

Fish, fish, fish, fish, tuna 12:50

The fish, it never cackles 49:68

Fisherman Peter on the sea 26:6

Five green and speckled frogs 59:1

Five little chickadees peeping at the door 38:77

Five little chickadees sitting on the floor 65:22

Five little ducks went out one day 60:47

Five little ducks went swimming one day 70:10

Five little monkeys running 'round the ring 17:18

Five little monkeys walked along the shore 50:52

Five little pumpkins sitting on a gate 59:6

Five little pussycats playing near the door 74:44

Five little speckled frogs 65:54

Flat foot floogee with the floy floy 66:140

Flea! Flea! 64:76

Flea flea-flea fly 49:77

Flow gently, sweet Afton 46:24

Fly, little butterfly, fly, fly, fly 3:23

Follow the drinking gourd 40:32

Follow the yellow brick road 66:37

Follow what the experts say 6:41

Following the leader, following the leader 14:9

The foolish man built his house upon the sand 26:12

For a bold bad man was this desperado 20:14

For friends and food 42:125

For God so loved the world 42:74

For she's got rings on her fingers 65:33

Fox went out in the chilly night
36:88, 66:88

Fox went out on a chilly night 33:42,
40:34

Foxes sleep in the forest 59:88

Free enterprise, let everybody do
whatever they do best 13:49

Freight train, freight train, going so
fast 40:36

Frere Jacques 1:114

Frere Jacques, Frere Jacques 25:24,
31:7, 38:134, 46:61, 62:109,
66:234

Frere Jacques, Frere Jacques, dormez
vous 36:91, 59:79

A friend of mine came by last night
and said 56:40

The friendly cow all red and white
68:24

The frog is a clever amphibian 3:21

A frog went a-courtin', he did ride
33:44, 66:182

The frog went a-courtin', he did ride
36:94

Froggie went a-courting and he did
ride, a-hum, a-hum 75:18

From Lucerne to Weggis fair 76:16

From the halls of Montezuma to the
shores of Tripoli 36:161

From the wide Pacific Ocean to the
broad Atlantic shore 19:8

From this valley they say you are
going 33:108, 40:85, 67:13

From under a shamrock one cold
winter's day 47:42

Frosty the snow man was a jolly,
happy soul 66:240

Frosty the snowman was a jolly,
happy soul 57:50

Fruit, fruit, give me some fruit 21:30

Fuzzy little caterpillar 38:22

Fuzzy Wuzzy was a bear 50:60

Galump! went the little green frog one
day 55:59

George Washington, George Washington 47:39

George Washington was a very good
man 13:22

Georgie Porgie, pudding and pie 44:13

Georgie Porgie, pudd'n' an' pie 31:67

Georgy Porgy, pudding and pie 75:33

Get up in the morning, what's the
first thing you do? 6:14

Giggle tickle fiddle little wiggle
around 56:39

Give a hip, hip hooray for the hippo
3:40

Give a little help to your neighbor
71:22

Give it rest and give it healthy food
18:29

Give me a heart of love, I pray 42:141

Give me joy in my heart 34:12

Give me that old-time religion 27:2

Give, said the little stream, Give, oh!
54:39

Glory to God in the highest! 42:110

Glory to Thee, my God 46:92

Go and hush the baby 56:165

Go for a natural high, high, high,
high 8:8

Go in and out the window 31:45,
33:47, 36:100

Go round and round the village
15:42, 38:85

Go tell Aunt Rhody 36:101, 38:116,
40:42, 67:4

Go tell it on the mountain 2:40, 40:43

Go to sleep, go to sleepy 63:65

Go to sleep now, my pumpkin 65:92

Go to sleep precious little baby 72:60

Go to sleepy, little baby 35:72, 36:102

Gobble strut, strut, gobble strut, strut
a little 3:13

God created ev'rything that's beautiful 68:26

God gave us the Bible 42:17

God is like my daddy 42:58

God is our wonderful God 42:92

God is so good 42:62, 48:12

God is stronger than the Devil 42:78

God knows ev'rything about me 42:59

God made heav'n and earth and sky
42:89

God made the fall for His beautiful
world 42:93

God made the world and ev'rything in
it 42:88

God made this world a lovely place
42:28

God of love, God above 42:112

God rest you merry, gentlemen 23:24,
28:54

God sees me in ev'rything I do 42:60

God who made the earth 42:139

God's own people waited many years 42:117

God's plan it is for me to be 42:96

Going on a picnic, leaving right away 59:64

The golden plates lay hidden 14:61

Golden slumbers kiss your eyes 25:28, 31:8, 38:16, 41:69, 74:6

Gonna jump down, turn around 36:190

Gonna jump down, turn around, pick a bale o'cotton 59:57

Gonna lay down my sword and shield 33:33

Gonna ride on the bus, cha-ka-cha 14:11

Gonna take a walk outside today 60:94

Good King Wenceslas look'd out 28:62

Good morning, Lord! It's a beautiful day 68:29

Good morning to you 38:115

Good night, ladies 31:73

Good night, toys, sleeping time is here 35:35

Goosey, goosey, gander, whither do you wander? 38:57

Goosey, goosey, gander, whither shall I wander? 31:10, 75:25

Gotta shake, shake, shake my sillies out 19:24, 59:31

Grandpapa, Grandpapa, I love my Grandpapa so 4:20

Great green gobs of greasy grimy gopher guts 51:30

Great Tom is cast 46:84

Groundhog Groundhog come on out and play 71:38

Guess what I'm doing. I'm playing charades 14:13

Guess who likes to throw a ball, my brother and I 4:16

A gust of fall wind 22:168

H A L L O HO HO 71:15

Ha ha thisaway 58:33

Ha, ha, this-a-way, ha, ha, that-a-way 66:168

Had a dog and his name was Blue 63:30

Had a little dog, his name was right 63:26

Had a little dog, skinny as a rail 55:39

Hambone, Hambone, where you been? 55:37

Hand in hand, you see us well 15:47

Hanu- Hanu- Hanukah 71:20

Hanukkah, Hanukkah, candle lights are glowing 47:20

Hanukkah is happiness 47:18

Happy birthday, happy birthday (name) dear friend 4:25

Happy birthday to you 31:7, 66:252

Happy, happy birthday, children, dear 54:9

Happy, happy, happy 42:70

Happy New Year to everyone at your house 5:20

Hark, hark! The dogs do bark 38:54

Hark! how the bells; Sweet silver bells 28:72

Hark! the herald angels sing 28:30, 36:114, 45:36, 52:96, 61:18

Haru ga kita haru ga kita 58:42

Haru korono 67:15

Have you ever heard of the Grease and Sweets? 6:10

Have you ever lived with a whiney child crying? 11:28

Have you ever thought to consider 56:112

Have you seen the ghost of Tom? 22:330

He does not have wings, but he flies thru the air 17:40

He escaped to America from a country where people aren't free 29:48

He goes on the prowl each night 66:206

He had a dream of peace and freedom 47:30

He is Lord; He is Lord 42:67

He owns the cattle on a thousand hills 42:132

He plants me like a seed and watches as I grow 42:142

He promised he'd buy me a fairing should please me 65:34

He rocks in the tree-tops all day long 20:42

He said, "Sing softer," 56:47

He'd fly through the air with the greatest of ease 24:28

He'll be comin' down the chimney when he comes 59:34

He's a dog with a bow-wow-wow-wow 3:10

He's got the whole world in His hands 20:48, 26:24, 36:118, 60:48

Head and shoulders, baby 64:54

Head and shoulders, baby 1 2 3 1:108

Head and shoulders, knees and toes 20:40, 42:53, 65:12

Head, shoulders, baby, one (clap) 49:33

Hear the jingle, hingle, jingle 2:51

Hear the wind blow, blow 4:30

Heavenly Father, I want to be 54:31

Heavenly sunshine, heavenly sunshine 27:22

Hecha lutz le'man avodah 34:22

Heigh-ho, heigh-ho, To make your troubles go 66:66

Hello, Hello 21:6

Hello, Hello! How are you? 42:86

Hello, Hello. You are beautiful 71:55

Hello there, farmer 55:60

Here are baby's eyes to look around 72:50

Here are my lady's knives and forks 38:24

Here comes a turtle 21:29

Here comes Peter Cottontail 66:243

Here comes Santa Claus 2:44

Here comes the ox cart 54:65

Here in America young men dared to dream 13:15

Here is the church, here is the steeple 35:53, 38:25

Here lie the bones of lazy Fred 51:50

Here stands a redbird 38:106

Here we are as friends together 68:38

Here we come a-caroling 2:6

Here we come a-caroling among the leaves so green 23:26

Here we come a wassailing 28:76

Here we come gath'ring nuts in May 38:81

Here we go cheerio, cheerio, cheerio 64:84

Here we go looby loo 24:26, 31:12, 36:116, 38:92, 64:83

Here we go round the mulberry bush 15:41, 33:84, 36:166, 38:80, 44:29, 65:14, 66:216, 74:45, 75:26

Here we go 'round the mulberry bush 31:6

Here we go sodeo, sodeo, sodeo 59:46

Here we sit like birds in the wilderness 50:35

Here's a song of Tinker and Peter 69:6

Here's my nose 42:104

Hevenu shalom Alechem 34:23

Hey, cross-eyed gopher 63:20

Hey diddle diddle, the cat and the fiddle 31:54, 38:67, 44:35, 66:226, 71:63, 75:28

Hey dum diddeley dum 64:12

Hey dum diddley dum 20:34

Hey ho, nobody home 36:119

Hey ho, to the greenwood now let us go 46:83

Hey Jack, what's in the sack? 56:82

Hey Jim along, Jim along Josie 36:141

Hey jim-a-long 1:66

Hey! There's a lizard on your head 5:30

Hey won't somebody come and play with me? 9:13

Hi-diddle-dee-dee,-an actor's life for me 66:70

Hi, ho, the rattlin' bog 64:44

Hi yo hi yo ip si ni ya 22:25

Hickety, pickety, my black hen 44:8

Hickory, dickory, dock 33:55, 35:61, 36:120, 44:2, 72:43

Hickory, dickory, dock, the mouse ran up the clock 31:23, 38:51, 66:232, 74:24

Higglety, pigglety, pop! 44:34

Higglety, Pigglety, pop! The dog had eaten the mop 65:48

High in the sky I go, walking in the sky I go 22:14

Himmel und Erde mussen ver-gehn 67:7

Hine ma tov umah nayim 34:51

Hippity hop to bed 38:13

Hippity hop to the barber shop 38:55

His shell's as green as pickles 68:21

Ho Ho Ho I'm the King of the jungle 71:44

The holly and the ivy 45:22

The holly and the ivy, When they are both full grown 28:57

Holy Bible, book divine 48:6

Holy, holy, holy 34:16

Holy, holy, holy, Lord God Almighty 34:10

Holy, Holy, ivy 47:21

Home is a place where I can be my-
    self 42:135
Hooray for Mister Lincoln 71:34
Hooray, Professor Un! Touche,
    Professor Un! 12:62
Hop, hop, hop, hop 3:14
Hop up and jump up and whirl
    'round 34:53
Hosanna! Hosanna! 42:64
Hot cross buns! 38:140, 44:40
Hot cross buns! Hot cross buns!
    31:16, 36:124, 66:224
How all the buildings come to be?
    10:43
How can we show our love today?
    42:38
How do you like to go up in a swing
    68:16
How do you obey God's word? 42:73
How many miles to Babylon? 44:27
How many people do you love? 4:13
How many roads must a man walk
    down 22:360
How much is that doggie in the
    window 66:82
How would you like a great big ice
    cream? 55:53
How would you like to go up in the
    swing, up in the air so blue?
    35:38
Huckleberry, gooseberry, raspberry
    pie 69:11
The human spirit oh where does it
    come from? 18:25
Humpty Dumpty sat on a wall 31:41,
    38:71, 44:35, 66:225, 75:29
Humpty Dumpty sat on the wall
    64:102
Hush a bye, don't you cry 22:268
Hush-a-by, don't you cry 77:18
Hush-a-bye baby, Thy cradle is green
    41:67
Hush-a-bye, baby, on the tree top
    44:60
Hush-a-bye, don't you cry 33:7, 38:11,
    72:59
Hush-a-bye, my darling 69:18
Hush, little baby, don't say a word
    22:98, 25:18, 31:20, 33:62,
    36:126, 38:12, 40:74, 65:91,
    66:181, 70:38, 72:57, 74:9, 77:10
Hush, little love-bugs, don't say a
    word 53:53

Hush, little rooster with your cock-a-
    doo-dle-doo 42:19
Hush'n bye, don't you cry 62:36
Hush-you-bye, don't you cry 46:56
Hut-sut Rawlson on the rillerah
    66:146

I always have a happy feeling 54:71
I am a child of God 14:7
I am a child of God, and He has sent
    me here 54:7
I am climbing up the tower 72:54
I am happy for my home 42:35
I am happy today for the sunshine
    54:47
I am learning how to spell, and I
    think I do it rather well 9:7
I am quiet, very quiet 42:25
I am slowly going crazy 50:69, 51:77,
    64:79
I am so glad that Jesus loves me 48:1
I am with thee and will keep thee
    42:122
I asked my mom to take me shopping
    56:199
I brush my teeth in the morning 72:29
I buyed me a little dog 63:28
I can hear the snow melting all
    around 68:11
I can say this Bible thought 42:16
I can sing the blues, write a poem to
    you 56:133
I can't tell when friends are true, but
    God can! 42:108
I come from Alabama with a banjo on
    my knee 40:79
I come from Alabama with my banjo
    on my knee 33:98, 36:179,
    38:126
I come from Salem City with my wash-
    pan on my knee 22:180
I come to town the other night 66:184
I could while away the hours 66:30
I danced in the morning when the
    world was begun 34:18
I don't brush my teeth and I never
    comb my hair 56:22
I don't care for underwear 51:53
I don't think my teacher likes me
    56:160
I don't wanna go to school 56:128
I don't want a pickle 40:77

I dreamed I saw Joe Hill last night 40:64

I eat baby chipmunks 56:35

I feel blue, I feel numb 49:86

I feel my Savior's love 54:37

I found happiness, I found peace of mind 42:144

I gave my love a cherry that had no stone 40:87

I gave my love a cherry that has no stone 33:110

I get angry at myself, I get mad, mad, mad 10:36

I got a camel for Christmas 35:84

I got a teacher, she's so mean 56:36

I got an old mule and her name is Sal 36:81

I got sheep 22:172

I had a baby brother, his name was Tiny Tim 55:14

I had a bed (I had a bed) 55:13

I had a cat and the cat pleased me 24:12, 40:6, 67:5

I had a friend named Jake, he was a happy kid 56:42

I had a hen, no eggs she gave 49:74

I had a horse, his name was Bill 49:18, 51:72

I had a little cow by the barnyard gate 55:61

I had a little dog and his name was Paul 49:9

I had a little dreidel 55:22

I had a little nut tree 38:53, 44:41

I had a little nut tree, nothing would it bear 33:65, 36:127, 75:64

I had a little rooster, and the rooster pleased me 35:82

I had a rooster and the rooster pleased me 50:22

I have a dear old daddy 19:16, 66:152

I have a dog and his name is Rags 64:42

I have a dog his name is Rags 20:38

I have a fam'ly here on earth 54:25

I have a Friend who loves me 42:5

I have a garden, a lovely garden 54:51

I have a little dreydel 59:20

I have a little shadow that goes in and out with me 68:12

I have a little sister who's not at all like me 42:137

I have a ship on the ocean 76:28

I have a small recorder here inside 9:44

I have hands that will clap, clap, clap! 42:45

I have ten little fingers and they all belong to me 35:60

I have two little hands folded snugly and tight 54:73

I hear a mumble 55:20

I hear thunder 65:56

I hear, I hear, I hear with my (ears) 21:18

I heard the bells on Christmas day 28:37

I hold in my hand a wonderful book 42:15

I just keep trusting my Lord 42:61

I know a little pussy 65:50

I know a little pussy, her coat is silver gray 36:128

I know a man named Dirty Bill 50:39, 51:35

I know a man named Michael Finnegan 51:79, 64:79

I know a name, a glorious name 54:23

I know an old lady who swallowed a fly 66:125

I know my Father lives and loves me too 14:7, 54:7

I know my Father loves me 54:25

I know where I'm goin' 46:55

I learned a trick, learned it quick 7:18

I like holidays, you do too 35:90

I like me. I'm okay, I'm all right 10:39

I like spring 68:10

I like to eat, eat, eat 19:32

I like to eat, eat, eat apples and bananas 60:70

I like to eat, eat, eat 55:19

I like to go bowling with my friend Bert 60:89

I like to play in the snow, you know 5:17

I like your eyes; I like your nose 66:14

I live at one house with my mother 11:68

I looked into the mirror-what did the mirror say? 56:182

I looked out the window and what did I see? 54:43

I lost my pants, has anybody seen them? 56:144

I love America; yes I do 13:9
I love it when I go sliding 35:46
I love Jesus, he loves me 42:71
I love little kitty, her coat is so warm 31:65
I love little pussy, her coat is so warm 33:66, 36:130, 38:46, 44:6, 66:101, 75:30
I love mother, she loves me 54:11
I love my daddy, though he always yells at me 56:162
I love the flowers, I love the flowers 4:28
I love to go awandering 36:112
I love to hear my father play the piano 30:22
I love to see the temple, I'm going there someday 14:25
I love you, every valentine says I do 5:21
I love your eyes, I love your ears 56:140
I may never march in the infantry 26:4
I miss Grandma, 'cause Grandma isn't here 56:138
I must learn to take the blame 42:48
I need a friend, you need a friend 8:22
I need you like a doughnut needs a hole 56:24
I never did like you, anyhow 56:28
I never have seen me a happier lass 66:246
I never thought I'd fall again, 'least not like this 56:99
I often go walking in meadows of clover 54:13
I open my Bible book and read 42:10
I pledge allegiance to America 5:43
I point to myself 55:18
I pushed my baby brother off the roller coaster 56:29
I remember Ellis Island as our ship rounded the Battery 29:20
I ride an old paint 40:52
I ride an old paint, I ride an old dam 36:131
I rock my doll, I rock my doll 35:25
I roll the ball to Daddy 35:27, 64:74
I sat next to the Duchess at tea 50:26
I saw a peanut stand, heard a rubber band 66:56
I saw three ships come sailing by 38:139, 44:43

I saw three ships come sailing in 45:30
I saw three ships come sailing in, On Christmas Day 28:44
I say the Rock Island Line is a mighty good road 40:89
I scream, you scream, we all scream for ice cream 66:143
I see you see we see the see-saw 35:47
I shall always love December 54:27
I sing a new song since Jesus 42:119
I sing a song of the saints of God 34:42
I sit down, then stand up 42:52
I sneaked into the kitchen in the middle of the night 56:32
I take a block, another block 35:26
I take my little hand and clap clap clap 72:18
I talk to God wherever I may be 42:80
I thank God for my father 42:41
I thank thee, dear Father in heaven above 54:21
I think I'm happy now, just look at me 11:30
I think I'm pretty lucky, I'm sure you'll agree 56:53
I think the world is glorious and lovely as can be 54:53
I think when I read that sweet story of old 54:33
I told the truth, I'm so happy I've got to start dancing 10:22
I used to have a sister, until just recently 56:64
I used to know a caterpillar 56:186
I used to live on the mountain-top 40:81
I want I want a malted 50:36
I want to be kind to everyone, for that is right you see 54:49
I want to be your friend 47:32
I want to go teach the Gospel 54:75
I was all alone 56:79
I was born about ten thousand years ago 40:54
I was standing by the window on one cold and cloudy day 40:133
I wash my hands before I eat 42:49
I watch the rain coming down 68:48
I wear my silk pajamas in the summer when it's hot 25:8
I went to a dance and the animals came 59:60

I went to the animal fair 36:22, 66:87, 70:18
I went to the dance and the animals come 31:18
I went to the movies tomorrow 55:30
I will listen 42:11
I will only have a sweet after I eat 6:44
I will sing of the love of the Lord forever 42:27
I will sing of the mercies of the Lord forever 42:127
I will sing praise to God 42:84
I wish I was a mole in the ground 63:25
I wish I was a ranasasorius 50:62
I wish I was in de land ob cotton 36:68
I wish I was in the land of cotton 33:31
I wish that I were a red balloon 35:44
I with I were a fithy in the thea 51:18
I with I were a wittle thugar bun 49:10
I wonder how it felt to wake up in the belly of a whale 42:120
I wonder if I'm growing 59:9
I wonder, when He comes again 54:37
I would be true for there are those who trust me 34:54
I wouldn't wanna be a movie star 56:180
I'd come to your house for tea, but your door is never locked 56:148
I'd fight a hundred dragons and not be afraid 11:4
I'd like the world to merrily sing a love song about Miss Liberty 29:36
I'd like to be under the sea 60:75
I'd like to dance and tap my feet 66:68
I'd like to ride on a sea horse 3:20
I'll find you a dress that is sewn with 11:23
I'll meet you in the middle on Valentine's Day 47:37
I'll obey my mother and father 42:134
I'll praise the Lord in the morning 42:128
I'll sing you one O! green grow the rushes O! 36:106
I'll sing you one-o? 33:48
I'll take the leg from some old table 49:90

I'm a fur fur furry squirrel 71:12
I'm a little acorn, small and round 51:78
I'm a little city cowboy, I wear real cowboy suits 30:14
I'm a little cookie, yes I am 31:4, 55:32
I'm a little teapot, short and stout 16:32, 35:52, 38:95, 66:109, 74:28
I'm a pumpkin round and plump 47:4
I'm a special person 42:100
I'm a 3-toed, triple-eyed, double-jointed dinosaur 56:20
I'm a V. I. P. in my family 4:7
I'm a very happy person 39:7
I'm a walkin' walkin', walkin' 72:9
I'm a work of art, but I haven't got a heart 73:31
I'm a'gonna wrap myself in paper 31:52, 66:130
I'm about to climb in the jungle, ungle gym 35:43
I'm being eaten by a boa constrictor 51:33
I'm bringing home a baby bumblebee 55:9
I'm Captain Dependable; you can always count on me 12:60
I'm Did (I'm Didn't) 10:9
I'm flashing red and green 73:22
I'm going to Australia to get a cute, cuddily koala 30:32
I'm going up, up, up 42:124
I'm gonna lay down my sword and shield 40:26
I'm gonna leave ol' Texas now 20:22
I'm gonna sing when the spirit says sing 26:28
I'm gonna wrap myself in paper 20:44
I'm in the mood for singing 60:52
I'm late, 'cause I missed my bus 56:159
I'm looking out the window 72:40
I'm my friend, my very special friend 12:53
I'm not one of the crowd 42:143
I'm not small, I'm so tall 55:25
I'm one inch taller than I used to be 42:102
I'm only an ingrate in an ingrate world 11:41
I'm peeling my banana, banana 55:50
I'm Popeye, the sailor man 49:26, 51:121, 66:77

I'm pressed and dressed and ready to go 12:35

I'm so glad when Daddy comes home 54:17

I'm standing naked on the kitchen table 56:166

I'm still a kid, barely eight years old 56:114

I'm the captain of a ship called Love 29:60

I'm the one who takes him dinner 11:58

I'm the phone girl, I'm the phone girl 30:38

I'm the Statue of Liberty, I stand with beauty and majesty 30:28

I'm trying to be like Jesus 54:61

I'm wild about horns on automobiles 50:67

I've a centipede body 53:1

I've always wanted a big brother 42:72

I've been workin' on the railroad 36:135

I've been working on the railroad 33:70, 38:132, 59:40, 66:158

I've been working on the railroad all the live-long day 40:59, 67:12

I've got a dog and my dog's name is Cat 56:69

I've got a home in glory land that out-shines the sun 26:22

I've got a little sister and my sister's name is Gail 56:72

I've got a mule, her name is Sal 22:116, 40:30

I've got a sausage pizza in my 12-string case 51:49

I've got my very own set of designer genes 8:19

I've got one head, one heart, too 49:8

I've got peace like a river 27:8

I've just had my orange juice 60:37

I've seen some mean and very hairy, scary dinosaurs 56:147

I've sung this song, but I'll sing it again 40:103

I've traveled all over this country 40:2

I've wandered all over this country 22:192

Ich weiss nicht 46:34

If a body meet a body 66:203

If a body meet a body comin' through the rye 70:24

If all the raindrops were lemon drops 65:57

If I could fly like a bird 35:40

If I could have a windmill 65:62

If I had a dinosaur, just think what we could do 59:36

If I had a hammer, I'd hammer in the morning 40:56

If I were a bunny, I'd tell you what I'd do 71:46

If I were a flower growing wild and free 56:61

If I were a little bird, high in the sky 74:46

If the cookie jar is empty 13:38

If there's a fire, we hear an alarm 21:35

If you believe in me, then you and I will always be a team 29:44

If you chance to meet a frown 54:41

If you don't answer my questions well 22:206

If you go down in the woods today 66:98

If you think your friend's in trouble 8:2

If you're bored and feeling tired 10:46

If you're happy and you know it 74:38

If you're happy and you know it, clap your hands! 49:28, 66:176, 70:20

If you're looking for a buddy with a hug to share 58:35

If you're wearing green, stand up 55:48

If you've got a kid who complains all the time 56:136

If your dad comes home and he's all worn out 9:4

Ilu hotci hotci onu 34:26

In a cabin in a wood 70:4

In a cabin in the wood 64:39

In a cavern, in a canyon 31:27, 33:26, 36:55, 40:20, 50:40, 51:87, 66:164, 67:6

In a minute, in a while 12:64

In come Daddy from the plow 63:22

In Dublin's fair city, where girls are so pretty 66:196

In eighteen hundred and forty-one 36:188

In our costumes prancing round 47:8

In Plymouth Town there lived a maid 46:18

In seventeen seventy-six, my friend,
    Americans were Englishmen
    13:12
In the beginning God made the
    heaven and earth 42:90
In the Big Rock Candy Mountain
    22:354
In the ev'ning the nightingale 39:9
In the garden under the hedge 47:44
In the house next door to me 66:94
In the leafy treetops the birds sing
    54:45
In the little village of Bethlehem 2:22
In the Scrubit Land of Clean all the
    children's teeth are white 12:40
In the town where I was born lived a
    man 66:74
The incey wincey spider went up the
    water spout 38:28
Indian brothers strong and brave
    47:13
Insure domestic tranquility 13:40
Irene, goodnight 40:48
Is this what it means to have courage,
    to do something when you're
    11:14
It ain't gonna rain 31:77
It came upon a midnight clear 61:8
It came upon the midnight clear
    28:15, 45:44
It happens when a baby's crying 18:39
It is wonderful to know that Jesus
    42:68
It isn't any trouble just to S M I L E
    49:65
It takes courage to do the things you
    should 11:9
It was last Monday morning 63:38
It was nothing less than a miracle
    13:24
It's a rosebud in June 76:25
It's always fun when Grandpa comes
    54:23
It's autumn time, it's autumn time
    54:55
It's fun to take the ferry to the Statue
    of Liberty 29:10
It's mine, but you can have some
    59:18
It's my responsibility to do my part
    42:95
It's not that easy bein' green 66:10
It's only through knowledge that you
    come to understanding 18:16

It's raining, it's pouring 31:55, 33:69
It's raining, it's pouring, the old man
    is snoring 36:134
It's spring outside my window 42:34
It's time to play the music 66:4
It's time to sing a song or two 60:67
It's time to take a break 17:21
Itchy scritchy, scratch my head 53:7
Itiskit, Itaskit, a green and yellow
    basket 36:133

Jack and Jill went up the hill 31:41,
    33:75, 36:138, 38:39, 44:14,
    65:26, 66:223, 75:36
Jack, be nimble 38:104
Jack, can I ride? 63:76
Jack was every inch a sailor 64:116
Jaiye kirumbe rumbe 1:70
Jamais on na vu vu vu 64:62
Janet lives in England 60:84
Jeremiah, blow the fiah 65:83
Jesse James was a lad, he killed many
    a man 40:62
Jesus came to John the Baptist 54:69
Jesus had a fam'ly just like you and
    me 42:98
Jesus has risen, Jesus, our friend
    54:35
Jesus is living in heaven today 42:1
Jesus, Jesus, I love Jesus 42:65
Jesus, Jesus, Jesus in the morning
    26:16
Jesus loves me, Jesus loves me 42:66
Jesus loves me, this I know 26:20
Jesus loves the little children 48:5
Jesus once was a little child 54:31
Jesus our brother, kind and good 2:41
Jesus, our brother, kind and good
    28:26, 36:92
Jesus said, "Eat this bread, and
    remember me" 42:14
Jesus said, "I will be with you" 42:77
Jesus said love every one, treat them
    kindly too 54:49
Jesus used his feet to walk, walk,
    walk 42:8
Jesus wants me for a sunbeam 27:28,
    54:39
Jesus worked in many ways 42:7
John Brown's baby had a cold upon
    his chest 51:22
John Brown's baby had a cold upon its
    chest 16:30, 66:177

John Jacob Jingleheimer Schmidt 50:90, 51:9, 64:75, 66:134

Jolly old Saint Nicholas 23:12

Jolly old Saint Nicholas, lean your ear this way 45:16

Jolly old St. Nicholas 2:60

Joseph dearest, Joseph mine 2:30

Joseph was an old man 28:69

Joshua fit the battle of Jericho 43:10

Joshua fought the Battle of Jericho 36:146

Joy fills my heart in the place where I stay 68:31

Joy to the world! 61:6

Joy to the world the Lord is come 45:34

Joy to the world! the Lord is come 23:16, 28:53

Joy to the world, the Lord is come 2:15

Joybells ringing, children singing 68:42

Joyful, joyful, joyful, we adore thee 34:14

Jump down, turn around 31:70

Jump, jump, (clap, clap) 55:10

June brings tulips 76:6

Junk food junkie, she's a junk food junkie 6:19

Just like the birds that keep on flying 58:45

Just walkin' along out in the woods 42:131

Just whistle while you work 66:62

Kangaroo, kangaroo, look at you 3:35

Keep the commandments; keep the commandments 54:63

The keeper would a-hunting go 36:148, 46:8

Kitten in the sun 3:8

Knock at the door, Peep in 38:25

Knock, knock, knock, then run, run, run 5:22

Kookaburra sits in the old gum tree 70:32

Kookaburra sits on an old gum tree 36:150, 46:75

Koom bachur atsel 1:118

Kum ba yah, my Lord 26:26

Kum-ba-ya, Lord, kum-ba-ya 19:22

Kumbaya, Lord, kumbaya 60:31

La la la la Tamzara 1:128

Lady bird, lady bird fly away home 75:31

Landlord, fill the flowing bowl 46:32

Late at night when Mommy and Daddy have gone out 56:50

Lavender's blue, diddle, diddle 44:54

Lavender's blue, dilly, dilly 20:18, 33:79, 36:151, 38:66, 75:38

Lazy days of summer 5:40

Lazy Mary, will you get up 31:64, 33:80, 35:56, 36:153, 38:62, 65:8, 72:24, 75:41

Lazy Mary, will you get up, will you get up 66:228

Left, right, left 53:17

Left, right, left, right, marching along pah, pah, pah, pah 4:24

Leroy is a late bloomer 56:102

Let us break bread together 27:12

Let us gather in a circle 54:21

Let's all sing a song together 39:7

Let's ban Halloween forever 73:11

Let's be friends, let's be friends 47:35

Let's do the numbers rumba 60:60

Let's get the wiggles out, one, two, three 4:22

Let's go bowling in Bowling Green 50:64

Let's go hunting, says Risky Rob 36:40

Let's go trick or treatin', Think of what we'll soon be eatin' 73:26

Let's hear the rhythm on the (instrument) 21:16

Let's make some noise, we girls and boys 58:26

Let's sing a song of a bear, bear, bear 3:32

Let's watch the man dance with (name) 21:20

The lightly rain, the sprightly rain 68:12

Lightly row, lightly row 38:138, 67:4, 76:10

Like an aimless traveler 56:68

Listen to the horses clipping, clopping 59:50

Listen to the noises, listen to them all 35:28

Listen to the plink, plink, plink 42:24

Little Arabella Miller found a furry caterpillar 50:43

Little Arabella Miller found a hairy caterpillar 74:23

Little Arabella Miller had a fuzzy caterpillar 64:37

Little barefoot boy, running through the sand 42:121

The little bells of Christmas say 2:49

Little Betty Blue lost her holiday shoe 71:24

The little black bull came down the meadow 63:54

Little Bo Peep has lost her sheep 36:156

Little Bo-Peep has lost her sheep 31:74, 38:65, 44:16, 66:221, 75:34

Little boxes on the hillside 40:69

Little Boy Blue, come blow on your horn 31:15

Little Boy Blue, come blow your horn 38:70, 44:15, 66:226, 75:44

Little bumble bee, little bumble bee 3:22

Little bunnies and lambs are home for the night 35:34

Little David, play on your harp 43:12

Little dolly, soft and pretty 35:24

Little drops of water, Little grains of sand 38:63

Little echo voice (little echo voice) 14:4

A little girl/boy went walking 55:55

Little Jack Horner sat in a corner 31:54, 38:36, 75:45

Little Jack Horner sat in the corner 36:157, 44:18, 65:71, 66:225

Little Jesus, sweetly sleep 2:42

Little Miss Muffet sat on a tuffet 31:66, 38:40, 66:227

Little Miss Muffet sat on her tuffet 71:61

Little Miss Muffet, she sat on a tuffet 44:18

Little Peter Possum had a fly upon his ear 24:2

Little Peter Rabbit had a flea upon his ear 64:36

Little Peter Rabbit had a fly upon his ear 50:19

Little Peter Rabbit had a fly upon his nose 35:76

Little pioneer children gath'ring berries for food 54:67

Little purple pansies touched with yellow gold 54:51

Little red bird of the lonely moor 46:40

Little Sally Saucer sitting in the water 64:86

Little Sally Saucer, sitting in the water 65:23

Little Sally Waters, sitting in the sun 38:101

Little Tommy Tinker sat upon a clinker 64:74

Little Tommy Tucker, sing for your supper 31:75

Little Tommy Tucker sings for his supper 38:35, 44:17, 75:48

Living in this crazy world 32:24

Lo, how a rose e'er blooming 28:38, 39:23

London Bridge is falling down 15:43, 31:61, 33:83, 38:105, 44:30, 65:24, 66:230, 75:58

London Bridge is falling down, falling down 36:160

The lone wild bird in lofty flight 34:48

Long, long ago God made this great big world 42:29

Loo loo loo little baby, close your eyes 4:15

Look all the world over, there's no one like me 42:50

Look at her, look at him 73:6

Look for a grandma or mother with children 7:28

Looking in a mirror, what do I see? 14:21

Lord, I want to be a Christian in my heart 42:140

The Lord is a great God 42:107

The Lord is great! Ev'rybody sing 26:18

The Lord is my shepherd 68:40

Lost my partner, what'll I do? 15:45, 31:21, 33:124

Lots of fish in Bonavist' Harbor 64:112

Lou, Lou, skip to my Lou 36:210

Love, love, fam'ly love 42:136

Lovely Lady of Liberty, how beautiful you are 29:40

The lowly germ is very small 12:18

The luckiest creature in all of the world is a fish 3:19

Lucy Locket lost her pocket 31:51, 44:19

Lulabel, where are you going? 50:50

Lullaby, and good night 31:11, 35:70, 38:17, 74:11, 77:31
Lullaby, my Jamie 46:60
Lullaby, my pretty one 41:67
Lullay, thou little tiny child 28:35, 61:16
Lulloo lullay, by night and day 77:12
Lully, lullay, thou little, tiny child 2:39

Mademoiselle, vou lez vous danser la bastringue 64:67
Mairzy doats and dozy doats and liddle lamze divey 66:138
Make channels for the streams of love 34:50
Mama don't allow no guitar playin' round here 40:71
Mama don't 'low no banjo playin' round here 49:59
Man and a woman bought a little pig 63:50
Marching! Marching! 42:51
Marianne, oh, Marianne, oh, won't you marry me? 66:191
Marvin doesn't like the new baby 56:154
Mary had a little lamb 31:58, 32:32, 36:163, 38:58, 44:20, 65:16, 75:60
Mary, Mary, quite contrary 44:21
Mary wore her red dress, red dress 31:24, 58:22
Masakari katsuida Kintaro 62:78
Matthew, Mark, Luke and John, went to bed with their britches on 64:18
May Day, May Day 5:33
May there always be sunshine 55:24
Maybe you know someone who is not as smart as you 9:28
Me and my horse go hippity hoppity 15:47
Me and my wife and my wife's pap 22:82
Me and you just singing on the train 56:38
Me stone is me stone 64:111
Meat, milk and grain 6:16
Meow, meow, come little kitty! 39:17
Merrily, caroling, singing joy for Christmas 2:48
Merrily we roll along 38:59

Merry-go-round, Merry-go-round 30:18
Michael, row the boat ashore 20:26, 27:10, 34:30, 40:73
Michael, row the boat ashore, Hallelujah 67:14
Michaud est mon te' dans un grand pommier 60:57
Michaud est monte dans un beau pommier 64:63
'Mid pleasure and palaces though we may roam 33:60
The midnight hour is creepin' 53:45
Mighty pretty motion too-do-la 1:2
Mine eyes have seen the glory of the coming of the Lord 36:32
Miss Lucy had a baby 49:40, 51:82, 65:78
Miss Mary Mack 1:78
Miss Polly had a dolly that was sick, sick, sick 49:39
Miss Polly had a dolly who was sick, sick, sick 55:41, 65:77
Miss Quiss! Look at this! 69:26
M-i-s-s-i-s-s-i-p-p-i, that used to be so hard to spell 66:157
Mister Earth, I love you Mister Earth 11:60
Mister Lister sassed his sister 69:24
Mister Rabbit, Mister Rabbit, yours ears mighty long 63:16
Mister Stand-On-One-Leg, I've seen you at the zoo 3:25
Mister Sunshine, Mister Sunshine 4:27
Mister wind is a mischief 4:31
Mistress Mary, quite contrary 38:38
Mistress Mary, quite contrary, how does your garden grow? 31:67
Mom and Dad are always right and I am always wrong 56:88
Mom came home from the store last night 56:70
Monkey in the treetops swinging with ease 3:29
The monkey married the baboon's sister 31:44
Monte sur un elephant 64:58
More than the rainbow loves the sky 9:39
The more we get together 31:28, 59:16
The more we serve, the more we love 12:11

Morning has broken like the first
  morning 34:8
The most chivalrous fish of the ocean
  46:46
Mother dear, I love you so 54:13
Mother, I love you, Mother I do 54:11
Mother needs two little hands to help
  her 5:36
Mud, mud, glorious mud 50:79, 51:31
Mummy's taking us to the zoo tomor-
  row 59:24
Muskrat, muskrat, dog-gone your
  daddy's soul 63:21
Muss i denn, muss i denn 46:36
My body machine is super keen 6:6
My Bonnie lies over the ocean 33:87
My brother thinks he's a banana
  56:57
My brother threw up on my stuffed
  toy bunny 56:62
My country, 'tis of thee 33:13
My dad's the biggest guy, and my
  dad's the strongest guy 9:10
My daddy is my fav'rite pal 54:17
My daddy said, "Wash your face"
  55:34
My daddy said, "Wash your face, wash
  your face" 56:60
My Dame hath a lame, tame crane
  46:87, 75:73
My dentist is an awfully nice man
  56:24
My dog's bigger than your dog 66:84
My father calls me his little child as
  he sits me on his knee 29:56
My father hunted a kangaroo 51:32
My home's in Montana, I wear a
  bandanna 67:7
My kite is white with stripes of blue
  30:46
My light is but a little one 54:79
My little pony likes to trot 3:9
My love's an arbutus 46:28
My mommy drives a dump truck
  56:66
My mommy said not to put beans in
  my ears 40:8
My mother and father know where I
  am 42:4
My mother ran away today 56:95
My old hen's a good old hen 63:44
My paddle's keen and bright 76:12
My teacher told me I should never tell
  a lie 9:42

My thumbs are starting to wiggle
  42:54
My tongue is such a little thing
  42:103
My uncle had an old mule 63:62
My wife and I lived all alone 66:166

(Name) had a little car 72:35
(Name) give it to (name) 21:10
(Name) move over, Make room for
  (name) 21:11
(Name) play your horn right now
  21:12
Namo Ganesha 62:65
Nancy's gone to the hospital, hospital,
  hospital 21:34
Nanny Banny Bumble bee 69:21
Nano hana batakeni 67:15
Never cook your sister in a frying
  pan 56:92
Nina nana cocolo della mama 1:74
No matter how young a prune may be
  50:27
No No No I like to say No 71:29
No one else can smile my smile 4:9
Nobody knows the trouble I've seen
  33:89
The north wind doth blow 44:10,
  75:66
The north wind doth blow, And we
  shall have snow 38:33
Now, didn't it rain, children 43:2
Now, go on, old 'gator 63:74
Now I lay me down to sleep 31:80
Now in a hole (now in a hole) 49:22
Now is the close of day 39:21
Now, Old King Cole was a merry old
  soul 31:30, 66:229
Now run along home and jump in the
  tub 49:62
Now the day is over 33:91, 34:32
Now the day is over, Night is drawing
  nigh 38:21, 77:29
Now the government works like a
  great 13:27
Now unto the King eternal 42:129
Now, you better not giggle, now don't
  you laugh 56:188
Now you may think 51:123
Now you may think (now you may
  think) 49:92
Numi numi yeldate 62:45

O beautiful for spacious skies 33:14, 36:20

O Christmas tree, O Christmas tree 2:9, 23:6, 28:66, 45:18

O come, all ye faithful 2:17, 28:41, 36:172, 45:20, 52:64, 61:4

O come, little children, o come, one and all 2:37, 45:40

O come, O come, Emmanuel 28:9

O hangman, O hangman, O hold up your rope 46:38

O Hanukkah, O Hanukkah, come light the menorah 36:110

O how lovely is the evening 48:7

O little town of Bethlehem 2:18, 28:46, 36:177, 61:14

O once upon a time in Arkansas 36:24

O pioneers! 5:45

O, the summer time is coming 76:22

O where, o where has my little dog gone? 36:248

Oats and beans and barley grow 60:13

Oats, peas, beans, and barley grow 24:8, 33:93, 36:171, 38:89, 66:228, 75:68

Obwisana, obwisana, obwisana 64:111

Of all the beast-es in the world 63:75

Off we go on a piggy back ride 69:14

Oh, a cowhand's life is a mighty fine life 71:50

Oh, a driving we will go 72:36

Oh, a-hunting we will go 38:88

Oh a-hunting we will go 36:19

Oh, Alouette, gentille Alouette 66:194

Oh Chester, have you heard about Harry 51:25

Oh chicken lips and lizard hips and alligator eyes 19:34

Oh, come, oh, come, let us worship today 42:23

Oh! dear, what can the matter be? 36:174

Oh, dear! what can the matter be? 67:9

Oh, dear, what can the matter be? 33:94, 44:52, 70:30

Oh, do you know the muffin man 36:165, 38:34, 75:47

Oh, do you know the muffin man, the muffin man 64:98

Oh, do you remember sweet Betsy from Pike 22:186

Oh, don't you remember sweet Betsy from Pike 33:128, 36:214, 40:108

Oh Dunderbeck, oh Dunderbeck, how could you be so mean? 36:76

Oh, every single morning and every single night 71:36

Oh freedom, oh freedom 47:31

Oh, give me a home where the buffalo roam 33:56, 36:121, 40:50, 67:7

Oh, give me some fruit, fruit 68:19

Oh, Hanukkah, Oh, Hanukkah 38:144

Oh, have you seen the muffin man, the muffin man 15:42

Oh hear the bells ringing 39:25

Oh, here sits a monkey in the chair, chair, chair 59:68

Oh, how I love Jesus 42:2

Oh, how lovely is the ev'ning 36:176

Oh, how lovely is the evening 33:96, 38:134

Oh, hush thee, my baby 54:29

Oh, I come from Alabama with a banjo on my knee 31:68

Oh, I dreamt I shore in a shearin' shed 46:80

Oh, I have a sniggle for my friend 71:25

Oh, I love trash, anything dirty or dingy or dusty 66:19

Oh I milked that cow with a squeeze, squeeze, squeeze 10:52

Oh, I stuck my head 51:42

Oh, I stuck my head in the little skunk hole 50:53

Oh, I wanna be a dog 56:111

Oh, I went down South for to see my gal 19:36

Oh, I went down South for to see my Sal 31:50, 66:174

Oh, I'm bringing home a baby bumble bee 50:8, 51:112

Oh, I'm ninety-nine miles from home 50:72

Oh, I'm riding in the car 72:37

Oh, I'm so embarrassed 12:46

Oh I'm walkin' round the corner 50:76

Oh, it ain't gonna rain no more, no more 51:60, 66:148

Oh, it's a shame to wash the car on a Sunday 55:29

Oh, it's beans, beans, beans 50:29

Oh, it's beans, beans, beans that turn us into fiends 51:43

Oh, John, the Rabbit, Yes, ma'am 22:216, 49:55

Oh me, oh my! 59:44

Oh Mister Sun, Sun, Mister Golden Sun 19:14

Oh, Mister Sun, Sun, Mister Golden Sun 59:12

Oh mules we find 51:52

Oh my goodness, oh my dear 69:10

Oh no! I like my sister! 56:184

Oh, no no no more mosquitoes 51:120

Oh oh yes 1:12

Oh, once upon a time in Arkansas 40:4

Oh, pretty Polly, don't you cry 31:13

Oh, rise and shine and give God your glory, glory 50:91

Oh, she sailed away on a sunny summer day 64:49

Oh, Shenandoah, I long to hear you 22:125, 33:119, 40:96

Oh, Shenandoah, I long to see you 46:72

Oh, Stewball was a good horse 40:106

Oh, the bear went over the mountain 36:34

Oh the big ship's sailing on the Allee Allee O 65:65

Oh, the Easter Bunny goes thump, thump, thump 38:141

Oh the fox went out on a chilly night 19:40

Oh, the grand old Duke of York 65:29

Oh, the horse went went around 50:16

Oh, the noble Duke of York 16:31, 38:88

Oh, the old bell'd yoe 'n' the little speckled wether 63:60

Oh, the Rock Island Line, it is a mighty good road 66:172

Oh they think I'm very pious 53:13

Oh, to be a robber fly 53:49

Oh, we can play on the big bass drum 74:36

Oh, we're marching shoulder to shoulder 56:104

Oh we're on our way, we're on our way 60:87

Oh, were you ever in Rio Grande? 46:70

Oh, what did Delaware, boys 49:48

Oh, what did Delaware, boys, oh, what did Delaware? 51:64

Oh, what do you do in the summertime 54:47

Oh, when I was a little kid I never liked to eat 32:39

Oh, when the saints go marching in 27:6

Oh, where have you been, Billy Boy 33:18, 66:220

Oh, where have you been, Billy Boy, Billy Boy? 36:42, 38:111

Oh where, oh where has my little dog gone? 31:42, 38:114, 44:9, 66:86, 70:36

Oh, will you wear blue 33:76

Oh, will you wear red, oh, my dear, oh, my dear 64:14

Oh, wolves are howling 63:79

Oh, you can't get to heaven 51:90

Oh, you can't get to heaven (oh, you can't get to heaven) 26:8

Oh, you can't say "psb" on the radio 56:81

Oh you lovely Augustine, Augustine 36:16

Ol' Dan Tucker, he came to town 22:88

Old Aunt Dinah went to town 63:47

The old cow died 63:56

An old cow-poke went riding out one dark and windy day 20:24

The old family toothbrush 25:6, 50:87, 51:34

Old fox walked out one moonshiny night 63:32

The old hen she cackled 63:42

Old Joe Clarke's a fine old man 50:44

Old King Cole was a merry old soul 36:182, 38:74, 44:42, 65:40, 75:70

Old lady goose, done turned her loose 63:40

Old MacDonald had a car, E I E I O 72:34

Old MacDonald had a farm 36:184

Old MacDonald had a farm E-I-E-I-O 31:48, 74:48

Old MacDonald had a farm, E-I-E-I-O 33:100, 38:118, 66:96

Old MacTavish is dead and his brother don't know it 51:15

Old McDonald had a band 59:22

Old Missus Lazibones and her dirty daughter 50:46

Old Mister Johnson had troubles of his own 49:52, 51:114

Old Mother Hubbard, she went to the cupboard 71:58

Old Mother Leary left a lantern in the shed 50:38

Old Roger is dead and he lies in his grave 64:88
Old Stewball, uh huh, was a red horse 63:68
Old toy trains, little toy tracks 57:74
Oliver Cromwell lay buried and dead 46:16
On a bright and summer's morning 63:34
On a hill far away stood an old rugged cross 27:26
On a summer day in the month of May 36:37
On December five and twenty, fum, fum, fum 2:23
On ev'ry blest Lord's Day I bow my head and pray 42:115
On foot I gaily take my way 76:18
On the first day of Christmas 36:231
On the first day of Christmas, my true love sent to me 2:12, 23:20
On the good ship Lollipop 66:42
On top of my pizza 51:98
On top of my pizza all covered with sauce 50:31
On top of Old Smokey all covered with snow 33:103
On top of Old Smoky 40:83, 67:6
On top of Old Smoky all covered with snow 31:25
On top of spaghetti 36:186, 37:38
On top of spaghetti all covered with cheese 66:128
On Veterans Day a tribute we pay 5:10
Once a jolly swagman camped by a billabong 66:200
Once an Austrian went yodeling on a mountain so high 55:33
Once I saw three goats and they were wearing coats 64:77
Once I stood on Liberty Island and heard freedom bells ring 29:66
Once in royal David's city 28:16
Once there lived a chicken who would say "chick-chick," 66:113
Once there was a little gal 49:81
Once there was a little kitty 35:92
Once there was a snowman, snowman, snowman 54:59
Once there was an elephant 38:124
Once three little kittens, they lost their mittens 31:22

Once upon a gentle breeze a seed came floating by 9:16
Once upon a time in a nursery rhyme 55:26
Once, when I was all alone 56:74
Once within a lowly stable 54:29
One bottle o' pop 64:24
One bottle pop 51:16
One bottle pop, Two bottle pop 50:80
One by one they enter the cage 17:29
One day as I was riding on the subway 64:72
One day I met a lion strolling down a shady lane 3:30
One day my best friend Barbara turned into a frog 56:54
One day when I was riding on the subway 70:28
One elephant went out to play 37:58, 64:9
One finger, one thumb 74:41
One finger, one thumb keep moving 64:46
One finger, one thumb, keep moving 35:64, 49:30
One flea fly flew up the flu 50:11
One light, one sun 60:100
One little girl was a very good girl 4:10
One little, two little, three little Indians 36:217, 66:217
One little, two little, three little toesies 72:45
One little two little three little witches 50:75
One misty, moisty morning, when cloudy was the weather 65:58
One night as I lay on my pillow 51:96
One song, I have but one song 66:64
One sparkling star in the evening sky 4:37
One time some kids at school 11:62
One, two, buckle my shoe 74:42
One, two, three, four, five 64:33
One, two, three, four, five people marching in a line 21:25
One, two, three, four, look who's comin' through the door 64:94
One voice is a solo 71:40
Only a boy named David, only a little sling 27:20
Onward, Christian soldiers, marching as to war 27:4

Ooey Gooey was a wiggle worm 55:15
Oooo, Boo! 47:7
Open my eyes that I may see 34:40
Open, shut them 72:55
Open, shut them, open, shut them 55:58
Oranges and lemons, say the bells of St. Clements 44:31, 75:74
Orleans Beaugency 1:24
The other day (the other day) I saw a bear 50:56
Our church is like a great big family 42:99
Our dog Bernard lived in the back-yard 56:58
Our Father who art in heaven 34:37
Out in the meadow you can hear them whistling 68:23
Over hill, over dale, we have hit the dusty trail 36:51
Over in the meadow in a nest in a tree 49:16
Over in the meadow in a pond in the sun 60:27
Over in the meadow in the sand 38:44
Over the river and through the wood 38:142
Over the winding trail we go 54:65

Pat-a-cake, pat-a-cake, baker's man 31:32, 35:50, 38:27, 44:59, 72:20
Peace is flowing like a river 34:34
A peanut butter sandwich made with jam 59:4
Peanut, peanut butter and jelly 50:30
Peanut, peanut butter! Jelly! 55:57
Pease porridge hot 31:14, 38:104, 44:28, 65:11, 75:77
Peek at a peacock 3:24
Peek-a-boo, peek-a-boo 74:20
Peek-a-boo, Where's the baby? 72:7
Peeking thru the window what do I see 71:26
Peep, squirrel, dah diddle um 63:18
The people in the bus go up and down 36:49, 38:130
People near and far who yearn to be free 29:70
Peter Piper picked a peck of pickled peppers 71:60
Phoebe in her petticoat 65:13
Picking the trash up off the street 71:10

The pilgrims and the Indians had a pow-wow 5:14
Pioneer children sang as they walked 54:65
Pioneers traveled westward long, long ago 5:44
Pitter patter, splash and splatter little raindrops 4:33
Playful little Jack Frost came last night 5:18
Please be quiet, oh, please be quiet 42:87
Polly, put the kettle on 31:39, 33:105, 36:192, 38:60, 44:22, 65:67, 75:14
Pony Boy, Pony Boy 65:32
Poor Roger is dead and gone to his grave 50:70
Pounding his chest and screaming violently 3:38
The power to love, the power to give 18:34
Praise and thanksgiving 42:126
Praise God, from whom all blessings flow 34:20, 48:3
Praise God with songs of joy 42:26
Praise Him, Praise Him 27:16, 42:81
Preacher went a-huntin' 66:170
Presidents are famous men 47:38
Pretty green grass and colored eggs too 47:43
Pretty white teeth so shiny and bright 72:14
Puff, the magic dragon, lived by the sea 19:44, 66:161
Pumpkins sitting on the wall 47:10
Pussy cat, pussy cat, where have you been? 38:50, 44:6, 66:108, 75:49
Pussycat, pussycat, where have you been? 31:35
Put your finger in the air, in the air 36:196, 66:132
Put your little foot, put your little foot 66:208
Put your right foot forward 66:211

Quack, quack, quack 3:7
Quack, quack quack quack quack 60:62
Queen Queen Caroline 1:6
Quick, quick, quick is the little squirrel 35:39

Rabbit ain't got no tail at all 49:85
Raccoon's got a ring-round tail 63:15
The rain falls down 69:15
Rain is falling all around 54:51
Rain, rain, go away 38:49, 65:60
Rain, rain, rain, rain 71:62
Reindeer are tapping on the rooftop 2:59
Rejoice in the Lord always 27:14
Rejoice! Rejoice! 42:130
Remember September, October, November 5:7
Remember your name and address 66:213
Reuben, Reuben, I've been thinking 50:68
Rev'rently, quietly, lovingly we think of thee 54:73
Ride a cockhorse to Banbury Cross 31:9, 38:52, 44:26, 66:186, 74:16
Ride Sally ride, spread your wings and fly to the sky 71:32
Ride your red horse down Vinegar Lane 69:22
Riding along, singing a cowboy song 64:16
Riding in an airplane, high above the ground 60:81
Riding in the buggy Miss (name) 72:39
Riding on that new river train 59:38
Riding on the City of New Orleans 40:16
Riding on the New River Train 55:31
Right foot, right foot 21:19
Ring a-long, ring a-long 47:27
Ring-a-ring o' roses 44:28, 65:21
Ring-a-round a rosy 72:13
Ring around a rosy 31:59, 38:107, 75:52
Ring! Hello 64:75
Ring, ring, ring the bells 2:49
Ring, ring, the joy bells are ringing 2:50
Ring the bell for Christmas 21:36
Ring those bells and turn around 2:58
Ringel ringel Rosen 1:124
Rise and shine and give God the glory 34:44
Rise with the blue-bird, Shine like the sun 60:35
Robin in the rain, what a saucy fellow 59:28
Rock, rock, sleep, my baby 69:23

Rock-a my soul in the bosom of Abraham 43:4
Rock-a-bye baby, on the tree top 25:22, 31:34, 33:112, 36:198, 41:66, 65:93, 66:221, 77:28
Rock-a-bye baby, so sweet and so fair 74:8
Rockabye, baby, on the tree top 38:20
Roll, roll, roll see those big wheels rolling 10:50
Roly poly, clap, clap, clap 4:23
The rooster's dead, oh what a shame 39:18
Roses are red, Violets are blue 71:8
Round and round on the merry-go-round 35:45
Row, row, row your boat 31:26, 36:199, 38:135, 60:64, 65:83, 66:234, 74:25, 75:53
Ru ru-que 1:20
Rub-a-dub-dub, three men in a tub 38:45, 72:46
Rubber Duckie, you're the one 66:16
Rudolph the red-nosed reindeer 57:68
Rules are things we all must follow 42:36

Safety Kids, I'm proud to be one, smile when you see one 8:6
A sailor went to sea sea sea 50:65, 51:63
Sakura sakura ya yoino sorawa 67:8
Sally eats shoelaces, straw and string 56:156
Sally go round the sun 5:42, 38:87, 65:23
The sandman comes 25:26, 74:7
The sandman comes, the sandman comes 38:15
Sandwiches are beautiful, sandwiches are fine 20:8
Santa Claus is coming 2:50
Santa's coming soon I know 47:28
Saturday is a special day 54:15
Savez-vous planter des choux a la mode 58:20
Savez-vous planter les choux? 64:68
Saw a snail chase a whale 20:12
Schlaf, Kindlein, Schlaf 62:38
Scraping up sand in the bottom of the sea 40:98
A seal and a walrus went out to play one day 3:26

The secret of happiness lies in your heart 11:32

See my fingers dance and play 72:53

See the pony galloping, galloping 38:98

See-saw, jump in the straw 69:25

See-saw, Margery Daw 31:75

See-saw, Margery Daw, Jacky shall have a new master 44:27

See-saw, Marjorie Daw 38:37

Seeds are planted deep, deep, deep 55:12

Seesaw Marjorie Daw, Jack shall have a new master 75:72

Service with a capital S- sharing a burden 12:16

Shall we gather at the river 40:92

Shalom, chaverim, shalom, chaverim 67:9

Shamrocks and leprechauns fit the Irish fancy 47:41

Sharing, sharing, everybody caring 4:12

She sailed away on a happy summer day 16:31

She sailed away on a sunny summer day 50:54

She went into the water, and she got her feet all wet 24:20

She'll be comin' 'round the mountain when she comes 31:37, 33:116, 36:201, 49:46, 64:22, 66:178, 67:6

She'll be coming around the mountain 15:46

She'll be coming round the mountain when she comes 20:6, 38:128, 40:94

She's about this high, she's taller than I 4:18

Sheep have lambs and goats have kids 5:28

Shh! The grass is sleeping 71:42

The shiny silver moon floats across the sky 35:36

Shizuka na yofu keni 67:12

Shoes, shoes, shoes 22:132

Shoo fly, don't bother me 24:14, 35:54, 36:203

Should old acquaintance be forgot 36:28, 45:46

Show me the path, Lord, that I should follow 42:101

Shut up in the library! 56:30

Si si si si tuna takaya 1:36

Silent night! Holy night! 45:42

Silent night, Holy night! 2:20, 23:14, 28:18, 36:206, 61:30

Simple Simon met a pieman, going to the fair 33:123, 38:48, 44:44, 65:31

Sing a song of sixpence, a pocket full of rye 31:38, 36:208, 38:30, 44:45, 66:222, 75:55

Sing a song, sing a song of September 71:6

Sing a song, today is May 71:54

Sing about Martin 71:30

Sing along with me, my song's about you 30:6

Sing! Sing a song 66:7

Sing we now of Christmas 23:10

Singing a song is fun to do 54:57

Sittin' on the ice till my feet get cold, honey 36:60

Sitting on the fence post chewing my bubble gum 55:44

Six little ducks that I once knew 24:18, 50:18, 59:52

Six little mice sat down to spin 44:3

Skies are fair above us 54:45

Skinnamarink-y dink-y dink 65:95

Skinnamarinky dinky dink 64:122

Skip, skip, skip to my Lou 38:90

Sleep, baby, sleep, thy father guards the sheep 38:18, 74:8, 77:7

Sleep, baby, sleep, thy father tends the sheep 36:59, 41:68

Sleep, my baby, on my bosom 77:24

Sleep my baby, Sleep my darling 41:69

Sleep, my child, and peace attend thee 77:8

Sleepers wake, sleepers wake 39:24

Sleigh bells ring, people sing carols in the snow 47:23

The slithery D slipped into the sea 50:94

Slow, slow snail 53:4

The snake baked a hoecake 63:24

Snows are a-fallin' on Douglas Mountain 57:72, 59:54

So many steps to the top of the tower 11:24

So many things to learn 10:29

Soft falls the snow, the coals burn low 69:30

Soldier, soldier, won't you marry me 65:36

Some have a little and some have a lot 56:152

Somebody loves (child's name) 4:8

Sometimes I get a feeling inside that makes me so warm all over 9:32

Sometimes you just gotta yell and scream 7:27

Somewhere over the rainbow 66:34

A song is a wonderful kind of thing 54:41

Soon as we all cook sweet potatoes 65:74

Sowing in the morning 33:22

A special gift is kindness 54:49

Speed, bonny boat, like a bird on the wing 33:127

Spell some names 21:8

Spin, spin, spin 47:19

A squirrel is a pretty thing 63:19

Standin' tall, You know I'm growing when I'm standin' tall 10:4

Stanley stole my shoelace and rubbed it in his armpit 56:163

Stars shining number, number one 64:25

Stepping over, crawling under 14:26

Still as the night when the wind drops 53:11

Still, still, still, the little Jesus sleeps 2:39

Stop! and let me tell you what the Lord has done for me 42:118

Stop moving about 56:106

Straight home, straight aim, straight arrow 12:70

Stretch up, stretch up, stretch up 21:23

Summer breeze, so softly blowing 76:21

Summer is a-coming in, loudly sing cuckoo 46:26

The sun'll come out tomorrow 66:25

Sur le pont d'Avignon 38:108, 59:80, 64:60

Surely, it is God who saves me 34:36

Susie, oh, Susie, oh, where is your goose? 50:15

The swan sings tir-e-li-o 1:102

Swans sing before they die 46:89

Sweet and low, sweet and low 62:40

Sweet Rosie O'Grady 50:42

Sweet water rolling 62:30

Sweetly sings the donkey at the break of day 46:88

Swing low, sweet chariot 22:148

Swing low, sweet chariot, comin' forth to carry me home 59:66

Ta ta ta li 62:63

Take me out to the ball game 22:296, 40:110, 60:72

Take three steps forward then one step back 11:12

Take time to look upon a flower 68:34

Take your hat off when the flag goes by 13:4

The tall giraffe whose neck is long 66:105

A tall lanky lawyer from Illinois 47:40

Tape tape petites mains 62:59

Tapping, tapping, little elf 2:61

Teach me to walk in the light of His love 54:79

Teddy bear, teddy bear, turn around 49:38

Tell me, dear Lord, in thine own way I pray 54:77

Tell me the stories of Jesus I love to hear 54:33

Tell me the tales that to me were so dear 67:9

Tell me why the stars do shine 32:6, 40:113

Ten in the bed, and the little one said 38:121

Ten more days of vacation 50:73

Tete, epaules, genoux et pieds-Head and shoulders, knees and feet 60:59

Thank you, God 42:9, 42:22

Thank you, I say thank you 11:53

Thank you, Lord, O thank you for the love I feel 68:39

Thanks a lot 60:19

Thanks to God for His love 39:22

Thanksgiving Day is coming 47:16

Theirs is a little house, theirs is 58:13

There are lots of things for me to do 59:58

There are many ways to travel 14:24

There are songs that make you smile 30:50

There are these kids all around 8:12

There are three ways to get peanut butter 50:33

There are three white gulls a-flying 38:97

There are two sides to forgiveness, it's important that you know 10:34
There came a girl from France 59:82
There I sat on Buttermilk Hill 22:66
There is a beautiful dance called the Thank You 11:56
There is a tree, (there is a tree) 24:4
There is a zoo, I'm going to 35:78
There lived a little princess 25:10
There once was a man named Michael Finnigin 75:62
There once was a woman who gobbled Swiss cheese 50:32
There was a bee-eye-ee-eye-ee 50:12
There was a crooked man 44:46
There was a crooked man and he walked a crooked mile 75:57
There was a farmer who had a dog 31:36, 33:21, 38:82, 51:26, 66:124
There was a farmer who had a dog and Bingo was his name-o 35:57, 36:44
There was a lady loved a swine 44:36
There was a little baby 57:80
There was a man 51:117
There was a man and he was mad 75:81
There was a man from Pleasantville 49:21, 51:39
There was a man lived in the moon 25:20, 44:38, 51:12, 59:30, 75:16
There was a tailor had a mouse 49:72
There was a wee cooper who lived in Fife 46:14
There was an old frog and he lived in a spring 22:226
There was an old frog and he lived in the spring 63:48
There was an old lady lived over the sea 22:54
There was an old lady who swallowed a fly 33:131, 36:221
There was an old man named Michael Finnegan 22:244, 37:59
There was an old sow had three little piggies 49:12
There was an old woman, all skin and bones 22:336, 49:14, 59:43
There was an old woman tossed up in a basket 38:42, 44:47, 75:82
There was an old woman who lived in a shoe 31:40, 66:227
There was cheese, cheese 59:76
There was no growl 53:29

There was one, there were two, there were three little angels 2:26
There were ten in the bed 25:14, 65:88, 70:34
There were three jolly fishermen 50:86
There were three little ships in the harbor 66:248
There're fruits and veggies 6:26
There's a big beautiful planet in the sky 60:50
There's a brown girl in the ring 64:104
There's a church in the valley by the wild wood 26:2
There's a hole in my bucket, dear Liza 36:218
There's a hole in the bucket, dear Liza 40:114, 50:88, 70:8
There's a line that goes around me 7:24
There's a little wheel a-turnin' in my heart 55:38
There's a little wheel a-turning in my heart 20:20, 38:120
There's a little white duck 58:40
There's a little white duck sitting in the water 36:158, 66:92
There's a special kind of love that makes a family 11:65
There's a spider on the floor, on the floor 59:21
There's a star in the East on Christmas morn 28:24
There's crickets and tadpoles 42:133
There's just one little nose like mine 12:44
There's no substitute for a cat 56:141
They are so funny and silly and sad 17:11
They came on ships from across the sea with the dream of being free 29:30
They said, "Eat the broccoli" 56:90
They tell you in the Army 22:356
Think about a thank you 11:50
Think positively, positively think 73:35
Thirty purple birds, sitting on the curb 51:51
This is for the people who never rode the train 66:116
This is going to be neat. This is going to be fun! 12:8

This is my commandment, that you love one another 42:75

This is my jumping song 14:6

This is the day we come to church 42:20

This is the night we've waited for 54:19

This is the way the ladies ride 74:12

This is the way we put on our pants 72:31

This land is your land 22:370

This land is your land, this land is my land 40:116, 66:188

This little light of mine 19:48, 26:10, 34:46, 60:65

This little light of mine, I'm gonna let it shine 40:119

This little pig found a hole in the fence 69:8

This little pig went to market 35:62, 38:26, 74:19, 75:11

This little piggy went to market 72:8

This little toe goes a rub-a-dub dub 72:44

This morning when the sun came up 5:27

This old man, he play one 65:59

This old man, he played one 19:38, 31:56, 36:223, 54:13, 66:218, 70:16, 72:17, 75:86

This old man, he plays one 60:29

Three blind mice 31:43, 44:2, 65:51, 66:233, 75:78

Three blind mice, three blind mice 36:224

Three crow sat upon a wall 64:114

Three geese in straw sat as blissfully as can be 39:16

Three great kings I met at early morn 2:28

Three green speckled frogs sat on a speckled log 50:21

Three little children lying in bed 31:76

Three little kittens, they lost their mittens 38:72, 44:4, 75:90

Three times around went the gallant ship 38:84

Through a still small voice the spirit speaks to me 54:69

Throw the ball, then catch the ball 10:17

Thumbelina, Thumbelina, tiny little thing 60:41

The thumbkins they can sing 55:52

Ticklely, Ticklely 72:52

Ting-a-lay-o, run my little donkey 19:12

Tinga Layo! Come, little donkey, come 24:16

Tingalayo come little donkey come 60:92

Tingalayo! Run, little donkey, run! 70:14

Tingalayo, come, little donkey come 37:39

Tingalayo, run m'little donkey 64:106

Tip-toe, here we go 47:5

Tippy tippy toe across the floor 14:16

Tiptoe, tiptoe, tiptoe 21:15

'Tis a gift to be simple 33:120

Tis a gift to be simple 40:122

Tis advertised in Boston, New York, and Buffalo 22:103

'Tis the far north lands that are calling me away 76:13

'Tis the gift to be simple 22:38, 46:48

Tis the gift to be simple 34:62

A tisket, a tasket, a green and yellow basket 24:6, 38:100

Tit galop, tit galop 22:50

To ev'ry thing (turn, turn, turn) there is a season 40:126

To everyone in all the world I reach my hand, I shake their hand 60:21

To market, to market, to buy a fat pig 31:33, 38:99, 65:44, 74:16

To my little one's cradle in the night 77:16

To Portsmouth! 46:74

Today is Monday 65:6

Today is the day fer the wearin' o' the green 5:24

The togetherness kids 7:14

Tom, he was a piper's son 44:24

Tom, Tom, the Piper's son 31:49, 38:56, 44:23, 65:44, 75:85

Train is a-comin', oh yes 49:50

Train whistle blowing, makes a sleepy noise 19:46, 60:33

Trot, trot, trot, go and never stop 62:71, 74:16

Trunk to tail, trunk to tail 17:15

Try to please a princess, try to make her smile 11:20

Tumbling, tumbling, tumbling, tumbling acrobats move fast 17:33

Turkey in the straw 51:84
Turkey run, turkey hide 47:14
Turn again Whittington 46:85
Turn out your toe! 38:93
Twas in the moon of wintertime 2:24, 28:70
Twinkle, twinkle, little star 19:42, 25:2, 31:47, 33:137, 36:235, 38:64, 41:68, 44:32, 60:99, 65:85, 66:202, 67:4, 75:93
Two and two are four 66:40
Tzena, Tzena, Tzena, how can anything be plainer 66:198

Un elephante se balanceaba 64:115
Uncle Reuben caught a 'coon 36:237
Under the spreading chestnut tree 36:239
Underwear is ev'rywhere but mostly underneath 56:174
Une poule blanche 62:32
Unite and unite, now let us unite 76:4
Uno, dos, y tres 38:137
Up and over and down 4:32
Up in the air, Junior Bird Man 51:10
Up on the housetop reindeer pause 2:46, 23:22, 57:53
Up one road and down another 68:15
Up to the barber shop I go 38:117
Up, up, up goes the baby 72:23
Up, up, up in the air 35:30
Uptown, downtown, wrong side to 69:28
Uurgh, eeegh, ugh 53:44

A Valentine for me 47:34
Valentine, Valentine 47:36
Valentines are special greetings 47:33
The very best part of Christmas time, the very best part I know 5:19
The very moment that I decided that ev'ry success I might have had 64:118
Voyez voyez les zombis la? 59:81

Waa waa waa, cried baby bear 71:52
Waddaly atcha, waddaly atcha 64:52
Waiting throughout the year 57:55
Wake, snake, day is a-breakin' 22:248
Wake up! Jonah you are the man 43:18

Wake up, little baby 72:26
Walk forward, walk forward 21:22
Walking down the pumpkin row 47:12
Wash your hair, wash your hair 12:20
Water in the rain clouds 71:53
The water is fine, fine, fine 58:4
Water started long ago 56:190
Way down south where the cotton grows 51:68
Way out on the ocean 32:36
We are all colors in a rainbow 68:37
We are climbing Jacob's ladder 34:31, 43:6
We are going to Grandma's house 4:19
We are soldiers marching along 74:29
We came to the seashore to swim in the waves 76:8
We come on the sloop John B. 40:100
We gather together to ask the Lord's blessing 33:138, 36:240, 66:251
We have a band, the very best band 64:20
We have a birthday party ev'ry October twenty-eighth 29:14
We have a dear old Daddy 25:16, 51:36
We have a friend that we all know 55:54
We hold these truths to be self-evident 13:18
We live in televised 18:4
We need people with the fire of invention 18:9
We need to do a little bit of service every day 12:14
We need to put our best selves forward 6:34
We shall overcome 34:28, 40:128
We sing now together our song of thanksgiving 34:60
We thank God for the starry sky 68:30
We thank thee, Father, for our homes 42:138
We thank you, Lord of heaven 34:56
We the people of the United States 13:32
We three kings of Orient are 2:16, 28:48, 48:10, 61:24
We used to live in an old fashioned house 38:146
We volunteer, we volunteer 12:6

We were forty miles from Albany
36:79
We wish you a merry Christmas 2:8,
23:28, 28:80, 36:244, 38:153,
45:10, 48:11, 54:27, 57:82
We're glad you're here, (name) 42:55
We're going to Kentucky 64:82
We're just two friends who like to say
thank you 11:37
We're the children of America 29:24
We're the Safety Kids 7:6
Wee Willie Winkie, runs through the
town 38:19, 71:16
Welcome April sunshine! 39:27
Well, come along friends, listen to my
tale 20:36
Well, did you feed my cow? 64:50
Well, Hello Mister Turkey 71:21
Well I always thought that cows
looked prettier in a field 56:46
Well I thought it was a kitten with a
stripe down its back 3:36
Well, last Monday mornin' 36:104
Well, ole Mister Johnson had troubles
all his own 40:14
Well, who built the ark? Noah, Noah
59:32
Well you can play with me, and you
can hold my hand 35:74
Were you ever in Quebec 36:71
Wet again, wet again 56:169
What are you going to be on
Halloween night 5:12
What can I do with five little fingers
72:51
What can I do? 71:18
What child is this, who laid to rest
2:35, 28:29, 61:26
What did you do in school today?
56:158
What do I have that Jesus wants?
42:113
What do we do when baby wakes up?
35:12
What do you do when someone else is
taunting you 11:16
What do you do when you're happy?
What do you do? 11:34
What do you know about water? 4:29
What do you like? 21:7
What does the clock say, "Tick-tock,
tick-tock" 35:20
What if a zebra had spots? 56:197
What is the answer? 68:41

What is the number that you have?
21:28
What kind of trees are found out
there? 39:13
What shall we do when we all go out
65:20
What shall we do with the baby-o?
55:43
What shall we do with the drunken
sailor 46:68
What will we do with the baby-o?
35:51
What will we do with the old sow's
hide? 63:52
The wheels on the bus go round
and round 16:32, 20:16,
49:44, 60:43
When an Indian boy had to prove that
he had courage 11:6
When good King Arthur ruled this
land 44:39
When I first came to this land 22:272
When I see a star twinkling in the
night 42:6
When I was a seeker 28:79
When I was bound apprentice in
famous Lincolnshire 46:30
When I was just a wee little lad
66:118
When I was one I sucked my thumb
55:8
When I was shipwrecked 63:72
When I was young, I used to wait
36:45
When I went out this morning 68:20
When I work and when I play 42:111
When I'm happy I can sing 42:85
When is the day to be happy? 42:56
When Israel was in Egypt land 36:98,
43:8
When Israel was in Egypt's land
22:128, 34:24, 42:79
When John Henry was a little baby
36:144, 40:67
When John Henry was a little baby
boy 22:152
When Johnny comes marching home
again 36:245
When Missus Miller isn't home be-
cause she's feeling bad 12:4
When my mother calls me 54:15
When November comes along 47:15
When Poppa put the paper on the
wall 49:76

When she says to wipe the dishes I will do it 10:14
When somebody makes you sad 10:42
When the days turn warm, and the ground turns green 5:29
When the fam'ly gets together 54:19
When the sun comes back and the first quail calls 22:140
When there is a task to do 54:49
When things aren't going exactly my way 9:19
When we're helping we're happy 54:15
When you come to the end of a lolli-pop 49:89
When you get in trouble and you don't know right from wrong 66:72
When you have a gratitude attitude 11:46
When you tell one lie it leads to another 10:25
When you wake up in the morning and it's quarter to one 19:26, 59:8
When your hands are feeling sticky 12:32
Whenever I am naughty, whenever I am bad 56:18
Whenever I feel afraid 66:48
Whenever I hear the song of a bird 54:53
Whenever love is in the air I always feel like God is there 11:70
Where are you going to, my pretty maid? 44:55
Where are your eyes? 35:14, 36:242, 52:28
Where is baby Moses 71:51
Where is John 1:96
Where is the baby, Jesus boy 2:33
Where is Thumbkin? 31:62, 35:66, 42:57, 65:19, 72:49
Where is Thumbkin? Where is Thumbkin? 36:247
Where is Thumbkin, where is Thumbkin? 38:29, 64:30
Where is your house? 21:32
Where love is, there God is also 54:81
Where, O where, has my little dog gone? 74:21
Where oh where is nice little Mary? 72:30
Where oh where is pretty little Sally? 15:44

Where, oh, where is sweet little Nellie? 64:96
Where, oh where, where can baby be? 35:33
Where's my pajamas? 65:87
While shepherds watch'd their flocks by night 28:12
Whisper a pray'r in the morning 27:18
Whistler and his dog 66:102
White coral bells upon a slender stalk 36:249
Who broke my window? Telling the truth isn't going to be easy 10:19
Who can name all of the days in the week? 21:31
Who carries his trunk where ever he goes? 3:42
Who killed Cock Robin? 75:88
Who made the beautiful rainbow? 42:33
Who made the cow "Moo" 42:32
Who made the trees and the birds and flow'rs? 42:94
Who stole my chickens and my hens? 1:16
Who would desire a pleasanter thing 42:30
Who's afraid of the big bad wolf 66:52
Who's got a beard that's long and white? 2:54, 57:70, 59:26
Who's tail is curly and who's plump and surly? 3:16
Who's the most important man this country ever knew? 66:135
Whoa, mule! Can't get the saddle on 63:64
Whoever shall have some good pea-nuts 49:56
Whooping up cattle, I'm setting up straddle 63:70
Why are there so many songs about rainbows 66:22
Why come ye hither, invaders, your mind what madness fills? 36:35
Why do we have an army in Amer-ica? 13:43
Why is the sky so blue today? 54:43
Why shouldn't my goose 46:86
Wiggle, wiggle, wiggle little finger 72:48
Will you wear white, O my dear? 22:74

Will you wear white, oh my dear, oh my dear? 36:139
Willie, take your little drum 2:38
Willoughby, wallaby, wee 19:20
Willoughby Wallaby Woo 59:7
Wind through the olive trees softly did blow 2:30
Winter's cold and summer's warm 68:9
Witches, ghosts and goblins flutter through the night 47:6
With a smile and a song 66:59
With his shiny blade 22:136
With my little broom I sweep, sweep, sweep 74:35
Won't you bring back 20:46, 22:236, 49:82
The words you speak, the words you say 9:36
Worms, worms, worms, crawling in the ground 71:56
Wriggledy jiggledy, here we go 49:36

Y'a un rat dans le grenier 59:86
Yankee Doodle came to town 44:48
Yankee Doodle went to town 22:62, 31:57, 33:140, 38:122, 40:135, 66:250
A Yankee ship came down the river 22:110
Ye saints who dwell on Europe's shore 22:176
Yesterday I heard a word and wondered what it meant 54:61
You are very special 42:44
You better watch out; you better not cry 66:238

You can be anything you want to be 9:26
You can make people laugh and wear a grin 18:20
You can't make a horse go fast 6:30
You can't make a turtle come out 49:63
You get a line and I'll get a pole, honey 40:24
You gotta sing when the spirit says sing 59:56
You gotta sing when your spirit says sing 19:6
You have the power to be 18:44
You know Dasher and Dancer 66:235
You ought to see me, Cindy 46:44
You put on a tall black hat 47:9
You put your right foot in 66:204
You sing a song, and I'll sing a song 59:63
You were where you said you'd be 12:68
You're as sweet as sugar on a stick 56:103
You're not gonna get rich on me 8:26
You've been playing hard all day long 6:38
Young folks, old folks 51:56
Your face is friendly, I admit 56:150
Your neck's so long, your neck's so long 3:37
Yu ya ke koyake no akato nbo 67:11

The zebra, the zebra has such a funny hide 3:33
Zipper up my coat 71:28
Zoom, zoom, zoom 64:51

The subject guide is a thesaurus of broad topics that will aid in the use of the subject index. This guide contains 275 topics with lists of pertinent headings from the subject index.

Abraham
JUDAISM

Action Songs
CIRCLE GAMES
DANCERS AND
    DANCING
EXERCISE GAMES
FINGER AND
    HAND PLAY
JUMP ROPE
    JINGLES
MARCHING
PLAY
RHYTHMS

Africa
CONGO

Airplanes
ASTRONAUTS
BALLOONS
    (AIRSHIPS)
FLYING

Alligators
CROCODILES

Alphabets
SIZE AND SHAPE

Animal Sounds
ANIMALS
BEES
CHICKENS
CIRCUSES
CUCKOOS
DUCKS
GEESE
SOUNDS
TURKEYS
ZOOS

Animals
ANTEATERS
BEARS
CAMELS
CATS
CIRCUSES
COWS
DEATH
DEER

DOGS
DONKEYS
ELEPHANTS
FOXES
GOATS
GOPHERS
HEDGEHOGS
HORSES
HUNTING
KANGAROOS
LIONS
MICE
MOLES
MONKEYS
MULES
MUSKRATS
NURSERY RHYMES
OPOSSUMS
PANTHERS
PETS
PIGS
RABBITS
RACCOONS
SEALS
SHEEP
SKUNKS
SNAILS
SQUIRRELS
WALLABIES
WOLVES
WOODCHUCKS
WORMS
ZEBRAS
ZOOS

Apples
FRUITS

Astronauts
AIRPLANES
FLYING
OUTER SPACE

Australia
WALLABIES

Automobiles
BUSES
TRANSPORTATION
WHEELS

Autumn
SEASONS
SEPTEMBER

Babies
CHILDREN
DOLLS
FAMILIES
HOME
NURSERY RHYMES
SLEEP

Ball Sports
BASEBALL

Balloons (Airships)
AIRPLANES
FLYING

Balls
TOPS
TOYS

Bananas
FRUITS

Baseball
BALL SPORTS

Beans
BARLEY

Bedtime
CLOSING SONGS
DREAMS
EVENING
NIGHT
PRAYERS
SLEEP

Bible Stories
ABRAHAM
ANGELS
APOSTLES
CHRISTIANITY
DANIEL
EZEKIEL
JESUS CHRIST
JOSHUA
JUDAISM
MOSES
NOAH
SAINTS

59

Birds
  CHICKENS
  CRANES
  CROWS
  CUCKOOS
  DUCKS
  FLYING
  GEESE
  KOOKABURRA
  NIGHTINGALES
  ROBINS
  SWANS
  TURKEYS

Boats
  FERRIES
  TRANSPORTATION

Boats and Boating
  CANOES AND
    CANOEING
  FISHERMEN AND
    FISHING
  SAILING

Bread
  BAKERS AND
    BAKING

Brooks
  RIVERS
  WATER

Brotherhood
  FRIENDSHIP
  NEIGHBORS

Buses
  AUTOMOBILES
  TRANSPORTATION
  WHEELS

Cakes and Cookies
  CANDY
  PIES

Camp Songs
  CIRCULAR SONGS
  CLOSING SONGS
  ECHO SONGS
  FOLK SONGS
  JOHN HENRY
  MINERS AND
    MINING

Candy
  CAKES AND
    COOKIES
  PIES

Canons
  CHANTS
  ROUNDS

Cartoons
  MOVING PICTURES
  TELEVISION

Caterpillars
  BUTTERFLIES

Children
  BABIES
  BASEBALL
  BICYCLES AND
    BICYCLING
  DOLLS
  DRUGS
  FAMILIES
  FEAR
  FRIENDSHIP
  GROWING UP
  HOME
  MAKE-BELIEVE
  NURSERY RHYMES
  PLAY
  PRAYERS
  SAFETY
    AWARENESS
  SCHOOL LIFE
  STRANGERS
  SWINGS AND
    SWINGING
  TOYS

Christianity
  APOSTLES
  BIBLE STORIES
  CHRISTMAS
  CHRISTMAS
    CAROLS
  CHURCHES
  EASTER
  FORGIVENESS
  HYMNS
  JESUS CHRIST
  SPIRITUALS

Christmas
  BELLS
  CHRISTMAS
    CAROLS
  CHRISTMAS SONGS
  DECEMBER
  SANTA CLAUS
  SNOW

Christmas Carols
  CHRISTIANITY
  CHRISTMAS
  CHRISTMAS SONGS
  DRUMS
  HYMNS
  JOY

Christmas Songs
  BELLS
  CHRISTMAS
  CHRISTMAS
    CAROLS
  NATIVE
    AMERICANS

Churches
  CHRISTIANITY

Circle Games
  ACTION SONGS
  CIRCULAR SONGS
  DANCERS AND
    DANCING
  EXERCISE GAMES
  FINGER AND
    HAND PLAY

Circular Songs
  CIRCLE GAMES

Circuses
  ANIMAL SOUNDS
  ANIMALS
  CLOWNS
  MERRY-GO-
    ROUNDS
  ZOOS

Civics
  CIVIL RIGHTS
  DEMOCRACY
  EQUAL RIGHTS
  FLAGS
  FREEDOM
  KING, MARTIN
    LUTHER, JR.
  PATRIOTIC SONGS
  PEACE AND
    JUSTICE
  SLAVERY
  UNITED STATES

Civil Rights
  AFRICAN-
    AMERICAN
  BROTHERHOOD

CIVIL WAR (U.S. 1861-1865)
EQUAL RIGHTS
FOLK SONGS
KING, MARTIN LUTHER, JR.
PEACE AND JUSTICE

Civil War (1861-1865)
LINCOLN, ABRAHAM
WAR SONGS AND CRIES

Civil War (U.S. 1861-1865)
SLAVERY

Clapping Games
FINGER AND HAND PLAY

Cleanliness
GROOMING, PERSONAL
HAIR
HANDS
HEALTH
SKIN
TEETH

Clocks and Watches
NUMBERS
TELLING TIME

Clothing and Dress
COLOR
COTTON
HATS
SHOES
WOOL

Clowns
CIRCUSES

Color
COTTON
SHOES
SIZE AND SHAPE
WOOL

Counting
DIMINISHING SONGS
MATHEMATICS

NUMBERS
TELLING TIME

Countries
AFRICA
AUSTRALIA
AUSTRIA
CONGO
DANCES
ENGLAND
FINLAND
FRENCH LANGUAGE
GERMAN LANGUAGE
GHANA
HUNGARY
IRELAND
ISRAEL
ITALY
JAMAICA
JAPAN
JAPANESE LANGUAGE
LATIN AMERICA
MEXICO
NORWAY
PUPPETS
RUSSIA
SCOTLAND
SPANISH LANGUAGE
TANZANIA
TRINIDAD
TURKEY
UNITED STATES
WALES
YIDDISH LANGUAGE

Courting
LOVE
POSTAL SERVICE

Covered Wagons
COWBOYS
FRONTIER LIFE
MORMONS AND MORMONISM
OX CART
PIONEERS
STAGECOACHES
WHEELS

Cowboys
COVERED WAGONS

FRONTIER LIFE
PIONEERS
TEXAS

Cows
COWBOYS

Crocodiles
ALLIGATORS

Crying
FEAR
FEELINGS

Cumulative Songs
DIMINISHING SONGS
MATHEMATICS

Dancers and Dancing
DANCES
SQUARE DANCING

Dances
DANCERS AND DANCING
SQUARE DANCING

Days
EVENING
MONTHS
MORNING
SUNRISE

Death
HUNTING

Democracy
CIVICS
EQUAL RIGHTS
FLAGS
FREEDOM
WASHINGTON, GEORGE

Dentists
TEETH

Devils
WITCHES

Diminishing Songs
CLOSING SONGS
CUMULATIVE SONGS
MATHEMATICS

Doctors
HOSPITALS
SICKNESS

Dolls
BALLS
TOPS
TOYS

Donkeys
MULES

Dragons
ELVES

Dreams
SLEEP

Drugs
SAFETY
AWARENESS
STRANGERS

Ears
SOUNDS

Echo Songs
CAMP SONGS
CIRCULAR SONGS
QUESTION AND
ANSWER
SONGS

Elves
FAIRIES, DWARFS,
AND GOBLINS

England
KINGS AND
RULERS
REVOLUTIONARY
WAR IN AMER-
ICA (1776-1781)

Entertainment
CARTOONS
CIRCUSES
CLOWNS
MERRY-GO-
ROUNDS
MOVING PICTURES
TELEVISION
ZOOS

Environment
FLOWERS
FORESTS
NATURE
TREES

Equal Rights
BROTHERHOOD
CIVIL RIGHTS

PEACE AND
JUSTICE

Erie Canal
MULES

Evening
CLOSING SONGS
NIGHT

Exercise Games
ACTION SONGS
CIRCLE GAMES
DANCERS AND
DANCING
FINGER AND
HAND PLAY
JUMP ROPE
JINGLES
WALKING

**Fairies, Dwarfs,
and Goblins**
ELVES

Fall
SEASONS

Families
BABIES
CHILDREN
GOOD BEHAVIOR
GREETINGS
GROWING UP
HAPPINESS
HOME
HOUSES
HUMAN
RELATIONS
KINDNESS
LOVE
SHARING

Fantasy World
DEVILS
DRAGONS
DREAMS
ELVES
FAIRIES, DWARFS,
AND GOBLINS
GHOSTS
IMAGINATION
MAKE-BELIEVE
WITCHES

Farms
ANIMAL SOUNDS

Fear
CRYING
FEELINGS

Feelings
CRYING
FAMILIES
FEAR
GOOD BEHAVIOR
HAPPINESS
HOME
HUMAN
RELATIONS
JOY
KINDNESS
LOVE
SMILES

**Finger and Hand
Play**
ACTION SONGS
CLAPPING GAMES
CUMULATIVE
SONGS
DIMINISHING
SONGS

Fire
SAFETY
AWARENESS

Fire Engines
FIREFIGHTERS
FIRES

Firefighters
FIRE ENGINES
FIRES

Fires
FIRE ENGINES
FIREFIGHTERS

Fish and Sea Life
CLAMS
CRABS
CRAYFISH
FISHERMEN AND
FISHING
OCEANS
SEA HORSE
SEASHORE
SHARKS
SHELLS
(MOLLUSKS)
WHALES

Flowers
FORESTS
GARDENERS AND
    GARDENING
MAY

Flying
AIRPLANES
ASTRONAUTS
BALLOONS
    (AIRSHIPS)
KITES
OUTER SPACE

Fog
WEATHER

Folk Songs
BANJOS
BOATS AND
    BOATING
CAMP SONGS
CIRCULAR SONGS
COURTING
COWBOYS
DEATH
DRILLING
FRONTIER LIFE
HUNTING
JOHN HENRY
MINERS AND
    MINING
MUSIC AND
    MUSICIANS
OUTLAWS
PEACE AND
    JUSTICE
PIONEERS
RAILROADS
SPIRITUALS
SQUARE DANCING
UNITED STATES
WHISTLES AND
    WHISTLING
WORK SONGS

Food and Eating
APPLES
BANANAS
BARLEY
BEANS
BREAD
CABBAGE
CAKES AND
    COOKIES

CANDY
CORN
FRUITS
PICNICS
PIES
PUMPKINS
TEA
VEGETABLES

Forests
FLOWERS
LUMBERJACKS
    AND
    LUMBERING
NATURE
TREES

Fourth of July
PATRIOTIC SONGS

Freedom
AFRICAN-
    AMERICAN
CIVICS
CIVIL RIGHTS
CIVIL WAR (U.S.
    1861-1865)
DEMOCRACY
EQUAL RIGHTS
FLAGS
KING, MARTIN
    LUTHER, JR.
LINCOLN,
    ABRAHAM
PEACE AND
    JUSTICE
REVOLUTIONARY
    WAR IN AMER-
    ICA (1776-1781)
SLAVERY
SPIRITUALS
STATUE OF
    LIBERTY
WASHINGTON,
    GEORGE

Friends
HUMAN
    RELATIONS

Friendship
BROTHERHOOD
GREETINGS
HAPPINESS
JOY
KINDNESS

LOVE
NEIGHBORS
PLAY
SCHOOL LIFE
SELF-IMAGE
SMILES
TRUTH
VOLUNTEERS

Friendships
GOOD BEHAVIOR
SHARING

Frogs
TOADS

Frontier Life
COVERED WAGONS
COWBOYS
DEATH
HUNTING
JAMES, JESSE
    WOODSON
LUMBERJACKS
    AND
    LUMBERING
MINERS AND
    MINING
MORMONS AND
    MORMONISM
NATIVE
    AMERICANS
OUTLAWS
OX CART
PIONEERS
PRISONERS AND
    PRISONS
STAGECOACHES
TEXAS

Fruits
APPLES
BANANAS

**Gardeners and
    Gardening**
FLOWERS

Gardens
FLOWERS
FORESTS
GARDENERS AND
    GARDENING
GRASS
MAY
TREES

Ghosts
DEVILS
HALLOWEEN
WITCHES

Good Behavior
FORGIVENESS
GREETINGS
KINDNESS
MANNERS
NEIGHBORS
SELF-IMAGE
SHARING
TRUTH
VOLUNTEERS

Greetings
NAMES

Grooming
EARS
HAIR
HANDS

**Grooming,
   Personal**
CLEANLINESS
GROWING UP
HEALTH
SKIN
TEETH

Growing Up
HOME
SCHOOL LIFE
VEGETABLES

Guessing Games
ECHO SONGS
QUESTION AND
   ANSWER
   SONGS
RIDDLES

Halloween
DEVILS
GHOSTS
PUMPKINS
WITCHES

Happiness
FEELINGS
JOY
SMILES

Harvest
AUTUMN
PUMPKINS

Health
CLEANLINESS
DENTISTS
DRUGS
EARS
GROOMING,
   PERSONAL
GROWING UP
HAIR
HANDS
HOSPITALS
SAFETY
   AWARENESS
SICKNESS
SKIN
STRANGERS
TEETH
VEGETABLES

Holidays
BIRTHDAYS
CHRISTMAS
CHRISTMAS SONGS
EASTER
FOURTH OF JULY
HALLOWEEN
HANUKKAH
LINCOLN,
   ABRAHAM
MAY DAY
NEW YEAR
PILGRIMS
SAINT PATRICK'S
   DAY
SANTA CLAUS
THANKSGIVING
   DAY
VALENTINE'S DAY
WASHINGTON,
   GEORGE

Home
FAMILIES
HOUSES

Horses
MULES
STAGECOACHES

Hospitals
SICKNESS

Houses
STAIRWAYS

Human Body
BABIES

CHILDREN
CLEANLINESS
CRYING
DEATH
DENTISTS
DREAMS
DRUGS
EARS
FINGER AND
   HAND PLAY
GROOMING,
   PERSONAL
GROWING UP
HAIR
HANDS
HATS
HEALTH
HOSPITALS
SELF-IMAGE
SHADOWS
SHOES
SICKNESS
SKIN
SLEEP
SOUNDS
TEETH
VEGETABLES

Human Relations
BABIES
BROTHERHOOD
CHILDREN
COURTING
DEATH
FAMILIES
FEELINGS
FORGIVENESS
FRIENDSHIP
GOOD BEHAVIOR
GREETINGS
HAPPINESS
HOME
KINDNESS
LOVE
MANNERS
NEIGHBORS
SELF-IMAGE
SHARING
SKIN
TRUTH
VOLUNTEERS

Hymns
CHRISTIANITY
PRAYERS

Imagination
DOLLS
ELVES
FAIRIES, DWARFS,
AND GOBLINS
MAKE-BELIEVE

Insects
ANTS
BEES
BEETLES
BUTTERFLIES
CATERPILLARS
CENTIPEDES
FLEAS
FLIES
GRASSHOPPERS
LADYBUGS
MAYFLIES
MOSQUITOES
PRAYING MANTIS
SPIDERS
WALKING STICKS

Ireland
SAINT PATRICK'S
DAY

Israel
JUDAISM

**James, Jesse
Woodson**
OUTLAWS

Jesus Christ
APOSTLES
CHRISTIANITY
CHRISTMAS
CHRISTMAS
CAROLS
EASTER
FORGIVENESS
HYMNS

Joy
FEELINGS
HAPPINESS
SMILES

Judaism
ABRAHAM
BIBLE STORIES
HANUKKAH
ISRAEL
MOSES
NOAH

Jump Rope Jingles
CHANTS
CLAPPING GAMES
RHYTHMS

Kindness
MANNERS
SHARING
VOLUNTEERS

**King, Martin
Luther, Jr.**
AFRICAN-
AMERICAN
CIVIL RIGHTS
FREEDOM
PEACE AND
JUSTICE

Kites
AIRPLANES

Learning Skills
ALPHABETS
CLOCKS AND
WATCHES
COLOR
COUNTING
IMAGINATION
MAKE-BELIEVE
MATHEMATICS
NAMES
NUMBERS
SCHOOL LIFE
SIZE AND SHAPE
SOUNDS
TELLING TIME

Lifestyles
FRONTIER LIFE
MILITARY LIFE
PRISONERS AND
PRISONS
RURAL LIFE
SCHOOL LIFE
URBAN LIFE

Lincoln, Abraham
CIVIL WAR (U.S.
1861-1865)
FREEDOM
SLAVERY

Literary Forms
LIMERICKS
NURSERY RHYMES

RIDDLES
STORIES
TONGUE
TWISTERS

Love
COURTING
FEELINGS
HAPPINESS

Lullabies
BABIES
BEDTIME
CLOSING SONGS
DREAMS
EVENING
MERRY-GO-
ROUNDS
NATIVE
AMERICANS
NIGHT
NURSERY RHYMES
PRAYERS
SLEEP

**Lumberjacks and
Lumbering**
TREES

Make-Believe
CLOWNS
DOLLS
ELVES
FAIRIES, DWARFS,
AND GOBLINS
IMAGINATION
PLAY
PUPPETS

Manners
FORGIVENESS
GOOD BEHAVIOR
GREETINGS
HUMAN
RELATIONS
KINDNESS
NAMES
SELF-IMAGE
SHARING
TRUTH

Marching
MILITARY LIFE
SOLDIERS
WAR SONGS AND
CRIES

Mathematics
COUNTING
CUMULATIVE
SONGS
DIMINISHING
SONGS
NUMBERS
TELLING TIME

Military Life
MARCHING
PATRIOTIC SONGS
REVOLUTIONARY
WAR IN AMER-
ICA (1776-1781)
SAILORS
SOLDIERS
WAR SONGS AND
CRIES

Miners and Mining
DRILLING

Money
NUMBERS

Months
APRIL
DAYS
DECEMBER
MAY
SEPTEMBER

Moon
ASTRONAUTS

Mormons and
Mormonism
COVERED WAGONS
OX CART

Morning
SUNRISE

Moving Pictures
CARTOONS
PUPPETS

Mules
ERIE CANAL

Music
CAMP SONGS
CANONS
CHRISTMAS
CAROLS
CHRISTMAS SONGS
CIRCULAR SONGS
CLOSING SONGS

DANCES
FOLK SONGS
HYMNS
NONSENSE SONGS
PATRIOTIC SONGS
QUESTION AND
ANSWER
SONGS
RHYTHMS
SEA SONGS
SINGING
SPIRITUALS
WAR SONGS AND
CRIES
WORK SONGS
YODELS

Musical Activities
ACTION SONGS
ANIMAL SOUNDS
CHANTS
CIRCLE GAMES
CLAPPING GAMES
CUMULATIVE
SONGS
DANCERS AND
DANCING
DANCES
DIMINISHING
SONGS
ECHO SONGS
EXERCISE GAMES
FINGER AND
HAND PLAY
GUESSING GAMES
HANDS
JUMP ROPE
JINGLES
MARCHING
QUESTION AND
ANSWER
SONGS
ROUNDS
SINGING GAMES
SQUARE DANCING
TONGUE TWISTERS

Musical
Instruments
BANJOS
BELLS
DRUMS
FLUTE
MUSIC AND
MUSICIANS

VIOLINS
WHISTLES AND
WHISTLING

Names
GREETINGS

Native Americans
COWBOYS
FRONTIER LIFE
PILGRIMS
PIONEERS

Nature
CAMP SONGS
FLOWERS
FORESTS
GRASS
MUD
PICNICS
TREES
WALKING

Needlework
SPINNING
WEAVING

Neighbors
FRIENDSHIP
VOLUNTEERS

Night
BEDTIME
CAMP SONGS
DREAMS
SLEEP

Nighttime Songs
BEDTIME
EVENING

Nonsense Songs
CAMP SONGS
CIRCULAR SONGS
CUMULATIVE
SONGS
DEATH
ECHO SONGS
LUMBERJACKS
AND
LUMBERING
MAKE-BELIEVE
MULES
NURSERY RHYMES
QUESTION AND
ANSWER
SONGS
RIDDLES

TONGUE
TWISTERS

Numbers
CLOCKS AND
WATCHES
COUNTING
CUMULATIVE
SONGS
DIMINISHING
SONGS
MATHEMATICS
SIZE AND SHAPE
TELLING TIME

Nursery Rhymes
CAKES AND
COOKIES
CIRCLE GAMES
COLOR
COURTING
JUMP ROPE
JINGLES
KINGS AND
RULERS
MAKE-BELIEVE
MUSIC AND
MUSICIANS
NEEDLEWORK
PIES
SHOES
STAIRWAYS
STREET CRIES
TONGUE
TWISTERS
WOOL

Occupations
DENTISTS
FISHERMEN AND
FISHING
MINERS AND
MINING
MUSIC AND
MUSICIANS
POLICE
POSTAL SERVICE
WORK AND LABOR

Oceans
SAILING
SEA SONGS
SEASHORE
WATER

Outer Space
ASTRONAUTS
FLYING

Outerspace
AIRPLANES

Outlaws
JAMES, JESSE
WOODSON
PRISONERS AND
PRISONS

Patriotic Songs
FLAGS
FOURTH OF JULY
MILITARY LIFE
SOLDIERS
STATUE OF
LIBERTY
UNITED STATES
WAR SONGS AND
CRIES

Peace and Justice
BROTHERHOOD
CIVICS
DEMOCRACY
EQUAL RIGHTS
FOLK SONGS
KING, MARTIN
LUTHER, JR.

People
ABRAHAM
AFRICAN-
AMERICAN
APOSTLES
BIBLE STORIES
CASEY JONES
COLUMBUS,
CHRISTOPHER
DANIEL
EZEKIEL
JAMES, JESSE
WOODSON
JESUS CHRIST
JOE HILL
JOHN HENRY
JOSHUA
KING, MARTIN
LUTHER, JR.
KINGS AND
RULERS
MOSES

NATIVE
AMERICANS
NOAH
OUTLAWS

Pets
ANIMAL SOUNDS

Physical World
BROOKS
GRASS
HUMAN BODY
MOON
MOUNTAINS
MUD
NATURE
OCEANS
OUTER SPACE
RIVERS
SEASHORE
SEASONS
SHADOWS
STARS
SUN
SUNRISE
WATER
WEATHER

Pies
CAKES AND
COOKIES
CANDY

Pilgrims
THANKSGIVING
DAY

Pioneers
COVERED WAGONS
FRONTIER LIFE
MORMONS AND
MORMONISM
OUTLAWS
OX CART

Places
CHURCHES
HOSPITALS
HOUSES
STAIRWAYS

Plants
BARLEY
FLOWERS
FORESTS
GARDENS
HARVEST
TREES

Play
ACTION SONGS
BALLS
BASEBALL
BICYCLES AND
BICYCLING
CIRCLE GAMES
CLOWNS
DOLLS
FRIENDSHIP
HANDS
KITES
MERRY-GO-
ROUNDS
MUD
PUPPETS
SCHOOL LIFE
SWINGS AND
SWINGING
TOPS
TOYS

**Presidents—
United States**
LINCOLN,
ABRAHAM
UNITED STATES
WASHINGTON,
GEORGE

Pumpkins
HALLOWEEN
WITCHES

**Question and
Answer Songs**
ECHO SONGS
GUESSING GAMES
RIDDLES

Railroads
CASEY JONES
DRILLING
STAGECOACHES
TRANSPORTATION
WHEELS
WHISTLES AND
WHISTLING

Rain
RAINBOW
THUNDERSTORMS
WATER
WEATHER
WIND

Religion
ANGELS
BIBLE STORIES
CHRISTIANITY
CHRISTMAS
CAROLS
CHURCHES
DEVILS
HYMNS
JOY
JUDAISM
LOVE
MORMONS AND
MORMONISM
PRAYERS
SAINTS
SPIRITUALS

Religious Music
ABRAHAM
ANGELS
BIBLE STORIES
JESUS CHRIST
MOSES
NOAH

**Reptiles and
Amphibians**
ALLIGATORS
CROCODILES
DINOSAURS
FROGS
LIZARDS
SNAKES
TOADS
TURTLES

**Revolutionary War
in America
(1776-1781)**
WAR SONGS AND
CRIES
WASHINGTON,
GEORGE

Rhythms
CHANTS
JUMP ROPE
JINGLES

Riddles
ECHO SONGS
GUESSING GAMES
LIMERICKS

QUESTION AND
ANSWER
SONGS
TONGUE TWISTERS

Rivers
BROOKS
CANOES AND
CANOEING
ERIE CANAL
FERRIES
WATER

Romance
VALENTINE'S DAY

Rounds
CANONS
CHANTS

Rural Life
ANIMAL SOUNDS
CHICKENS
DUCKS
FARMERS AND
FARMING
GEESE
MUD
MULES
NATURE
TURKEYS

Safety Awareness
CRYING
DRUGS
FEAR
FIRE ENGINES
FIREFIGHTERS
FIRES
HEALTH
POLICE
STRANGERS

Sailing
BOATS AND
BOATING
SAILORS
SEA SONGS
SHIPS

Sailors
BOATS AND
BOATING
MILITARY LIFE
SAILING
SEA SONGS
SHIPS

Santa Claus
CHRISTMAS
CHRISTMAS SONGS

Sea Songs
BOATS AND
BOATING
SAILING
SAILORS

Seashore
OCEANS

Seasons
AUTUMN
DAYS
MONTHS
SPRING
SUMMER
WINTER

Self-Image
CHILDREN
CRYING
FEAR
FORGIVENESS
GROOMING,
PERSONAL
GROWING UP
HEALTH
HUMAN
RELATIONS
MANNERS
SMILES
STRANGERS

Senses
EARS

Sharing
MANNERS
NEIGHBORS
VOLUNTEERS

Sheep
WOOL

Ships
BOATS AND
BOATING
FERRIES
FISHERMEN AND
FISHING
SAILING
SAILORS
TRANSPORTATION

Sickness
HEALTH
HOSPITALS

Singing
YODELS

Singing Games
ACTION SONGS

Slavery
AFRICAN-
AMERICAN
CIVIL RIGHTS
CIVIL WAR (U.S.
1861-1865)
FREEDOM
LINCOLN,
ABRAHAM

Slavery
SPIRITUALS

Sleep
BEDTIME
DREAMS
NIGHT

Smiles
CRYING

Snow
WEATHER

Soldiers
MARCHING
MILITARY LIFE

Sounds
EARS

Spiders
SPINNING

Spinning
NEEDLEWORK
WEAVING

Spirituals
AFRICAN-
AMERICAN
CIVIL RIGHTS
CIVIL WAR (U.S.
1861-1865)
FOLK SONGS
HYMNS
SLAVERY

**Sports and
Recreation**
BALL SPORTS

BASEBALL
BICYCLES AND
BICYCLING
BOATS AND
BOATING
CANOES AND
CANOEING
DANCERS AND
DANCING
FISHERMEN AND
FISHING
FLYING
HUNTING
PICNICS
PLAY
SAILING
SEESAWS
SWINGS AND
SWINGING
WALKING

Spring
APRIL
MAY
MAY DAY
ROBINS
SEASONS

Stars
NIGHT

Storms
THUNDERSTORMS
WEATHER
WIND

Strangers
FEAR
SAFETY
AWARENESS

Street Cries
SHELLS
(MOLLUSKS)

Summer
BASEBALL
SEASONS

Sun
SUNRISE

Technology
MONEY
TELEPHONES
TRANSPORTATION

Teeth
DENTISTS

Television
CARTOONS
MOVING PICTURES
PUPPETS

Telling Time
CLOCKS AND
WATCHES
DAYS
MATHEMATICS
MONTHS
MORNING
NUMBERS
SIZE AND SHAPE

Thanksgiving Day
PILGRIMS
PUMPKINS
TURKEYS

Thunderstorms
RAIN
WEATHER
WIND

Time Measurement
BEDTIME
CLOCKS AND
WATCHES
DAYS
EVENING
MONTHS
MORNING
NEW YEAR
NIGHT
TELLING TIME
TIME

Toads
FROGS

Tops
BALLS

Toys
BALLS
DOLLS
KITES
PLAY
PUPPETS
SWINGS AND
SWINGING
TOPS

Transportation
AIRPLANES
AUTOMOBILES

BALLOONS
(AIRSHIPS)
BUSES
COVERED WAGONS
ERIE CANAL
FERRIES
OX CART
RAILROADS
SHIPS
STAGECOACHES
TRAVEL
WAGONS
WHEELS

Trees
FORESTS

United States
ALABAMA
ARKANSAS
CALIFORNIA
CIVICS
DEMOCRACY
FLAGS
HAWAII
MISSISSIPPI
NEW YORK
OKLAHOMA
STATUE OF
LIBERTY
TEXAS

United States History
CIVICS
CIVIL WAR (U.S.
1861-1865)
DEMOCRACY
EQUAL RIGHTS
FOLK SONGS
FOURTH OF JULY
FREEDOM
KING, MARTIN
LUTHER, JR.
LINCOLN,
ABRAHAM
MORMONS AND
MORMONISM
PATRIOTIC SONGS
PILGRIMS
RAILROADS
REVOLUTIONARY
WAR IN AMER-
ICA (1776-1781)
SAILORS
SLAVERY

SOLDIERS
STATUE OF
LIBERTY
THANKSGIVING
DAY
UNITED STATES
WASHINGTON,
GEORGE

Vegetables
CABBAGE
CORN
GARDENERS AND
GARDENING

Volunteers
FRIENDSHIP
MANNERS
NEIGHBORS

Wagons
WHEELS

Wake-Up Songs
MORNING
SUNRISE

War Songs and Cries
MARCHING
MILITARY LIFE
PATRIOTIC SONGS
REVOLUTIONARY
WAR IN AMER-
ICA (1776-1781)
SOLDIERS

Washington, George
REVOLUTIONARY
WAR IN AMER-
ICA (1776-1781)

Water
BROOKS
CANOES AND
CANOEING
FERRIES

Weather
FROST
MUD
RAIN
RAINBOW
SNOW
THUNDERSTORMS
WATER
WIND

Weaving
NEEDLEWORK
SPINNING

Wheels
BICYCLES AND
BICYCLING
BUSES

**Whistles and
Whistling**
RAILROADS

Winter
BELLS
CHRISTMAS SONGS
DECEMBER
FROST
SANTA CLAUS
SEASONS
SNOW
WIND

Witches
DEVILS
ELVES
FAIRIES, DWARFS,
AND GOBLINS
HALLOWEEN

Work and Labor
ASTRONAUTS

BAKERS AND
BAKING
BROTHERHOOD
COWBOYS
DENTISTS
DRILLING
ERIE CANAL
FAMILIES
FARMERS AND
FARMING
FIRE ENGINES
FIREFIGHTERS
FISHERMEN AND
FISHING
GARDENERS AND
GARDENING
LUMBERJACKS
AND
LUMBERING
MINERS AND
MINING
MUSIC AND
MUSICIANS
NEEDLEWORK
OCCUPATIONS
PIONEERS
POLICE
POSTAL SERVICE
RAILROADS
SAILORS

SOLDIERS
SPINNING
STREET CRIES
WEAVING
WHISTLES AND
WHISTLING
WORK SONGS

Work Songs
DRILLING
JOHN HENRY
MARCHING
MINERS AND
MINING
OCCUPATIONS
RAILROADS
SPINNING
STREET CRIES
WEAVING
WHISTLES AND
WHISTLING
WORK AND LABOR

Yiddish Language
ISRAEL
JUDAISM

Zoos
ANIMAL SOUNDS
ANIMALS
CIRCUSES

ABE LINCOLN. *See* **LINCOLN, ABRAHAM**

ABRAHAM
Rock-a My Soul 43:4

ACTION SONGS
A-Driving We Will Go 72:36
A Paris 62:73
All of Me 42:104
All the Fish 72:42
Alley Cat Song 66:206
Amen 1:60
Aserrin, Aserran 62:75
Baby Bear's Chicken Pox 71:52
Baby Cakewalk 69:16
Baby Moses 71:51
Baby's Face 72:50
Baby's Going Bye-Bye 35:22
Back of a Crocodile 64:49. *See also* Crocodile, The; Smile on the Crocodile
Barnyard Stomp 56:68
Bassez Down 64:92
Bim Bom 1:56
Biscuits in the Oven 60:9
Bluebird 38:83, 65:9
Boci Tarka 1:88
Boom da li-da 1:84
Bow Belinda 38:102
Bunny Hop 66:211
Bus Song 20:16, 36:49, 38:130. *See also* Wheels on the Bus
Car Car 72:38
Charades 14:13
Charlie over the Ocean 64:95
Cheerio 64:84
Choose the Animal 14:19
Christopher Columbus 47:1
Christopher McCracken 50:48
Cinnamon Ship, The 55:8
Circle Games 21:26
Clap Your Hands 21:14, 38:86
Climbing Up the Tower 72:54
Clipety Clop 72:12
Clothes Clothes 72:32
Did You Ever See a Lassie? 24:24, 33:28, 36:64, 38:96

Diddle Diddle Dumpling 38:76, 71:48, 72:28
Do Your Ears Hang Low? 16:30, 38:113, 50:66, 51:75, 70:6
Down at the Station 74:37
Down by the Station 33:37, 36:73, 38:129, 66:116
Dr. Knickerbocker 64:90
Easter Bunny 38:141, 71:46
Easter Eggs 47:44
Everybody Says Sit Down 55:49
Everybody Stand Up 10:16
Fingers 14:22
First-Last 21:25
Five Little Fingers 72:51
Following the Leader 14:9
Freedom 47:31
French Cathedrals 1:24
Giggle Tickle Fiddle Little Wiggle Around 56:39
Go In and Out the Window 31:45, 33:47, 36:100
Go Round and Round the Village 38:85
Gogo 38:93
Going Out to Play 71:28
Going to Kentucky 64:82
Grand Old Duke of York 65:29
Groundhog 22:92, 71:38
Haiye Kirumbe 1:70
Halloween Capers 47:8
Halloween Is Here! 47:11
Hambone 55:37
Head and Shoulders, Baby 64:54. *See also* Head and Shoulders; Head, Shoulders, Baby; Tete, Epaules
Head, Shoulders, Baby 49:33. *See also* Head and Shoulders; Head and Shoulders, Baby; Tete, Epaules
Here Stands a Redbird 38:106
Here We Go Looby Loo 31:12, 36:116. *See also* Looby Loo
Here We Go Round the Mulberry Bush 15:41, 44:29, 74:45, 75:26. *See also* Mulberry Bush
Hippity Hop 3:14
Hippity Hop to Bed 38:13

ACTION SONGS (*cont.*)

Hippity Hop to the Barber Shop 38:55

Hokey-Pokey 66:204

Hop Up and Jump Up 34:53

Huff and Puff 11:24

I Am Learning How to Work 10:52

I Am Slowly Going Crazy 50:69, 51:77, 64:79

I Brush My Teeth 72:29

I Got a Letter 1:12

I Love God 42:63

I Sit Down 42:52

I'm a Little Teapot 16:32, 35:52, 38:95, 66:109, 74:28

I'm a Walkin 72:9

I'm Going Up, Up, Up 42:124

I'm in the Mood 60:52

I'm Not Small 55:25

I'm Peeling My Banana 55:50

If I Were a Little Bird 74:46

If You're Happy 74:38. *See also* If You're Happy and You Know It

If You're Happy and You Know It 49:28, 66:176, 70:20. *See also* If You're Happy

In and Out the Window 15:42

Incey Wincey Spider 38:28. *See also* Eency Weency Spider; Eensy Weensy Spider; Eentsy Weentsy Spider

Intermission Rag 17:21

Jack and Jill 31:41, 33:75, 36:138, 38:39, 44:14, 65:26, 66:223, 75:36

Jack, Be Nimble 38:104

Jack-O'-Lantern 47:4

Jaws 55:46

Jim Along Josie 36:141. *See also* Jim-a-long Josie

Jim-a-long Josie 1:66. *See also* Jim Along Josie

John Brown's Baby 16:30, 51:22, 66:177

Jungle Gym 35:43

La Bamba 20:28

Lazy Mary 33:80, 35:56, 36:153, 38:62, 65:8, 72:24, 75:41. *See also* Lazy Mary, Will You Get Up?

Lazy Mary, Will You Get Up? 31:64, 66:228. *See also* Lazy Mary

Lazy Susan 55:10

Left Right 4:24

Let's Be Friends 47:35

Let's Make Some Noise 58:26

Little Girl/Boy Went Walking 55:55

Little Green Frog 55:59

Little Man 1:46

Little Tommy Tinker 64:74. *See also* Little Tommy Tucker

London Bridge 31:61, 33:83, 36:160, 38:105, 44:30, 65:24, 66:230, 75:58. *See also* London Bridge Is Falling Down

London Bridge Is Falling Down 15:43. *See also* London Bridge

Looby Loo 24:26, 38:92, 64:83. *See also* Here We Go Looby Loo

Looking In a Mirror 14:21

Looking Out the Window 72:40

Many Ways to Travel 14:24

Marching Song 42:51

Mary Had a Little Car 72:35

Me and My Horse 15:47

Mighty Pretty Motion 1:2

Miss Mary Mack 1:78

Monkey See and Monkey Do 55:51

Monte Sur un Elephant 64:58

Move Over 21:11

Mulberry Bush 31:6, 33:84, 36:166, 38:80, 65:14, 66:216. *See also* Here We Go Round the Mulberry Bush

My Dog Rags 20:38, 64:42

My Jumping Song 14:6

My Pony Boy 65:32

No No No 71:29

Oh, I'm Riding in the Car 72:37

Oh, We Can Play 74:36

Ol' Dan Tucker 22:88

Old Mother Hubbard 71:58

Old Roger 64:88

On Halloween 47:5

One Finger, One Thumb 35:64, 49:30, 64:46, 74:41

One Little Girl 4:10

One, Two, Buckle My Shoe 74:42

Open, Shut Them 55:58, 72:55

Pair of Feet 14:14

Pawpaw Patch 15:44, 64:96

Peanut Butter 64:48

Peanut Butter and Jelly 55:57. *See also* Peanut Butter Song

Peanut Butter Sandwich 59:4

Peanut Butter Song 50:30. *See also* Peanut Butter and Jelly

Peep Squirrel 63:18
Peter Piper 71:60
Pick a Bale o' Cotton 31:70, 59:57.
    See also Pick a Bale of Cotton
Pick a Bale of Cotton 36:190. *See*
    also Pick a Bale o' Cotton
Plant a Little Tree 5:32
Please Sit Down 55:48
Polly-Wolly-Doodle 19:36, 31:50,
    66:174
Presidents Are Famous Men 47:38
Pretty White Teeth 72:14
Pumpkins 47:10
Punchinello 47 64:94
Put Your Finger in the Air 36:196,
    66:132
Put Your Little Foot Right Out
    66:208
Queen Caroline 1:6
Rain 71:62
Rattlin' Bog 64:44
Ride on a Bus 14:11
Riding in the Buggy 72:39
Rig-A-Jig-Jig 20:10, 25:4, 38:94,
    65:30
Right Foot, Left Foot 21:19
Ring Around a Rosy 31:59, 38:107,
    75:52. *See also* Ring Around the
    Rosy; Ring-a-Ring o' Roses
Ring Around the Rosy 72:13:13
Ring Those Bells 2:58
Ring-a-Long Bells 47:27
Ring-a-Ring o' Roses 44:28, 65:21.
    See also Ring Around a Rosy;
    Ring Around the Rosy
Ringel Rosen 1:124
Roly Poly 4:23
Sarasponda 1:30, 22:40, 67:10
Saturday Night 1:40
Savez-vous Planter des Choux?
    58:20. *See also* Savez-vous
    Planter les Choux?
Savez-vous Planter les Choux?
    64:68. *See also* Savez-vous
    Planter des Choux?
See My Fingers 72:53
See-saw, Margery Daw 31:75,
    44:27. *See also* See-Saw, Mar-
    jorie Daw; Seesaw, Marjorie
    Daw
See-Saw, Marjorie Daw 38:37. *See*
    also See-saw, Margery Daw;
    Seesaw, Marjorie Daw

See the Pony Galloping, Galloping
    38:98
Shake My Sillies Out 19:24, 59:31
She'll Be Comin' 'Round the Moun-
    tain 31:37, 33:116, 49:46,
    64:22, 66:178, 67:6. *See also*
    She'll Be Coming 'Round the
    Mountain; She'll Be Coming
    Around the Mountain; She'll Be
    Coming Round the Mountain
She'll Be Coming 'Round the Moun-
    tain 36:201. *See also* She'll Be
    Comin' 'Round the Mountain;
    She'll Be Coming Around the
    Mountain; She'll Be Coming
    Round the Mountain
She'll Be Coming Around the Moun-
    tain 15:46. *See also* She'll Be
    Comin' 'Round the Mountain;
    She'll Be Coming 'Round the
    Mountain; She'll Be Coming
    Round the Mountain
She'll Be Coming Round the Moun-
    tain 20:6, 38:128, 40:94. *See*
    also She'll Be Comin' 'Round
    the Mountain; She'll Be Com-
    ing 'Round the Mountain;
    She'll Be Coming Around the
    Mountain
Shiloh, Liza Jane 40:98
Shoe Shoe Patch 72:30
Si-si-si 1:36
Simon Says 14:28
Sing a Song of September 71:6
Six Little Ducks 24:18, 50:18, 59:52
Skinnamarink 64:122, 65:95
Skip to My Lou 15:45, 31:21,
    33:124, 36:210, 38:90
Sodeo 59:46
Sourwood Mountain 36:212
Squirrel, The 35:39
St. Patrick's Day 47:42
Stretch and Bend 21:23
Sur le Pont d'Avignon 38:108,
    59:80, 64:60
Ten Fingers 35:60
Thank You Dance 11:56
There Came a Girl from France
    59:82
Things Unseen 47:3
This Is the Way 72:31
This Is the Way the Ladies Ride
    74:12

ACTION SONGS (*cont.*)

This Little Toe 72:44
Three Steps Forward 11:12
Three Ways to Get Peanut Butter
    Off the Roof of Your Mouth
    50:33
Three White Gulls 38:97
Throw the Ball 10:17
Ticklely 72:52
Time to Sing 60:67
Tippy-Tippy Toes 14:16
Trot, Trot, Trot 62:71, 74:16
Turkey Run 47:14
Turtles 21:29
Up Goes the Baby 72:23
Walk Forward and Backward 21:22
Walking Song 14:26, 76:16
We Are Soldiers 74:29
We're Glad You're Here 42:55
Wheels on the Bus 16:32, 49:44,
    60:43. *See also* Bus Song
When Is the Day? 42:56
Where Are Your Eyes? 35:14
Where Is John? 1:96
Whistling Cowhand 71:50
Who Stole My Chickens? 1:16
Wiggle Song 4:22, 42:54
Windmill 65:62
Witch, The 47:7
Witches, Ghosts, and Goblins 47:6
With My Little Broom 74:35
Worms 71:56
Wriggledy Jiggledy Song 49:36
You Gotta Sing 19:6, 59:56

AFRICA

Che Che Koolay 64:105
Haiye Kirumbe 1:70
Obwisana 64:111
Saturday Night 1:40
Si-si-si 1:36

AFRICAN-AMERICAN

Martin Luther King, Junior 47:30

AIRPLANES

Riding in an Airplane 60:81

ALABAMA

Oh, Susanna! 31:68, 33:98, 36:179,
    38:126, 40:79

ALLIGATORS

Animal Song 63:80
Go On, Old 'gator 63:74

ALPHABETS

ABC Song 65:17
Alfabet Song 56:119
Alphabet Song 31:72, 50:63, 66:212
B-I-B-L-E, The 26:14
Bingo 31:36, 33:21, 35:57, 36:44,
    38:82, 66:124. *See also* Bingo
    Was His Name
Bingo Was His Name 51:26. *See
    also* Bingo
Clock Without a "C" Is Still a Lock
    56:116
C-O-F-F-E-E 39:29
Halloween 71:15
I Am Learning How to Spell 9:7
M-I-S-S-I-S-S-I-P-P-I 66:157
Spell Some Names 21:8

ANGELS

Angel Band 2:26
Angels We Have Heard on High
    23:2, 28:22, 61:28
First Noel 2:14, 23:18, 28:10,
    36:86, 45:32, 57:62, 61:22
Hark! The Herald Angels Sing
    28:30, 36:114, 45:36, 52:96,
    61:18

ANIMAL SOUNDS

Barnyard Song 24:12, 40:6, 67:5
Bought Me a Cat 22:264
By the Barnyard Gate 55:61
Chickens in the Barnyard 3:12
Choose the Animal 14:19
Clever Amphibian 3:21
Cocky Doodle Doodle Doo 72:21
Ducks Like Rain 60:62
Farmer in the Dell 15:40, 31:26,
    33:41, 36:84, 38:79, 66:232. *See
    also* Farmer's in the Dell
Farmer's in the Dell 74:40, 75:20.
    See also Farmer in the Dell
Gobble Strut, Strut 3:13
He's a Dog 3:10
I Had a Little Rooster 35:82. *See
    also* I Had a Rooster
I Had a Rooster 50:22. *See also* I
    Had a Little Rooster
King of the Jungle 71:44
Listen to the Horses 59:50
Old MacDonald 31:48, 33:100,
    36:184, 74:48. *See also* Old Mac-
    Donald Had a Farm

Old MacDonald Had a Farm 38:118, 66:96. *See also* Old Mac-Donald
Quack, Quack, Quack 3:7
Six Little Ducks 24:18, 50:18, 59:52
Whistler and His Dog 66:102
Wolves A-Howling 63:79

ANIMALS
All Things Bright and Beautiful 42:91, 48:2
Anansi 59:72
And We Hunted and We Hunted 63:36
Animal Fair 36:22, 66:87, 70:18
Animal Song 63:80
Animals Are My Friends 71:19
Baa, Baa, Black Sheep 31:3, 33:17, 33:32, 36:31, 38:47, 44:7, 59:14, 66:223, 75:32
Babies 5:28
Baby Beluga 19:18, 60:7
Baby Bumble Bee 50:8, 51:112
Barnyard Song 24:12, 40:6, 67:5
Bear, Bear, Bear 3:32
Big Sheep, The 63:58
Black Sheep, Black Sheep 63:57
Boom Boom 51:68, 59:70. *See also* Boom, Boom Ain't It Great to Be Crazy
Boom, Boom Ain't It Great to Be Crazy 20:30. *See also* Boom Boom
Born This Night 2:31
Bought Me a Cat 22:264
Bronx Zoo Is for Me and You 30:10
By the Barnyard Gate 55:61
Cat Came Back 40:14, 49:52, 51:114
Chicken Lips and Lizard Hips 19:34, 32:39
Chickens in the Barnyard 3:12
Circus Is Coming 17:3
Circus, The 17:45
Clever Cow 3:15
Cluck, Cluck, Red Hen 20:32, 59:84
Crocodile Song 63:72
Cross-Eyed Gopher 63:20
Cute, Cuddily Koala 30:32
Daddy Shot a Bear 63:78
Deer Song, The 63:34
Down by the Bay 19:28, 24:22, 49:71, 59:2
Down by the Creek Bank 42:133
Down on Grandpa's Farm 60:87

Dromedaries 3:34
El Coquito 38:136
Farmer in the Dell 15:40, 31:26, 33:41, 36:84, 38:79, 66:232. *See also* Farmer's in the Dell
Farmer's in the Dell 74:40, 75:20. *See also* Farmer in the Dell
Five Little Frogs 59:1
Fooba-Wooba John 20:12
Fox in a Box 15:44
Fox, The 19:40, 33:42, 36:88, 40:34, 66:88. *See also* Old Fox
Friendly Beasts 2:41, 28:26, 36:92
Frog Went A-Courtin' 33:44, 36:94, 66:182. *See also* Froggie Went A-Courting
Froggie Went A-Courting 75:18. *See also* Frog Went A-Courtin'
Furry Squirrel 71:12
Go On, Old 'gator 63:74
Gobble Strut, Strut 3:13
Going to the Zoo 40:45, 59:24, 66:90
Good Night, Irene 59:88. *See also* Goodnight, Irene
Great Ape 3:38
Groundhog 22:92, 71:38
He's a Dog 3:10
Hello There, Farmer 55:60
Here Sits a Monkey 59:68
Hippity Hop 3:14
Hooray for the Hippo 3:40
Hop Up, My Ladies 63:66
Hush! 42:19
Hushabye 69:18
I Got a Camel for Christmas 35:84
I Had a Little Rooster 35:82. *See also* I Had a Rooster
I Had a Rooster 50:22. *See also* I Had a Little Rooster
I Know an Old Lady 66:125
I Wish I Were a Fish 3:19
I've Got a Dog and My Dog's Name Is Cat 56:69
If I Were a Little Bird 74:46
Jack, Can I Ride? 63:76
Jig Along Home 31:18, 59:60
Just Like the Sun 58:45
Kangaroo, Kangaroo 3:35
Kicking Mule 63:62
Kitten in the Sun 3:8
Listen to the Horses 59:50
Little Black Bull, The 63:54
Little Brown Dog 63:28
Little Dog Named Right 63:26

ANIMALS (*cont.*)

Little Lap-Dog Lullaby 63:27

Little Peter Possum 24:2

Little Peter Rabbit 35:76, 50:19, 64:36

Little Pig 63:50

Little White Duck 36:158, 58:40, 66:92

Mister Rabbit 63:16

Mole in the Ground 63:25

Muskrat 63:21

My Little Pony 3:9

My Old Hen's a Good Old Hen 63:44

Nine Little Reindeer 71:26

Of All the Beast-es 63:75

Oh, Blue 63:30

Oh, John the Rabbit 22:216, 49:55

Ol' Dan Tucker 22:88

Old Bell'd Yoe 63:60

Old Cow Died 63:56

Old Fox 63:32. *See also* Fox, The

Old Ground Hog 63:22

Old Hen Cackled and the Rooster Laid the Egg 63:42

Old Joe Clark 40:81. *See also* Old Joe Clarke

Old Joe Clarke 50:44. *See also* Old Joe Clark

Old MacDonald 31:48, 33:100, 36:184, 74:48. *See also* Old MacDonald Had a Farm

Old MacDonald Had a Farm 38:118, 66:96. *See also* Old MacDonald

Old Sow 63:52

Once I Saw Three Goats 64:77

Over in the Meadow 38:44, 49:16, 60:27

Peep Squirrel 63:18

Possum on the Flying Trapeze 24:28. *See also* Man on the Trapeze

Raccoon and Possum 63:15

Reindeer Are Tapping 2:59

Reptile World 56:148

Riddle 3:42

Riding Round the Cattle 63:70

Robin in the Rain 59:28

Seal and a Walrus 3:26

Shake That Little Foot, Dinah-O 63:47

She Went into the Water 24:20

Six Little Ducks 24:18, 50:18, 59:52

Slow, Slow Snail 53:4

Snake Baked a Hoecake 63:24

Squirrel Is a Pretty Thing 63:19

Stewball 40:106, 63:68

Sweetly Sings the Donkey 46:88

There Was an Old Frog 63:48

There Was an Old Lady 33:131, 36:221

Ting-a-lay-o 19:12. *See also* Tinga Layo; Tingalayo

Tinga Layo 24:16. *See also* Ting-a-lay-o; Tingalayo

Tingalayo 37:39, 60:92, 64:106, 70:14. *See also* Ting-a-lay-o; Tinga Layo

Tit Galop Pour Mamou 22:50

Truth About Lions 3:30

Turkey Song 63:46

Walk Outside 60:94

What If a Zebra Had Spots? 56:197

What Shall We Do with the Baby-O? 55:43. *See also* What Will We Do with the Baby-O?

What Will We Do with the Baby-O? 35:51. *See also* What Shall We Do with the Baby-O?

Where Is Your Goose? 50:15

Who Built the Ark? 59:32

Who Made the Animals? 42:32

Whoa, Mule! Can't Get the Saddle On 63:64

Whose Tail Is Curly? 3:16

Willie the Whistling Giraffe 66:105

Willoughby Wallaby Woo 19:20, 59:7

Wolves A-Howling 63:79

Words 42:47

You Better Not Giggle, Now Don't You Laugh, But I'm in Love with a Giraffe 56:188

Your Neck's So Long 3:37

Zebra, The 3:33

Zoo, The 35:78

ANTEATERS

Animal Song 63:80

ANTS

Ants Go Marching 24:10, 50:6, 64:78

March of the Worker Ants 53:17

APOSTLES

Green Grow the Rushes-O 33:48, 36:106

APPLES

Apples and Bananas 19:32, 55:19, 60:70
Fruit 21:30
Fruit Song 68:19
Oliver Cromwell 46:16

APRIL

I Played a Joke on You 5:30

ARKANSAS

Arkansas Traveler 36:24, 40:4

ASTRONAUTS

Betty Wants to Be an Astronaut 30:42
Ride Sally Ride 71:32

AUSTRALIA

Botany Bay 46:78
Cute, Cuddily Koala 30:32
Kookaburra 36:150, 46:75, 70:32
Shearer's Dream 46:80
Streets of Forbes 46:76
Waltzing Matilda 66:200

AUSTRIA

All That Has Life and Breath, Sing to the Lord 39:20
Bless This Meal 39:20
Bona Nox 39:30
C-O-F-F-E-E 39:29
Come Meet a Little Birdy Friend 39:12
Cuckoo in the Forest 39:10
Fire! Fire! 39:6
I'm a Very Happy Person 39:7
In the Ev'ning the Nightingale 39:9
Let's All Sing 39:7
Meow, Meow 39:17
Now Is the Close of Day 39:21
Oh Hear the Bells Ringing 39:25
Rooster's Dead 39:18
Sleepers Wake 39:24
Thanks to God for His Love 39:22
Three Geese in Straw 39:16
Welcome April Sunshine 39:27
What Kind of Trees Are Found Out There? 39:13

AUTOMOBILES

A-Driving We Will Go 72:36
Big Wheels 10:50
Car Car 72:38
I'm a Nut 50:67, 51:78
Mary Had a Little Car 72:35
Oh, I'm Riding in the Car 72:37
Old MacDonald Had a Car 72:34

AUTUMN

Autumn Day 54:55
Autumn Leaves Are Now Falling 48:9
Beautiful Autumn 5:8
Bringing in the Sheaves 33:22
It's Autumn Time 54:55
Remember September 5:7
Seasons 42:34, 42:93, 68:9
Summer's End 76:30

BABIES

Babies 5:28
Baby Bear's Chicken Pox 71:52
Baby Bye 65:81
Baby's Going Bye-Bye 35:22
Bath, The 35:32
Bye, Baby Bunting 35:68, 38:14, 41:67, 77:15
Bye-Low, My Baby 48:8
Communication 18:39
Cradle Is Warm 41:66
Dance to Your Daddy 44:58, 65:80, 77:26
Go and Hush the Baby 56:165
Hush-a-Bye Baby 41:67, 44:60
Hush, Little Baby 22:98, 25:18, 31:20, 33:62, 36:126, 38:12, 65:91, 66:181, 70:38, 72:57, 74:9, 77:10
Jeremiah 65:83
John Brown's Baby 16:30, 51:22, 66:177
Lullaby 4:15, 38:17. See also Brahms' Lullaby; Cradle Song; Cradlesong
Lullabye 69:23, 72:60
Marvin Doesn't Like the New Baby 56:154
Mockingbird Song 40:74
Pretty White Teeth 72:14
Rock-a-Bye Baby 25:22, 31:34, 33:112, 36:198, 41:66, 65:93, 66:221, 74:8, 77:28. See also All the Pretty Little Horses; Go to Sleepy; Hush A Bye; Hush'n Bye; Hush-You-Bye; Rockabye, Baby
Rockabye, Baby 38:20. See also All the Pretty Little Horses; Go to Sleepy; Hush A Bye; Hush'n Bye; Hush-You-Bye; Rock-a-Bye Baby
Shiny Silver Moon 35:36
Sleep My Baby 41:69

BABIES (*cont.*)

There Was a Little Baby 57:80
Tiny Tim 65:78
Up in the Air 35:30
Wake Up, Little Baby 72:26
What Do We Do? 35:12
What Does Baby Hear 35:20
What Does Baby See 35:16
What Shall We Do with the Baby-O? 55:43. *See also* What Will We Do with the Baby-O?
What Will We Do with the Baby-O? 35:51. *See also* What Shall We Do with the Baby-O?
Where Are Your Eyes? 35:14
Where Can Baby Be? 35:33

BABY. *See* **BABIES**

BAKERS AND BAKING

Biscuits in the Oven 60:9
Hot Cross Buns! 31:16, 36:124, 38:140, 44:40, 66:224
Muffin Man 15:42, 36:165, 38:34, 64:98, 75:47
Pat-a-Cake 31:32, 35:50, 38:27, 72:20. *See also* Pat-a-Cake, Pat-a-Cake
Pat-a-Cake, Pat-a-Cake 44:59. *See also* Pat-a-Cake
Simple Simon 33:123, 38:48, 44:44, 65:31

BALL ROLLING. *See* **BALL SPORTS**

BALL SPORTS

I Roll the Ball 35:27
Let's Go Bowling in Bowling Green 50:64
My Brother and I 4:16
The Bowling Song 60:89
Throw the Ball 10:17

BALLOONS (AIRSHIPS)

Balloon, The 35:44

BALLS

My Brother and I 4:16

BANANAS

Apples and Bananas 19:32, 55:19, 60:70
I'm Peeling My Banana 55:50

BANJOS

Mama Don't 'Low 49:59. *See also* Mama Don't Allow

Mama Don't Allow 40:71. *See also* Mama Don't 'Low

BARLEY

Oats and Beans and Barley 60:13. *See also* Oats, Peas, and Beans; Oats, Peas, Beans; Oats, Peas, Beans and Barley Grow
Oats, Peas, and Beans 33:93. *See also* Oats and Beans and Barley; Oats, Peas, Beans; Oats, Peas, Beans and Barley Grow
Oats, Peas, Beans 24:8, 36:171, 38:89, 75:68. *See also* Oats and Beans and Barley; Oats, Peas, and Beans; Oats, Peas, Beans and Barley Grow
Oats, Peas, Beans and Barley Grow 66:228. *See also* Oats and Beans and Barley; Oats, Peas, and Beans; Oats, Peas, Beans

BASEBALL

Take Me Out to the Ball Game 22:296, 40:110, 60:72

BEANS

Beans in My Ears 40:8
Oats and Beans and Barley 60:13. *See also* Oats, Peas, and Beans; Oats, Peas, Beans; Oats, Peas, Beans and Barley Grow
Oats, Peas, and Beans 33:93. *See also* Oats and Beans and Barley; Oats, Peas, Beans; Oats, Peas, Beans and Barley Grow
Oats, Peas, Beans 24:8, 36:171, 38:89, 75:68. *See also* Oats and Beans and Barley; Oats, Peas, and Beans; Oats, Peas, Beans and Barley Grow
Oats, Peas, Beans and Barley Grow 66:228. *See also* Oats and Beans and Barley; Oats, Peas, and Beans; Oats, Peas, Beans
Quartermaster Corps 50:29, 51:43

BEARS

Animal Song 63:80
Bear Song 50:56
Bear Went over the Mountain 36:34, 38:112, 70:22
Bear, Bear, Bear 3:32
Benjy Met a Bear 51:48

Daddy Shot a Bear 63:78
Fuzzy Wuzzy 50:60
Jazzy Three Bears 55:26
Teddy Bear Hug 58:35

BEDTIME
All the Pretty Little Horses
    22:268, 33:7, 35:72, 38:11,
    77:18. *See also* Go to Sleepy;
    Hush A Bye; Hush'n Bye; Hush-
    You-Bye; Rock-a-Bye Baby;
    Rockabye, Baby
Baby Doll 35:24
Bona Nox 39:30
Brahms' Lullaby 77:31. *See also*
    Cradle Song; Cradlesong; Lulla-
    by; Lullaby, and Good Night
Bye, Baby Bunting 35:68, 38:14,
    41:67, 77:15
Bye-Low, My Baby 48:8
Cradle Is Warm 41:66
Cradle Song 35:70, 36:59. *See also*
    Brahms' Lullaby; Cradlesong;
    Lullaby; Lullaby, and Good
    Night; Schlaf, Kindlein, Schlaf;
    Sleep, Baby, Sleep
Cradlesong 31:11. *See also*
    Brahms' Lullaby; Cradle Song;
    Lullaby; Lullaby, and Good
    Night
Did You Say Your Prayers Last
    Night? 9:22
Go to Sleep 63:65
Go to Sleep Now, My Pumpkin
    65:92
Go to Sleepy 36:102. *See also* All
    the Pretty Little Horses; Hush
    A Bye; Hush'n Bye; Hush-You-
    Bye; Rock-a-Bye Baby; Rock-
    abye, Baby
Golden Slumbers 25:28, 31:8,
    38:16, 41:69, 74:6
Good Night 35:35
Good Night, Irene 59:88. *See also*
    Goodnight, Irene
Good Night Song 4:39
Hippity Hop to Bed 38:13
Hush'n Bye 62:36. *See also* All the
    Pretty Little Horses; Go to
    Sleepy; Hush A Bye; Hush-You-
    Bye; Rock-a-Bye Baby; Rock-
    abye, Baby
I Rock My Doll 35:25
I Was Only Foolin' 25:8

Lullaby 4:15, 38:17. *See also*
    Brahms' Lullaby; Cradle Song;
    Cradlesong
Lullaby, and Good Night 74:11.
    See also Brahms' Lullaby; Cra-
    dle Song; Cradlesong
Lullaby, My Jamie 46:60
Lullaby, My Pretty One 41:67
Lullabye 69:23, 72:60
Lulloo Lullay 77:12
Me and My Teddy Bear 66:94
Mockingbird Song 40:74
Morningtown Ride 19:46, 60:33
Now I Lay Me Down to Sleep
    25:12, 31:80
Now the Day Is Over 33:91, 34:32,
    38:21, 77:29
Rig-A-Jig-Jig 20:10, 25:4, 38:94,
    65:30
Rock-a-Bye Baby 25:22, 31:34,
    33:112, 36:198, 41:66, 65:93,
    66:221, 74:8, 77:28. *See also* All
    the Pretty Little Horses; Go to
    Sleepy; Hush A Bye; Hush'n
    Bye; Hush-You-Bye; Rockabye,
    Baby
Roll Over 25:14, 38:121. *See also*
    Roll Over, Roll Over; Ten in the
    Bed
Roll Over, Roll Over 70:34. *See
    also* Roll Over; Ten in the Bed
Sandman Comes 25:26, 38:15, 74:7
Schlaf, Kindlein, Schlaf 62:38. *See
    also* Cradle Song; Sleep, Baby,
    Sleep
Shiny Silver Moon 35:36
Sleep, Baby, Sleep 38:18, 41:68,
    74:8, 77:7. *See also* Cradle
    Song; Schlaf, Kindlein, Schlaf
Sleep My Baby 41:69
Sleeping Time 35:34
Soft Falls the Snow 69:30
Ten in the Bed 65:88. *See also* Roll
    Over; Roll Over, Roll Over
Wee Willie Winkie 38:19, 71:16
Where's My Pajamas? 65:87

BEES
Baby Bumble Bee 50:8, 51:112
Bumblebee Song 56:112
Busy Bee 53:33
Cluck, Cluck, Red Hen 20:32, 59:84
Fiddle-De-De 75:22. *See also*
    Fiddle-dee-dee

BEES (*cont.*)

Fiddle-dee-dee 31:29. *See also* Fiddle-De-De

Little Bumble Bee 3:22

Nanny Banny 69:21

Return of the Baby Bumblebee 55:9

There Was a Bee-Eye-Ee-Eye-Ee 50:12

BEETLES

Battle of the Stags 53:29

BELLS

Are You Sleeping 39:26, 72:25. *See also* Frere Jacques

Bells Are Ringing 2:36

Carol of the Bells 28:72

Christmas Bells 2:50, 54:27

Christmastime Is Here 47:25

Climbing Up the Tower 72:54

Ding, Dong, Bell 31:14

French Cathedrals 1:24

Frere Jacques 1:114, 25:24, 31:7, 36:91, 38:134, 46:61, 59:79, 62:109, 66:234. *See also* Are You Sleeping

Great Tom Is Cast 46:84

Hear the Jingle Bells 2:51

I Heard the Bells on Christmas Day 28:37

Jingle Bells 2:10, 23:4, 31:78, 36:142, 38:150, 45:26, 57:60, 61:20

Little Bells of Christmas 2:49

O How Lovely Is the Evening 48:7

Oh Hear the Bells Ringing 39:25

Oh, How Lovely Is the Evening 33:96, 36:176, 38:134

Oranges and Lemons 44:31, 75:74

Ring, Ring, Ring the Bells 2:49

Ring the Bell 21:36

Ring Those Bells 2:58

Ring-a-Long Bells 47:27

Sleigh Bells Ring 47:23

BIBLE. *See* **BIBLE STORIES**

BIBLE STORIES

Baptism 54:69

B-I-B-L-E, The 26:14

I Think When I Read That Sweet Story 54:33

I Wonder How It Felt 42:120

Jesus Went About Doing Good 42:8

Joshua Fit the Battle of Jericho 43:10. *See also* Joshua Fought the Battle of Jericho

Joshua Fought the Battle of Jericho 36:146. *See also* Joshua Fit the Battle of Jericho

My Bible 42:12

Rise and Shine 34:44, 50:91, 60:35

Tell Me the Stories of Jesus 54:33

BICYCLES AND BICYCLING

Bike Song 68:15

BIRDS

Alouette 66:194

Birds in the Wilderness 50:35

Bluebird 38:83, 65:9

Come Meet a Little Birdy Friend 39:12

Cuckoo in the Forest 39:10

Dream Song 22:14

Five Little Chickadees 38:77, 65:22

Here Stands a Redbird 38:106

If I Could Fly 35:40

If I Were a Little Bird 74:46

In the Ev'ning the Nightingale 39:9

In the Leafy Tree Tops 54:45

Kookaburra 36:150, 46:75, 70:32

Little House, The 58:13

Little Red Bird 46:40

Lone Wild Bird 34:48

Mister Stand-On-One-Leg 3:25

My Dame Hath a Lame, Tame Crane 46:87, 75:73

North Wind Doth Blow 38:33, 44:10, 75:66

Peek at a Peacock 3:24

Quack, Quack, Quack 3:7

Robin in the Rain 59:28

Rockin' Robin 20:42

Sing a Song of Sixpence 31:38, 36:208, 38:30, 44:45, 66:222, 75:55

Thirty Purple Birds 51:51

Three Crow 64:114

Three White Gulls 38:97

Who Killed Cock Robin? 75:88

BIRTHDAYS

Good Morning to You 38:115

Happy Birthday 4:25

Happy Birthday Miss Liberty 29:14

Happy Birthday to You 31:7, 54:9, 66:252

Happy, Happy Birthday 54:9

Martin Luther King, Junior 47:30

BOATS AND BOATING

Belly and Tubs 69:19
Dark Brown Is the River 35:87
E-ri-e, The 36:79
Lightly Row 38:138, 67:4, 76:10
Michael, Row the Boat Ashore
    20:26, 27:10, 34:30, 40:73, 67:14
My Bonnie Lies over the Ocean
    33:87
Oh, You Can't Get to Heaven 26:8.
    See also You Can't Get to
    Heaven
Row, Row, Row 60:64. *See also*
    Row, Row, Row Your Boat
Row, Row, Row Your Boat 31:26,
    36:199, 38:135, 65:83, 66:234,
    74:25, 75:53. *See also* Row,
    Row, Row
Skye Boat Song 33:127
Walloping Windowblind 50:83
Where Go the Boats? 35:87
Yellow Submarine 66:74
You Can't Get to Heaven 51:90.
    See also Oh, You Can't Get to
    Heaven

BODY. *See* HUMAN BODY

BREAD

Biscuits in the Oven 60:9
Hot Cross Buns! 31:16, 36:124,
    38:140, 44:40, 66:224
Muffin Man 15:42, 36:165, 38:34,
    64:98, 75:47

BROOKS

Down by the Creek Bank 42:133
Down by the River 65:66

BROTHERHOOD

Blessing the Earth 68:48
Do You Know That You're a
    Person? 42:105
Everybody Needs to Be Someone
    42:106
Give a Little Love 32:24
I Would Be True 34:54
If I Had a Hammer 40:56
More We Get Together 31:28, 59:16
To Everyone in All the World 60:21
We Are One 68:37
World in Harmony 29:36
Your Power to Dream 18:9

BUGS. *See* INSECTS

BUNNIES. *See* RABBITS

BUSES

Bus Song 20:16, 36:49, 38:130. *See
    also* Wheels on the Bus
I'm Late 56:159
Ride on a Bus 14:11
Wheels on the Bus 16:32, 49:44,
    60:43. *See also* Bus Song

BUTTERFLIES

Caterpillar 38:22, 56:186
Creepy Crawly Caterpillar 53:41
Fly Little Butterfly 3:23

CABBAGE

Savez-vous Planter des Choux?
    58:20. *See also* Savez-vous
    Planter les Choux?
Savez-vous Planter les Choux?
    64:68. *See also* Savez-vous
    Planter des Choux?

CAKES AND COOKIES

I'm a Little Cookie 31:4, 55:32
Junk Food Junkie 6:19
Pat-a-Cake 31:32, 35:50, 38:27,
    72:20. *See also* Pat-a-Cake,
    Pat-a-Cake
Pat-a-Cake, Pat-a-Cake 44:59. *See
    also* Pat-a-Cake

CALIFORNIA

Oh, Susanna! 31:68, 33:98, 36:179,
    38:126, 40:79
Oh, Susannah 22:180

CAMELS

Alison's Camel 64:93
Dromedaries 3:34
I Got a Camel for Christmas 35:84

CAMP SONGS

Chester 64:53
Down in the Valley 40:28, 67:5
Kookaburra 36:150, 46:75, 70:32
Michael, Row the Boat Ashore
    20:26, 27:10, 34:30, 40:73, 67:14
Peanut Butter 64:48
Peanut Butter and Jelly 55:57. *See
    also* Peanut Butter Song
Peanut Butter Sandwich 59:4
Peanut Butter Song 50:30. *See
    also* Peanut Butter and Jelly
Tall Silk Hat 64:72
Ticka-Tacka 64:75
Vista 64:76
Waddaly Atcha 64:52

CANDY
Big Rock Candy Mountain 22:354, 36:37
Cotton Candy 17:6
Gum Song 50:34
Hippity Hop to the Barber Shop 38:55
Huckleberry, Gooseberry 69:11
I Will Only Have a Sweet 6:44
I'm a Little Cookie 31:4, 55:32
If All the Raindrops 65:57
Junk Food Junkie 6:19
On the Good Ship Lollipop 66:42
Tit Galop Pour Mamou 22:50
When You Come to the End of a Lollipop 49:89

CANOES AND CANOEING
Canoe Round 76:12

CANONS
All That Has Life and Breath, Sing to the Lord 39:20
Are You Sleeping 39:26, 72:25. See also Frere Jacques
Bless This Meal 39:20
Bona Nox 39:30
C-O-F-F-E-E 39:29
Come Here and Sing! 46:90
Come Meet a Little Birdy Friend 39:12
Cuckoo in the Forest 39:10
Dona Nobis Pacem 34:33, 46:91
Epigram on Singers 46:89
Family Love 42:136
Fire! Fire! 39:6
Frere Jacques 1:114, 25:24, 31:7, 36:91, 38:134, 46:61, 59:79, 62:109, 66:234. See also Are You Sleeping
Great Tom Is Cast 46:84
Hey Ho, to the Greenwood 46:83
In the Ev'ning the Nightingale 39:9
Jesus and the Children 42:123
Kookaburra 36:150, 46:75, 70:32
Let's All Sing 39:7
Lo, How a Rose E'er Blooming 28:38, 39:23
Meow, Meow 39:17
My Dame Hath a Lame, Tame Crane 46:87, 75:73
My Goose 46:86
Now Is the Close of Day 39:21
Oh Hear the Bells Ringing 39:25
Praise and Thanksgiving 42:126

Rooster's Dead 39:18
Row, Row, Row 60:64. See also Row, Row, Row Your Boat
Row, Row, Row Your Boat 31:26, 36:199, 38:135, 65:83, 66:234, 74:25, 75:53. See also Row, Row, Row
Sleepers Wake 39:24
Sweetly Sings the Donkey 46:88
Thanks to God for His Love 39:22
Three Geese in Straw 39:16
To Portsmouth 46:74
Turn Again Whittington 46:85
We Praise Thy Name 42:125
Welcome April Sunshine 39:27
What Kind of Trees Are Found Out There? 39:13

CARS. See **AUTOMOBILES**

CARTOONS
Casper the Friendly Ghost 66:80
Heigh-Ho 66:66
I'm Popeye the Sailor Man 66:77. See also Popeye, the Sailor Man
Octopus's Garden 60:75
One Song 66:64
Popeye, the Sailor Man 49:26, 51:121. See also I'm Popeye the Sailor Man
Silly Song 66:68
Whistle While You Work 66:62
With a Smile and a Song 66:59

CASEY JONES
Casey Jones 40:11, 46:52

CATERPILLARS
Arabella Miller 50:43, 64:37. See also Little Arabella Miller
Caterpillar 38:22, 56:186
Creepy Crawly Caterpillar 53:41
Little Arabella Miller 74:23. See also Arabella Miller

CATS
Alley Cat Song 66:206
Barnyard Song 24:12, 40:6, 67:5
Black Cat, The 71:14
Bought Me a Cat 22:264
Cat Came Back 40:14, 49:52, 51:114
Ding, Dong, Bell 31:14
Five Little Pussycats 74:44
Hey, Diddle, Diddle 31:54, 38:67, 44:35, 66:226, 71:63, 75:28

I Know a Little Pussy 36:128, 65:50. *See also* I Love Little Kitty; I Love Little Pussy

I Love Little Kitty 31:65. *See also* I Know a Little Pussy; I Love Little Pussy

I Love Little Pussy 33:66, 36:130, 38:46, 44:6, 66:101, 75:30. *See also* I Know a Little Pussy; I Love Little Kitty

Kitten in the Sun 3:8

Long Time Ago 35:92

Marvin Doesn't Like the New Baby 56:154

Meow, Meow 39:17

Pussy Cat, Pussy Cat 31:35, 38:50, 44:6, 66:108, 75:49

There's No Substitute for a Cat 56:141

Three Little Kittens 31:22, 38:72, 44:4, 75:90

CENTIPEDES
Hundred Feet Ahead 53:1

CHANTS
Che Che Koolay 64:105
Jazzy Three Bears 55:26

CHICKENS
Barnyard Song 24:12, 40:6, 67:5
Chick, Chick, Chicken 65:69
Chickens in the Barnyard 3:12
Chickery Chick 66:113
Cluck, Cluck, Red Hen 20:32, 59:84
Cock-a-Doodle-Doo! 38:68, 75:43
Hickety, Pickety, My Black Hen 44:8
I Had a Little Rooster 35:82. *See also* I Had a Rooster
I Had a Rooster 50:22. *See also* I Had a Little Rooster
My Old Hen's a Good Old Hen 63:44
Old Hen Cackled and the Rooster Laid the Egg 63:42
Rooster Came into Our Yard 49:74
Rooster's Dead 39:18
Where Is John? 1:96
Who Stole My Chickens? 1:16

CHILDREN
Boys and Girls Come Out to Play 44:12
Children All over the World 54:77
Children Who Love Jesus 42:37

Children, Go Where I Send Thee 2:34
Don't Leave Me in the House Alone 56:114
I Don't Think My Teacher Likes Me 56:160
I Got a Teacher, She's So Mean 56:36
I Roll the Ball 35:27
I'm Standing Naked on the Kitchen Table 56:166
If You've Got a Kid Who Complains All the Time 56:136
Inequality Makes the World Go 'Round 56:152
Jesus and the Children 42:123
Jesus Loves the Little Children 48:5
Jesus Once Was a Little Child 54:31
Like Me and You 60:84
Listen to the Noises 35:28
Little Bitty Baby 36:154
Little Pioneer Children 54:67
Marching Shoulder to Shoulder 56:104
Mother and Son 46:58
Pioneer Children 54:65
Stanley Stole My Shoelace and Rubbed It in His Armpit 56:163
Swing, The 35:38, 68:16
We Don't Have to Share 56:122
When Suzie Sneezed 56:40
When the House Is Dark and Quiet 56:50

CHRISTIANITY
Away in a Manger 2:19, 28:32, 36:30, 45:24, 52:78, 61:10
Baptism 54:69
Bells Are Ringing 2:36
B-I-B-L-E, The 26:14
Birthday of a King 2:22
Born This Night 2:31
Christmas Cradle Song 54:29
Did Jesus Really Live Again? 54:35
Do Lord 26:22
Fairest Lord Jesus 48:4
Friendly Beasts 2:41, 28:26, 36:92
Fum, Fum, Fum 2:23
Go Tell It on the Mountain 2:40, 28:79, 40:43

CHRISTIANITY (*cont.*)

Hark! The Herald Angels Sing
28:30, 36:114, 45:36, 52:96,
61:18

Heavenly Sunshine 27:22

I Am So Glad 48:1

I Feel My Savior's Love 54:37

I Have a Friend 42:5

I Just Keep Trusting My Lord
42:61

I Love Jesus 42:71

I Sing a New Song 42:119

I Think When I Read That Sweet
Story 54:33

I Will Sing 42:27

I Will Sing of the Mercies of the
Lord 42:127

I'll Be a Sunbeam 27:28

I'm Trying to Be Like Jesus 54:61

Jesus 26:16

Jesus and the Children 42:123

Jesus Has Risen 54:35

Jesus Is Living in Heaven Today
42:1

Jesus, Jesus 42:65

Jesus Loves Me 26:20

Jesus Loves Me, Jesus Loves Me
42:66

Jesus Loves the Little Children
48:5

Jesus Once Was a Little Child
54:31

Jesus Said Love Everyone 54:49

Jesus Wants Me for a Sunbeam
54:39

Jesus Went About Doing Good 42:8

Jesus Worked 42:7

Joseph Dearest, Joseph Mine 2:30

Last Supper 42:14

Little Drummer Boy, The 2:32

March of the Kings 2:28

May Jesus Christ Be Praised
42:115

My Bible 42:12

O Come, Little Children 2:37, 45:40

O Little Town of Bethlehem 2:18,
28:46, 36:177, 61:14

Oh, How I Love Jesus 42:2

Once Within a Lowly Stable 54:29

Rocking 2:42

Still, Still, Still 2:39

Tell Me the Stories of Jesus 54:33

There Was a Little Baby 57:80

Twas in the Moon of Wintertime
2:24, 28:70

What Child Is This? 2:35, 28:29,
61:26

What Do I Have? 42:113

When He Comes Again 54:37

Where Is the Baby? 2:33

Wind Through the Olive Trees 2:30

Wonderful Things to Know 42:68

CHRISTMAS

Angels We Have Heard on High
23:2, 28:22, 61:28

Away in a Manger 2:19, 28:32,
36:30, 45:24, 52:78, 61:10

Bring a Torch, Jeannette, Isabella!
28:60

Carol of the Bells 28:72

Cherry Tree Carol 28:69

Christmas Cradle Song 54:29

Christmas Is Coming 2:48, 36:54,
45:14, 47:26

Coventry Carol 2:39, 28:35, 61:16

Deck the Halls 2:7, 23:8, 28:58,
36:62, 45:12, 61:12

First Noel 2:14, 23:18, 28:10,
36:86, 45:32, 57:62, 61:22

Friendly Beasts 2:41, 28:26, 36:92

Frosty the Snow Man 66:240. *See
also* Frosty the Snowman

Frosty the Snowman 57:50. *See
also* Frosty the Snow Man

Fum, Fum, Fum 2:23

Go Tell It on the Mountain 2:40,
28:79, 40:43

God Rest You Merry, Gentlemen
23:24, 28:54

Good King Wenceslas 28:62

Hark! The Herald Angels Sing
28:30, 36:114, 45:36, 52:96,
61:18

Here We Come A-Caroling 2:6,
23:26

I Got a Camel for Christmas 35:84

I Heard the Bells on Christmas
Day 28:37

I Saw Three Ships 28:44, 38:139,
44:43, 45:30

It Came upon a Midnight Clear
61:8. *See also* It Came upon the
Midnight Clear

It Came upon the Midnight Clear
28:15, 45:44. *See also* It Came
upon a Midnight Clear

Jolly Old Saint Nicholas 23:12, 45:16. *See also* Jolly Old St. Nicholas

Jolly Old St. Nicholas 2:60. *See also* Jolly Old Saint Nicholas

Joy to the World 2:15, 23:16, 28:53, 45:34, 61:6

Little Jack Horner 31:54, 36:157, 38:36, 44:18, 65:71, 66:225, 75:45

Lo, How a Rose E'er Blooming 28:38, 39:23

March of the Kings 2:28

North Pole 47:29

O Christmas Tree 2:9, 23:6, 28:66, 45:18

O Come, All Ye Faithful 2:17, 28:41, 45:20, 52:64, 61:4. *See also* Oh Come, All Ye Faithful

O Come, Little Children 2:37, 45:40

O Come, O Come Emmanuel 28:9

O Little Town of Bethlehem 2:18, 28:46, 36:177, 61:14

Oh Come, All Ye Faithful 36:172. *See also* O Come, All Ye Faithful

Oh, Jolly Santa Claus 47:22

Once in Royal David's City 28:16

Once Within a Lowly Stable 54:29

Ring-a-Long Bells 47:27

Rise Up, Shepherd, and Follow 28:24

Rudolph the Red-Nosed Reindeer 57:68, 66:235

Santa Claus Is Comin' to Town 66:238

Santa Claus Is Coming 2:50

Santa's Coming 47:28

Silent Night 2:20, 23:14, 28:18, 36:206, 45:42, 61:30

Sleigh Bells Ring 47:23

Still, Still, Still 2:39

There Was a Little Baby 57:80

Very Best Part of Christmas Time 5:19

Wassail Song 28:76

We Wish You a Merry Christmas 2:8, 23:28, 28:80, 36:244, 38:153, 45:10, 48:11, 54:27, 57:82

What Child Is This? 2:35, 28:29, 61:26

While Shepherds Watched Their Flocks by Night 28:12

CHRISTMAS CAROLS

Angels We Have Heard on High 23:2, 28:22, 61:28

Away in a Manger 2:19, 28:32, 36:30, 45:24, 52:78, 61:10

Bring a Torch, Jeannette, Isabella! 28:60

Carol of the Bells 28:72

Cherry Tree Carol 28:69

Christmas Cradle Song 54:29

Christmas Joybells 68:42

Coventry Carol 2:39, 28:35, 61:16

First Noel 2:14, 23:18, 28:10, 36:86, 45:32, 57:62, 61:22

Friendly Beasts 2:41, 28:26, 36:92

Fum, Fum, Fum 2:23

Go Tell It on the Mountain 2:40, 28:79, 40:43

Good King Wenceslas 28:62

Hark! The Herald Angels Sing 28:30, 36:114, 45:36, 52:96, 61:18

I Heard the Bells on Christmas Day 28:37

It Came upon a Midnight Clear 61:8. *See also* It Came upon the Midnight Clear

It Came upon the Midnight Clear 28:15, 45:44. *See also* It Came upon a Midnight Clear

Joy to the World 2:15, 23:16, 28:53, 45:34, 61:6

Little Bitty Baby 36:154

O Come, All Ye Faithful 2:17, 28:41, 45:20, 52:64, 61:4. *See also* Oh Come, All Ye Faithful

O Come, Little Children 2:37, 45:40

O Come, O Come Emmanuel 28:9

O Little Town of Bethlehem 2:18, 28:46, 36:177, 61:14

Oh Come, All Ye Faithful 36:172. *See also* O Come, All Ye Faithful

Once in Royal David's City 28:16

Once Within a Lowly Stable 54:29

Rise Up, Shepherd, and Follow 28:24

Silent Night 2:20, 23:14, 28:18, 36:206, 45:42, 61:30

Sing Noel, Noel 23:10

Spirit of Christmas Is Here 68:44

Twas in the Moon of Wintertime 2:24, 28:70

Wassail Song 28:76

CHRISTMAS CAROLS (*cont.*)
We Three Kings   2:16, 36:242,
    48:10, 52:28. *See also* We Three
    Kings of Orient Are
We Three Kings of Orient Are
    28:48, 61:24. *See also* We Three
    Kings
What Child Is This?   2:35, 28:29,
    61:26
While Shepherds Watched Their
    Flocks by Night   28:12

CHRISTMAS SONGS
Alfie the Elf   2:56
Angel Band   2:26
Bells Are Ringing   2:36
Birthday of a King   2:22
Born This Night   2:31
Children, Go Where I Send Thee
    2:34
Christmas Bells   2:50, 54:27
Christmas Day   2:53
Christmas Decorations   47:21
Christmas Eve   47:24
Christmas Is Coming   2:48, 36:54,
    45:14, 47:26
Christmas Time's a Coming   57:75
Christmastime Is Here   47:25
Comin' Down the Chimney   59:34
December   54:27
Deck the Halls   2:7, 23:8, 28:58,
    36:62, 45:12, 61:12
Every Little Wish   57:65
Frosty the Snow Man   66:240. *See
    also* Frosty the Snowman
Frosty the Snowman   57:50. *See
    also* Frosty the Snow Man
God Rest You Merry, Gentlemen
    23:24, 28:54
Hear the Jingle Bells   2:51
Here Comes Santa Claus   2:44
Here We Come A-Caroling   2:6,
    23:26
Holly and the Ivy   28:57, 45:22
I Got a Camel for Christmas   35:84
I Saw Three Ships   28:44, 38:139,
    44:43, 45:30
Jingle Bells   2:10, 23:4, 31:78,
    36:142, 38:150, 45:26, 57:60,
    61:20
Jolly Old Saint Nicholas   23:12,
    45:16. *See also* Jolly Old St.
    Nicholas
Jolly Old St. Nicholas   2:60. *See
    also* Jolly Old Saint Nicholas

Joseph Dearest, Joseph Mine   2:30
Little Bells of Christmas   2:49
Little Drummer Boy, The   2:32
Lo, How a Rose E'er Blooming
    28:38, 39:23
March of the Kings   2:28
Merrily Caroling   2:48
Must Be Santa   2:54, 57:70, 59:26
Nine Little Reindeer   71:26
North Pole   47:29
O Christmas Tree   2:9, 23:6, 28:66,
    45:18
O Come, Little Children   2:37, 45:40
Oh, Jolly Santa Claus   47:22
Old Toy Trains   57:74
On Christmas Morning   57:55
Pat-a-Pan   2:38, 38:152
Petit Papa Noel   57:57
Reindeer Are Tapping   2:59
Ring, Ring, Ring the Bells   2:49
Ring the Bell   21:36
Ring Those Bells   2:58
Ring-a-Long Bells   47:27
Rocking   2:42
Rudolph the Red-Nosed Reindeer
    57:68, 66:235
Santa Claus Is Comin' to Town
    66:238
Santa Claus Is Coming   2:50
Santa's Chimney   38:146
Santa's Coming   47:28
Tapping   2:61
There Was a Little Baby   57:80
Twas in the Moon of Wintertime
    2:24, 28:70
Twelve Days of Christmas   2:12,
    23:20, 36:231
Up on the Housetop   2:46, 23:22,
    57:53
We Three Kings   2:16, 36:242,
    48:10, 52:28. *See also* We Three
    Kings of Orient Are
We Wish You a Merry Christmas
    2:8, 23:28, 28:80, 36:244,
    38:153, 45:10, 48:11, 54:27,
    57:82
Where Is the Baby?   2:33
Wind Through the Olive Trees   2:30

CHURCHES
Little Brown Church, The   26:2

CIRCLE GAMES
Al Citron   64:110
Alison's Camel   64:93

Aloha 71:9
Bluebird 38:83, 65:9
Cheerio 64:84
Christopher Columbus 47:1
Circle Games 21:26
Dr. Knickerbocker 64:90
Gallant Ship 38:84
Giving Song 21:10
Go Round and Round the Village 38:85
Going to Kentucky 64:82
Good-Bye Winter, Hello Spring 71:42
Halloween Fun 47:9
Here Stands a Redbird 38:106
Here We Go Looby Loo 31:12, 36:116. See also Looby Loo
Here We Go Round the Mulberry Bush 15:41, 44:29, 74:45, 75:26. See also Mulberry Bush
Hokey-Pokey 66:204
Indian Brothers 47:13
Little Girl/Boy Went Walking 55:55
London Bridge 31:61, 33:83, 36:160, 38:105, 44:30, 65:24, 66:230, 75:58. See also London Bridge Is Falling Down
London Bridge Is Falling Down 15:43. See also London Bridge
Looby Loo 24:26, 38:92, 64:83. See also Here We Go Looby Loo
Lucy Locket 31:51, 44:19
Me Stone 64:111
Move Over 21:11
Mulberry Bush 31:6, 33:84, 36:166, 38:80, 65:14, 66:216. See also Here We Go Round the Mulberry Bush
Nuts in May 38:81
Obwisana 64:111
Old Cow Died 63:56
Old Roger 64:88
Pair of Feet 14:14
Pop! Goes the Weasel 31:46, 33:106, 36:194, 38:32, 50:58, 65:47, 66:187, 70:26, 75:50
Punchinello 47 64:94
Rig-A-Jig-Jig 20:10, 25:4, 38:94, 65:30
Ring Around a Rosy 31:59, 38:107, 75:52. See also Ring Around the Rosy; Ring-a-Ring o' Roses

Ring Around the Rosy 72:13. See also Ring Around a Rosy; Ring-a-Ring o' Roses
Ring-a-Ring o' Roses 44:28, 65:21. See also Ring Around a Rosy; Ring Around the Rosy
Ringel Rosen 1:124
Sally, Go Round 38:87. See also Sally Go Round the Sun
Sally Go Round the Sun 65:23. See also Sally, Go Round
Shamrocks and Leprechauns 47:41
Sharing 4:12
Skip to My Lou 15:45, 31:21, 33:124, 36:210, 38:90
Teddy Bear, Teddy Bear 49:38
Thanksgiving Time 47:17
Tzena, Tzena, Tzena 66:198
Valentine 47:36
Valentine Friends 47:34
Valentine's Dance 47:37
We Are Going to Grandma's House 4:19
What Is the Number? 21:28
What Shall We Do When We All Go Out? 65:20
Your Easter Basket 47:43

CIRCULAR SONGS

Around the Corner 50:74, 51:8
John Jacob Jingleheimer Schmidt 50:90, 51:9, 64:75, 66:134
Little Sally Saucer 64:86, 65:23. See also Little Sally Waters
Little Sally Waters 38:101. See also Little Sally Saucer
Michael Finnegan 22:244, 37:59, 51:79, 64:79. See also Michael Finnigin
Michael Finnigin 75:62. See also Michael Finnegan

CIRCUSES

Acrobats, The 17:33
As He Walks on High 17:36
Circus Is Coming 17:3
Circus, The 17:45
Clowns, The 17:11
Cotton Candy 17:6
Dancing Horses 17:25
Five Little Monkeys 17:18, 50:52
Flea Circus 53:26
Intermission Rag 17:21
Lions 17:29

CIRCUSES (*cont.*)
Man on the Trapeze 17:40. *See also* Possum on the Flying Trapeze
Trunk to Tail 17:15

CITIES. *See* **URBAN LIFE**

CIVICS
Big Words 13:40
Blowin' in the Wind 22:360
Checks and Balances 13:27
Fall Apart 13:35
Free Enterprise 13:49
Here in America 13:15
Military Song 13:43
Miracle in Philadelphia 13:24
We Hold These Truths 13:18
We the People 13:32
Your Power to Dream 18:9

CIVIL RIGHTS
Martin Luther King, Junior 47:30
We Shall Overcome 34:28, 40:128

CIVIL WAR (U.S. 1861-1865)
Dixie 33:31, 36:68
When Johnny Comes Marching Home 36:245

CLAMS
Acres of Clams 22:192, 40:2

CLAPPING GAMES
Bim Bom 1:56
Bingo 31:36, 33:21, 35:57, 36:44, 38:82, 66:124. *See also* Bingo Was His Name
Bingo Was His Name 51:26. *See also* Bingo
Christopher McCracken 50:48
Clap Your Hands 21:14, 38:86
Cookie Jar 64:51
Dr. Knickerbocker 64:90
Ev'rybody Loves Saturday Night 49:34
Head, Shoulders, Baby 49:33. *See also* Head and Shoulders; Head and Shoulders, Baby; Tete, Epaules
I Got a Letter 1:12
I Take My Little Hand 72:18
Jack, Can I Ride? 63:76
Lazy Susan 55:10
Let's Clap Hands for ... 55:45
Let's Make Some Noise 58:26
Monkey See and Monkey Do 55:51

My Home 42:135
Namo Ganesha 62:65
Pease Porridge Hot 31:14, 38:104, 44:28, 65:11, 75:77
Ride on a Bus 14:11
She Went into the Water 24:20
Si-si-si 1:36
Skip to My Lou 15:45, 31:21, 33:124, 36:210, 38:90
Ta Ta Ta Li 62:63
Tamzara 1:128
Tape Tape Petites Mains 62:59
What Do We Do? 35:12

CLEANLINESS
Aunt Anna Came to Our House 56:130
Bath, The 35:32
Bathtime 58:4
Black Socks 51:54
Bubble Toes 12:29
Dirty Bill 50:39, 51:35
Fingernails 12:24
GIGO 12:38
Grandpa Gum 12:22
Helping God 42:49
Here We Go Round the Mulberry Bush 15:41, 44:29, 74:45, 75:26. *See also* Mulberry Bush
I Brush My Teeth 72:29
Little Seed 9:16
Look Ma! No Cavities 71:36
Lowly Germ 12:18
Mulberry Bush 31:6, 33:84, 36:166, 38:80, 65:14, 66:216. *See also* Here We Go Round the Mulberry Bush
Old Mrs. Lazibones 50:46
Pressed and Dressed 12:35
Rubber Duckie 66:16
Run Along Home 49:62
Scrubit Land of Clean 12:40
Skatter-Brak-Flath Who Lives in My Bath 56:53
Tomorrow 55:34, 56:60, 66:25
Wash the Stickies down the Drain 12:32
Wash Your Hair 12:20
With My Little Broom 74:35

CLOCKS AND WATCHES
Five More Minutes 56:198
Hickory, Dickory, Dock 31:23, 33:55, 35:61, 36:120, 38:51, 44:2, 66:232, 72:43, 74:24

CLOSING SONGS

Now You May Think 49:92, 51:123
Praise God from Whom All Blessings Flow 34:20, 48:3

CLOTHING AND DRESS

All by Myself 42:43
Baby's Going Bye-Bye 35:22
Clothes Clothes 72:32
Diddle Diddle Dumpling 38:76, 71:48, 72:28
Going Out to Play 71:28
I Lost My Pants 56:144
I Was Only Foolin' 25:8
I've Got a Cold in My Nose-Kerchoo! 49:86
Jennie Jenkins 33:76, 36:139. *See also* Jenny Jenkins
Jenny Jenkins 22:74, 64:14. *See also* Jennie Jenkins
Little Betty Blue 71:24
Mary Wore Her Red Dress 31:24, 58:22
Matthew, Mark, Luke and John 64:18
Phoebe in Her Petticoat 65:13
Pressed and Dressed 12:35
Shoe Shoe Patch 72:30
Soldier and the Maid 65:36
Tall Silk Hat 64:72
This Is the Way 72:31
Three Little Kittens 31:22, 38:72, 44:4, 75:90
Underwear 56:174
Where's My Pajamas? 65:87

CLOWNS

Clowns, The 17:11
Down Derry Down 69:27

COLOR

A-Tisket, A-Tasket 15:41, 24:6, 31:63, 38:100, 66:110, 70:12. *See also* Itiskit, Itaskit
All the Pretty Little Horses 22:268, 33:7, 35:72, 38:11, 77:18. *See also* Go to Sleepy; Hush A Bye; Hush'n Bye; Hush-You-Bye; Rock-a-Bye Baby; Rockabye, Baby
Autumn Leaves Are Now Falling 48:9
Colores, De 60:96

Go to Sleepy 36:102. *See also* All the Pretty Little Horses; Hush A Bye; Hush'n Bye; Hush-You-Bye; Rock-a-Bye Baby; Rockabye, Baby
Green 66:10
Hush'n Bye 62:36. *See also* All the Pretty Little Horses; Go to Sleepy; Hush A Bye; Hush-You-Bye; Rock-a-Bye Baby; Rockabye, Baby
Hush-You-Bye 46:56. *See also* All the Pretty Little Horses; Go to Sleepy; Hush A Bye; Hush'n Bye; Rock-a-Bye Baby
Itiskit, Itaskit 36:133. *See also* A-Tisket, A-Tasket
Jennie Jenkins 33:76, 36:139. *See also* Jenny Jenkins
Jenny Jenkins 22:74, 64:14. *See also* Jennie Jenkins
Lavender's Blue 20:18, 33:79, 36:151, 38:66, 44:54, 75:38
Mary Wore Her Red Dress 31:24, 58:22
Please Sit Down 55:48
Roses Are Red 71:8

COLUMBUS, CHRISTOPHER

Christopher Columbus 47:1
Columbus 5:9, 47:2
Nina, the Pinta, the Santa Maria, The 66:248

CONGO

Si-si-si 1:36

CORN

Shuckin' of the Corn 76:28

COTTON

Pick a Bale o' Cotton 31:70, 59:57. *See also* Pick a Bale of Cotton
Pick a Bale of Cotton 36:190. *See also* Pick a Bale o' Cotton

COUNTING

Alison's Camel 64:93
Angel Band 2:26
Ants Go Marching 24:10, 50:6, 64:78
By'm Bye 77:14. *See also* Bye 'n' Bye; Bye'm Bye
Bye'm Bye 22:196, 72:58. *See also* By'm Bye; Bye 'n' Bye
Bye 'n' Bye 49:66, 64:25. *See also* By'm Bye; Bye'm Bye

COUNTING (*cont.*)

Children, Go Where I Send Thee 2:34
Cinnamon Ship, The 55:8
Eight Piggies in a Row 58:23
Father Fell Off 72:15
First-Last 21:25
Five Little Chickadees 38:77, 65:22
Five Little Ducks 60:47, 70:10
Five Little Fingers 72:51
Five Little Frogs 59:1
Five Little Monkeys 17:18, 50:52
Five Little Pumpkins 59:6
Five Little Pussycats 74:44
Five Speckled Frogs 65:54
Great Tom Is Cast 46:84
Green Grow the Rushes-O 33:48, 36:106
Head and Shoulders 1:108, 20:40, 42:53, 65:12. *See also* Head and Shoulders, Baby; Head, Shoulders, Baby; Tete, Epaules
I Am Slowly Going Crazy 50:69, 51:77, 64:79
I've Got One Head 49:8
Inch Worm 66:40
Keeper, The 36:148, 46:8
Let's Do the Numbers Rumba 60:60
Little Bitty Baby 36:154
Mexican Counting Song 38:137
Nine Little Reindeer 71:26
Ninety-nine Miles from Home 50:72
One Bottle Pop 50:80, 51:16
One Elephant, Deux Elephants 37:58, 64:9
One Finger, One Thumb 35:64, 49:30, 64:46, 74:41
One Sparkling Star 4:37
One, Two, Buckle My Shoe 74:42
1,2,3,4,5 64:33
Over in the Meadow 38:44, 49:16, 60:27
Roll Over 25:14, 38:121. *See also* Roll Over, Roll Over; Ten in the Bed
Roll Over, Roll Over 70:34. *See also* Roll Over; Ten in the Bed
Sereno, El 64:108
Ten in the Bed 65:88. *See also* Roll Over; Roll Over, Roll Over
Ten Little Indians 36:217, 66:217
Ten Little Toesies 72:45

This Old Man 19:38, 31:56, 36:223, 54:13, 60:29, 65:59, 66:218, 70:16, 72:17, 75:86
Three Green Speckled Frogs 50:21
Three Little Witches 50:75
Twelve Days of Christmas 2:12, 23:20, 36:231
Un Elephante 64:115
United 71:40
We Don't Want to Go Home 50:73
Who Built the Ark? 59:32

COURTING

A-Roving 46:18
All I Want Is You 56:61
Apple of My Eye 56:74
Charlie Is My Darling 46:20
Cindy 46:44
Goodnight, Irene 40:48. *See also* Good Night, Irene
Greensleeves 33:53, 46:12
I Know Where I'm Goin' 46:55
Mail Myself to You 20:44, 31:52, 66:130
Marianne 66:191
Muss I Denn 46:36
My Love's an Arbutus 46:28
One Song 66:64
Soldier and the Maid 65:36
You Better Not Giggle, Now Don't You Laugh, But I'm in Love with a Giraffe 56:188

COVERED WAGONS

Covered Wagons 54:67
Westward Ho over the Oregon Trail We Go 54:65
White Covered Wagons 5:44

COWBOYS

Buffalo Gals 36:47, 40:9
City Cowboy 30:14
Cowboy's Lament 40:22
Get Along, Little Dogies 36:96. *See also* Git Along, Little Dogies
Ghost Riders in the Sky 20:24
Git Along, Little Dogies 22:290, 40:40. *See also* Get Along, Little Dogies
Home on the Range 33:56, 36:121, 40:50, 67:7
I Ride an Old Paint 36:131, 40:52
Jesse James 40:62
My Home's in Montana 67:7
Ol' Texas 20:22

Old Chisholm Trail 20:36
Red River Valley 33:108, 40:85,
    67:13
Riding Along 64:16
Riding Round the Cattle 63:70
Whistling Cowhand 71:50

COWS
Clever Cow 3:15
Cluck, Cluck, Red Hen 20:32, 59:84
Did You Feed My Cow? 64:50
Friendly Cow, The 68:24
Get Along, Little Dogies 36:96. See
    also Git Along, Little Dogies
Ghost Riders in the Sky 20:24
Git Along, Little Dogies 22:290,
    40:40. See also Get Along,
    Little Dogies
Hey, Diddle, Diddle 31:54, 38:67,
    44:35, 66:226, 71:63, 75:28
I Am Learning How to Work 10:52
Little Black Bull, The 63:54
Little Boy Blue 31:15, 38:70,
    44:15, 66:226, 75:44
Old Chisholm Trail 20:36
Old Cow Died 63:56
Riding Round the Cattle 63:70
Where Is John? 1:96

CRABS
Christopher McCracken 50:48

CRANES
My Dame Hath a Lame, Tame
    Crane 46:87, 75:73

CRAYFISH
Crawdad 36:60. See also Crawdad
    Song
Crawdad Song 40:24. See also
    Crawdad

CROCODILES
Back of a Crocodile 64:49. See also
    Crocodile, The; Smile on the
    Crocodile
Crocodile, The 16:31. See also
    Back of a Crocodile; Smile on
    the Crocodile
Crocodile Song 63:72
Smile on the Crocodile 50:54. See
    also Back of a Crocodile; Croco-
    dile, The

CROWS
Three Crow 64:114

CRYING
Whiney Child 11:28

CUCKOOS
Cuckoo in the Forest 39:10
Summer Is A-Coming In 46:26

CUMULATIVE SONGS
Green Grass Grew All Around
    49:22. See also Green Grass
    Grows All Around, The
I Had a Little Rooster 35:82. See
    also I Had a Rooster
I Had a Rooster 50:22. See also I
    Had a Little Rooster
I Know an Old Lady 66:125
Mockingbird Song 40:74
Once an Austrian Went Yodeling
    55:33
Rattlin' Bog 64:44
There Was an Old Lady 33:131,
    36:221
Twelve Days of Christmas 2:12,
    23:20, 36:231

DANCERS AND DANCING
Buffalo Gals 36:47, 40:9
Dance to Your Daddy 44:58, 65:80,
    77:26
Dancing Horses 17:25
Fiddlers 46:42
Haiye Kirumbe 1:70
Jig Along Home 31:18, 59:60
La Bamba 20:28
La Bastringue 64:67
Let's Watch 21:20
Lord of the Dance 34:18
Silly Song 66:68
Unite and Unite 76:4

DANCES
Ah Si Mon Moine 64:66
Alley Cat Song 66:206
Baby Cakewalk 69:16
Bassez Down 64:92
Bow Belinda 38:102
Brown Girl in the Ring 58:9, 64:104
Buffalo Gals 36:47, 40:9
Bunny Hop 66:211
Camptown Races 66:150
Come Dance and Sing 34:52
Did You Ever See a Lassie? 24:24,
    33:28, 36:64, 38:96
Flat Foot Floogee 66:140
Going to Kentucky 64:82

DANCES (*cont.*)
Ha, Ha, This-a-Way 66:168. *See also* Ha, Ha, Thisaway
Ha, Ha, Thisaway 58:33. *See also* Ha, Ha, This-a-Way
Here We Go Looby Loo 31:12, 36:116. *See also* Looby Loo
Hokey-Pokey 66:204
Hop Up and Jump Up 34:53
Hundred Feet Ahead 53:1
In and Out the Window 15:42
Intermission Rag 17:21
Jig Along Home 31:18, 59:60
La Bamba 20:28
La Bastringue 64:67
Let's Do the Numbers Rumba 60:60
Looby Loo 24:26, 38:92, 64:83. *See also* Here We Go Looby Loo
Lots of Fish in Bonavist' Harbor 64:112
Marianne 66:191
Mary Ann 67:16
Old Joe Clark 40:81. *See also* Old Joe Clarke
Old Joe Clarke 50:44. *See also* Old Joe Clark
Put Your Little Foot Right Out 66:208
Rig-A-Jig-Jig 20:10, 25:4, 38:94, 65:30
Right Foot, Left Foot 21:19
Rockin' Robin 20:42
Saturday Night 1:40
Shake My Sillies Out 19:24, 59:31
Sodeo 59:46
Sur le Pont d'Avignon 38:108, 59:80, 64:60
Thank You Dance 11:56
There Came a Girl from France 59:82
Turkey in the Straw 36:228, 40:124, 51:84
Tzena, Tzena, Tzena 66:198
Valentine's Dance 47:37
Waltz of the Witch 73:6
Wearin' o' the Green 5:24

DANIEL
Daniel 60:45
Didn't My Lord Deliver Daniel? 43:16

DAYS
Ev'rybody Loves Saturday Night 49:34

Everybody Happy 65:6
Name the Days 21:31
On a Sunday 55:29
Saturday 54:15
Saturday Night 1:40
This Is the Day We Come to Church 42:20
Twelve Days of Christmas 2:12, 23:20, 36:231
When Is the Day? 42:56

DEATH
Clementine 33:26, 36:55, 40:20, 50:40, 51:87, 66:164, 67:6. *See also* My Darling Clementine
Cowboy's Lament 40:22
Epigram on Singers 46:89
Every Night When the Sun Goes In 46:50
Freight Train 40:36
Joe Hill 40:64
John Henry 22:152, 36:144, 40:67
Living a Day 53:37
My Darling Clementine 31:27. *See also* Clementine
Old MacTavish Is Dead 51:15
Oliver Cromwell 46:16
Poor Roger Is Dead and Gone to His Grave 50:70
Streets of Forbes 46:76
Sweet Rosie O'Grady 50:42
Will the Circle Be Unbroken 40:133

DECEMBER
December 54:27

DEER
Deer Song, The 63:34
Hey Ho, to the Greenwood 46:83
Keeper, The 36:148, 46:8
Mairzy Doats 66:138
Nine Little Reindeer 71:26
Reindeer Are Tapping 2:59
Rudolph the Red-Nosed Reindeer 57:68, 66:235
Up on the Housetop 2:46, 23:22, 57:53

DEMOCRACY
Always Remember You Were Born in America 29:56
Big Words 13:40
Checks and Balances 13:27
Fall Apart 13:35
Here in America 13:15

I'm the Statue of Liberty 30:28
Military Song 13:43
Miracle in Philadelphia 13:24
We Hold These Truths 13:18
We the People 13:32
Where's the Justice 13:38

DENTISTS
My Dentist Is an Awfully Nice
    Man 56:24

DEVILS
Devil's Questions, The 22:206

DIMINISHING SONGS
Cabin in the Wood 64:39
Five Little Chickadees 38:77, 65:22
Five Little Ducks 60:47, 70:10
Five Little Frogs 59:1
Five Little Monkeys 17:18, 50:52
Horse Went Around, The 50:16
Little Peter Rabbit 35:76, 50:19,
    64:36
Ninety-nine Miles from Home
    50:72
Roll Over 25:14, 38:121. *See also*
    Roll Over, Roll Over; Ten in the
    Bed
Roll Over, Roll Over 70:34. *See
    also* Roll Over; Ten in the Bed
Ten in the Bed 65:88. *See also* Roll
    Over; Roll Over, Roll Over
We Don't Want to Go Home 50:73

DINOSAURS
Baby Bumble Bee 50:8, 51:112
Dinosaur Song 56:147
I'm a 3-Toed, Triple-Eyed, Double-
    Jointed Dinosaur 56:20
If I Had a Dinosaur 59:36

DOGS
Bingo 31:36, 33:21, 35:57, 36:44,
    38:82, 66:124. *See also* Bingo
    Was His Name
Bingo Was His Name 51:26. *See
    also* Bingo
Groundhog 22:92, 71:38
Had a Little Dog 55:39. *See also* I
    Had a Little Dog
Hark, Hark! 38:54
He's a Dog 3:10
He's My Responsibility 11:58
I Had a Little Dog 49:9. *See also*
    Had a Little Dog
I Wanna Be a Dog 56:111

I've Got a Dog and My Dog's Name
    Is Cat 56:69
Little Brown Dog 63:28
Little Dog Named Right 63:26
My Dog Rags 20:38, 64:42
My Dog's Bigger Than Your Dog
    66:84
Oh, Blue 63:30
Oh Where, Oh Where Has My Little
    Dog Gone? 44:9, 66:86. *See
    also* Where Has My Little Dog
    Gone?; Where, O Where;
    Where, Oh Where, Has My
    Little Dog Gone?
Old Mother Hubbard 71:58
Our Dog Bernard 56:58
That Doggie in the Window 66:82
Where Has My Little Dog Gone?
    31:42, 70:36. *See also* Oh
    Where, Oh Where Has My
    Little Dog Gone?; Where, O
    Where; Where, Oh Where, Has
    My Little Dog Gone?
Where, O Where 74:21. *See also*
    Oh Where, Oh Where Has My
    Little Dog Gone?; Where Has
    My Little Dog Gone?; Where,
    Oh Where, Has My Little Dog
    Gone?
Where, Oh Where, Has My Little
    Dog Gone? 36:248, 38:114. *See
    also* Oh Where, Oh Where Has
    My Little Dog Gone?; Where
    Has My Little Dog Gone?;
    Where, O Where
Whistler and His Dog 66:102

DOLLS
Baby Doll 35:24
I Rock My Doll 35:25
Miss Polly 55:41. *See also* Miss
    Polly Had a Dolly
Miss Polly Had a Dolly 49:39,
    65:77. *See also* Miss Polly

DONKEYS
Sweetly Sings the Donkey 46:88
Ting-a-lay-o 19:12. *See also* Tinga
    Layo; Tingalayo
Tinga Layo 24:16. *See also* Ting-a-
    lay-o; Tingalayo
Tingalayo 37:39, 60:92, 64:106,
    70:14. *See also* Ting-a-lay-o;
    Tinga Layo

DRAGONS
Puff, the Magic Dragon 19:44, 66:161

DREAMS
Betty Wants to Be an Astronaut 30:42
Dream Song 22:14
Little Seed 9:16
Over the Rainbow 66:34
Rainbow Connection 66:22

DRILLING
Drill, Ye Tarriers 22:158, 36:74
John Henry 22:152, 36:144, 40:67

DRUGS
All You Gotta Say Is No 8:15
Designer Genes 8:19
Go for a Natural High 8:8
It's Bad, Bad Stuff 8:12
You're Not Gonna Get Rich on Me 8:26

DRUMS
Little Drummer Boy, The 2:32
Pat-a-Pan 2:38, 38:152

DUCKS
Barnyard Song 24:12, 40:6, 67:5
Be Kind to Your Web-Footed Friends 51:124, 66:190
Ducks Like Rain 60:62
Five Little Ducks 60:47, 70:10
Little White Duck 36:158, 58:40, 66:92
Quack, Quack, Quack 3:7
She Went into the Water 24:20
Six Little Ducks 24:18, 50:18, 59:52

EARS
Do Your Ears Hang Low? 16:30, 38:113, 50:66, 51:75, 70:6
Listen to the Noises 35:28
What Does Baby Hear 35:20

EASTER
Easter Bunny 38:141, 71:46
Easter Eggs 47:44
It's Easter Time 5:29
Jesus Has Risen 54:35
Peter Cottontail 66:243
Your Easter Basket 47:43

ECHO SONGS
All Hid 64:19
Bear Song 50:56
Candy Man, Salty Dog 64:26

Charlie over the Ocean 64:95
Green Grass Grew All Around 49:22. See also Green Grass Grows All Around, The
Green Grass Grows All Around, The 24:4. See also Green Grass Grew All Around
Koom Bachur Atsel 1:118
Little Echo Voice 14:4
Now You May Think 49:92, 51:123
Oh, You Can't Get to Heaven 26:8. See also You Can't Get to Heaven
Sing About Martin 71:30
Vista 64:76

ELEPHANTS
Monte Sur un Elephant 64:58
One Elephant, Deux Elephants 37:58, 64:9
Riddle 3:42
Trunk to Tail 17:15
Un Elephante 64:115
When I See an Elephant Fly 66:56
Willoughby Wallaby Woo 19:20, 59:7

ELVES
Alfie the Elf 2:56
Tapping 2:61

EMOTIONS. See FEELINGS

ENGLAND
Botany Bay 46:78
Grand Old Duke of York 65:29
Hail to Britannia 64:102
Hush, Little Baby 22:98, 25:18, 31:20, 33:62, 36:126, 38:12, 65:91, 66:181, 70:38, 72:57, 74:9, 77:10
Lincolnshire Poacher 46:30
London Bridge 31:61, 33:83, 36:160, 38:105, 44:30, 65:24, 66:230, 75:58. See also London Bridge Is Falling Down
London Bridge Is Falling Down 15:43. See also London Bridge
Oh, Dear, What Can the Matter Be? 33:94, 36:174, 44:52, 65:34, 67:9, 70:30
Oliver Cromwell 46:16
Scarborough Fair 33:114
Turn Again Whittington 46:85
Under the Spreading Chestnut Tree 36:239

Unite and Unite 76:4
When Good King Arthur Ruled This
    Land 44:39

EQUAL RIGHTS
Inequality Makes the World Go
    'Round 56:152
Ride Sally Ride 71:32

ERIE CANAL
E-ri-e, The 36:79
Erie Canal 22:116, 36:81, 40:30

ETIQUETTE. *See* **MANNERS**

EVENING
Every Night and Every Morn 34:38
O How Lovely Is the Evening 48:7
Oh, How Lovely Is the Evening
    33:96, 36:176, 38:134

EXERCISE GAMES
Head and Shoulders 1:108, 20:40,
    42:53, 65:12. *See also* Head and
    Shoulders, Baby; Head, Shoul-
    ders, Baby; Tete, Epaules
Head and Shoulders, Baby 64:54.
    See also Head and Shoulders;
    Head, Shoulders, Baby; Tete,
    Epaules
Head, Shoulders, Baby 49:33. *See
    also* Head and Shoulders; Head
    and Shoulders, Baby; Tete,
    Epaules
Hokey-Pokey 66:204
Huff and Puff 11:24
I Sit Down 42:52
I'm a Walkin 72:9
If You're Happy 74:38. *See also* If
    You're Happy and You Know It
If You're Happy and You Know It
    49:28, 66:176, 70:20. *See also* If
    You're Happy
Monkey See and Monkey Do 55:51
Shake My Sillies Out 19:24, 59:31

EZEKIEL
Ezekiel Saw the Wheel 43:14

**FAIRIES, DWARFS, AND
    GOBLINS**
Baloo Baleerie 77:20
Heigh-Ho 66:66
One Song 66:64
Silly Song 66:68
Thumbelina 60:41
Whistle While You Work 66:62

White Coral Bells 36:249
With a Smile and a Song 66:59

FAMILIES
All I Really Need 60:23
Aunt Anna Came to Our House
    56:130
But I'm Just Thirteen 56:70
Children, Obey Your Parents 42:97
Christian Families 42:98
Dad Says That I Look Like Him
    56:100
Daddy's Homecoming 54:17
Dearest Names 54:23
Do It Song 10:14
Don't Forget the Family 12:14
Down on Grandpa's Farm 60:87
Early Sunday Morning 56:44
Families Can Be Together Forever
    54:25
Family 54:19
Family Love 42:136
Family Night 54:19
Family Prayer 54:21
Father Fell Off 72:15
Fathers Are Forever 5:35
Follow the Rules! 42:36
For My Sister, Wherever I May
    Find Her 56:64
God Is Like My Daddy 42:58
God's Plan for Families 42:96
Going to the Zoo 40:45, 59:24, 66:90
Great Big Family 42:99
Happy Family 54:11
Helping Mother 42:42
Here We Are 68:38
Home Sweet Home 33:60
Honor Your Parents 66:246
Honoring Mother and Father
    42:134
I Am Learning How to Spell 9:7
I Didn't Mean To 56:126
I Know Where I'm Goin' 46:55
I Love My Daddy 56:162
I Love My Family 54:25
I Love My Grandpa 4:20
I Love to Hear My Father Play the
    Piano 30:22
I Miss Grandma 56:138
I Never Did Like You, Anyhow
    56:28
I Often Go Walking 54:13
I Roll the Ball 35:27
I Sneaked into the Kitchen in the
    Middle of the Night 56:32

FAMILIES (*cont.*)

I Wonder If I'm Growing 59:9

I'm a V.I.P. 4:7

I'm Standing Naked on the Kitchen Table 56:166

I've Got a Little Sister 56:72

If You've Got a Kid Who Complains All the Time 56:136

Later 56:199

Let's Clap Hands for ... 55:45

Like Me and You 60:84

Little Brown Jug 66:166

Marvin Doesn't Like the New Baby 56:154

Mom and Dad Are Always Right 56:88

Mother and Son 46:58

Mother Dear 54:13

Mother Dear, I Love You 9:39

Mother, I Love You 54:11

Mother Needs Me 5:36

My Brother and I 4:16

My Brother Thinks He's a Banana 56:57

My Brother Threw Up on My Stuffed Toy Bunny 56:62

My Dad 9:10, 54:17

My Happy Home 42:35

My Home 42:135

My Mommy Drives a Dump Truck 56:66

My Mother Ran Away Today 56:95

My Responsibility 42:95

Never Cook Your Sister in a Frying Pan 56:92

O Hangman, O Hangman 46:38

Oh No! I Like My Sister! 56:184

Old Family Toothbrush 25:6, 50:87, 51:34

Old Mrs. Lazibones 50:46

Over the River and Through the Wood 38:142

Quickly I'll Obey 54:15

Service with a Smile 12:16

She's My Sister 4:18

Show a Little Love 9:4

Special Kind of Love 11:65

Still We Have Love 11:68

To Mommy 56:29

Tomorrow 55:34, 56:60, 66:25

Up in the Air 35:30

We Are Going to Grandma's House 4:19

We Don't Have to Share 56:122

Wet Again 56:169

When Grandpa Comes 54:23

When the House Is Dark and Quiet 56:50

When We're Helping 54:15

You're Something Special 42:137

FAMILY. *See* **FAMILIES**

FANTASY WORLD

Baloo Baleerie 77:20

Thumbelina 60:41

White Coral Bells 36:249

FARM LIFE. *See* **RURAL LIFE**

FARMERS AND FARMING

Farmer in the Dell 15:40, 31:26, 33:41, 36:84, 38:79, 66:232. *See also* Farmer's in the Dell

Farmer's in the Dell 74:40, 75:20. *See also* Farmer in the Dell

Hello There, Farmer 55:60

Oats and Beans and Barley 60:13. *See also* Oats, Peas, and Beans; Oats, Peas, Beans; Oats, Peas, Beans and Barley Grow

Oats, Peas, and Beans 33:93. *See also* Oats and Beans and Barley; Oats, Peas, Beans; Oats, Peas, Beans and Barley Grow

Oats, Peas, Beans 24:8, 36:171, 38:89, 75:68. *See also* Oats and Beans and Barley; Oats, Peas, and Beans; Oats, Peas, Beans and Barley Grow

Oats, Peas, Beans and Barley Grow 66:228. *See also* Oats and Beans and Barley; Oats, Peas, and Beans; Oats, Peas, Beans

FEAR

Beware 73:18

Don't Leave Me in the House Alone 56:114

I Whistle a Happy Tune 66:48

Is This What It Means to Have Courage 11:14

Thump, Thump, Thump 56:79

Who Broke My Window 10:19

Who's Afraid of the Big Bad Wolf? 66:52

FEAST OF LIGHTS. *See* **HANUKKAH**

FEELINGS
Communication 18:39
Do You Want to Feel Happy? 9:34
Every Night When the Sun Goes In 46:50
Everybody Happy 65:6
Everybody Needs to Feel Love 8:22
Family Love 42:136
Forgiveness 10:42
Giggle and a Hug and a Tickle and a Kiss 56:99
Give Me a Heart of Love 42:141
Great Ape 3:38
Happiness 42:144, 54:47
Happy Family 54:11
Happy, Happy! 42:70
Heart Song 73:31
How Many People Do You Love? 4:13
I Get Angry at Myself 10:36
I Never Did Like You, Anyhow 56:28
I Think I'm Happy Now 11:30
I'm a Very Happy Person 39:7
If I Were the Hero 11:4
If You're Happy 74:38. *See also* If You're Happy and You Know It
If You're Happy and You Know It 49:28, 66:176, 70:20. *See also* If You're Happy
If You've Got a Kid Who Complains All the Time 56:136
Indian Boy 11:6
Ingrate Song 11:41
Is This What It Means to Have Courage 11:14
It Isn't Any Trouble Just to Smile 49:65
It Takes Courage 11:9
Joy 68:31
Little Miss Muffet 31:66, 38:40, 44:18, 66:227, 71:61
Long, Long Ago 67:9
Make People Laugh 18:20
My Love's an Arbutus 46:28
Now, Now, Now 36:168
Oh, I'm So Embarrassed 12:46
Power to Love 18:34
Repentance 54:61
Secret of Happiness 11:32
Shining 68:46
Smile, Dear Princess 11:23
Still We Have Love 11:68

There's a Little Wheel A-Turnin' in My Heart 55:38. *See also* There's a Little Wheel A-Turning; There's a Little Wheel A-Turning in My Heart
There's a Little Wheel A-Turning 38:120. *See also* There's a Little Wheel A-Turnin' in My Heart; There's a Little Wheel A-Turning in My Heart
There's a Little Wheel A-Turning in My Heart 20:20. *See also* There's a Little Wheel A-Turnin' in My Heart; There's a Little Wheel A-Turning
Try to Please a Princess 11:20
Two Sides to Forgiveness 10:34
What Do You Do When You're Happy 11:34
When Suzie Sneezed 56:40
Whiney Child 11:28
Who Broke My Window 10:19
Who's Complaining? 55:20
You're as Sweet as Sugar on a Stick 56:103

FERRIES
It's Fun to Take the Ferry to the Statue of Liberty 29:10

FINGER AND HAND PLAY
All the Fish 72:42
Arabella Miller 50:43, 64:37. *See also* Little Arabella Miller
Baby Bye 65:81
Cabin in the Wood 64:39
Caterpillar 38:22, 56:186
Clap Your Hands 21:14, 38:86
Easter Bunny 38:141, 71:46
Eency Weency Spider 36:78. *See also* Eensy Weensy Spider; Eentsy Weentsy Spider; Incey Wincey Spider
Eensy Weensy Spider 31:60, 33:38, 65:61, 66:231, 72:19, 74:22. *See also* Eency Weency Spider; Eentsy Weentsy Spider; Incey Wincey Spider
Eentsy Weentsy Spider 35:58; Eency Weency Spider; Eensy Weensy Spider; Incey Wincey Spider
Fingers 14:22
Five Little Chickadees 38:77, 65:22

FINGER AND HAND PLAY
   (*cont.*)
   Five Little Ducks 60:47, 70:10
   Five Little Fingers 72:51
   Five Little Monkeys 17:18, 50:52
   Hambone 55:37
   Here Are My Lady's Knives and
      Forks 38:24
   Here Is the Church 35:53, 38:25
   Hickory, Dickory, Dock 31:23,
      33:55, 35:61, 36:120, 38:51,
      44:2, 66:232, 72:43, 74:24
   Hooray for Mr. Lincoln 71:34
   Hot Cross Buns! 31:16, 36:124,
      38:140, 44:40, 66:224
   I Have Two Little Hands 54:73
   In a Cabin 70:4
   Incey Wincey Spider 38:28. *See
      also* Acrobats, The; Arabella
      Miller; All the Fish; Eency
      Weency Spider; Eensy Weensy
      Spider; Eentsy Weentsy Spider;
      All the Little Fishies Do a
      Hoochie Koochie Dance
   Jaws 55:46
   John Brown's Baby 16:30, 51:22,
      66:177
   Knock at the Door 38:25
   Little Arabella Miller 74:23
   Little Peter Rabbit 35:76, 50:19,
      64:36
   Oh, Chester! 51:25
   One Finger, One Thumb 35:64,
      49:30, 64:46, 74:41
   1,2,3,4,5 64:33
   Open, Shut Them 55:58, 72:55
   Pat-a-Cake 31:32, 35:50, 38:27,
      72:20. *See also* Pat-a-Cake,
      Pat-a-Cake
   Pat-a-Cake, Pat-a-Cake 44:59. *See
      also* Pat-a-Cake
   Pease Porridge Hot 31:14, 38:104,
      44:28, 65:11, 75:77
   Petites Marionettes 59:49. *See also*
      Petites Marionnettes
   Petites Marionnettes 62:112. *See
      also* Petites Marionettes
   Put Your Finger in the Air 36:196,
      66:132
   Read Read Books Books 71:18
   Ride on a Bus 14:11
   Roly Poly 4:23
   Shoo Fly 24:14, 35:54, 36:203
   Ten Fingers 35:60

   This Little Pig 35:62, 38:26, 74:19,
      75:11. *See also* This Little Piggy
   This Little Piggy 72:8. *See also*
      This Little Pig
   This Old Man 19:38, 31:56, 36:223,
      54:13, 60:29, 65:59, 66:218,
      70:16, 72:17, 75:86
   Thumbkins 55:52
   Up in the Air, Junior Bird Man
      51:10
   What Shall We Do with the Baby-
      O? 55:43. *See also* What Will
      We Do with the Baby-O?
   What Will We Do with the Baby-
      O? 35:51. *See also* What Shall
      We Do with the Baby-O?
   Where Is Thumbkin? 31:62, 35:66,
      36:247, 38:29, 42:57, 64:30,
      65:19, 72:49
   Wiggle Wiggle 72:48

FINGER PLAY. *See* **FINGER
   AND HAND PLAY**

FINLAND
   Sarasponda 1:30, 22:40, 67:10

FIRE ENGINES
   Fire Drill 21:35

FIREFIGHTERS
   Fire Drill 21:35

FIRES
   Fire Drill 21:35
   Fire! Fire! 39:6
   Old Mother Leary 50:38

FISH. *See* **FISH AND SEA LIFE**

FISH AND SEA LIFE
   All the Fish 72:42
   All the Little Fishies Do a Hoochie
      Koochie Dance 55:23
   Baby Beluga 19:18, 60:7
   Chivalrous Shark 46:46
   I Wish I Were a Fish 3:19
   Lots of Fish in Bonavist' Harbor
      64:112
   Octopus's Garden 60:75
   1,2,3,4,5 64:33
   Seahorse Merry-Go-Round 3:20
   Three Little Fishies 66:154

FISHERMEN AND FISHING
   Can of Worms 53:21
   Christopher McCracken 50:48
   Crawdad 36:60. *See also* Crawdad Song

Crawdad Song 40:24. *See also* Crawdad
Dance to Your Daddy 44:58, 65:80, 77:26
Fisherman Peter 26:6
There Were Three Jolly Fishermen 50:86

FLAGS
America, I Love You 5:43, 13:58
Take Your Hat Off 13:4
That's My Flag 5:42

FLEAS
Flea Fly Song 50:11
Had a Little Dog 55:39. *See also* I Had a Little Dog
Itchy Flea 49:77, 51:120
Little Peter Rabbit 35:76, 50:19, 64:36
Vista 64:76

FLIES
Baby Bye 65:81
Blue-Tail Fly 36:45
Fiddle-De-De 75:22. *See also* Fiddle-dee-dee
Fiddle-dee-dee 31:29. *See also* Fiddle-De-De
Lament of the House Flies 53:49
Little Peter Possum 24:2
Little Peter Rabbit 35:76, 50:19, 64:36
Shoo Fly 24:14, 35:54, 36:203

FLOWERS
I Love the Flowers 4:28
I Often Go Walking 54:13
It's a Rosebud in June 76:25
Little Purple Pansies 54:51
Mother Goose Summer 76:6
Popcorn Popping 54:43
Summer Breeze 76:21
Take Time 68:34
Welcome April Sunshine 39:27
White Coral Bells 36:249
Wild Mountain Thyme 76:22

FLUTE
Pat-a-Pan 2:38, 38:152

FLYING
Balloon, The 35:44
If I Could Fly 35:40
Lone Wild Bird 34:48
Ride Sally Ride 71:32

FOLK SONGS
Blowin' in the Wind 22:360
Camptown Races 66:150
Clementine 33:26, 36:55, 40:20, 50:40, 51:87, 66:164, 67:6. *See also* My Darling Clementine
Dixie 33:31, 36:68
Down in the Valley 40:28, 67:5
Goodnight, Irene 40:48. *See also* Good Night, Irene
Home on the Range 33:56, 36:121, 40:50, 67:7
Joe Hill 40:64
Kicking Mule 63:62
Little Brown Jug 66:166
Michael, Row the Boat Ashore 20:26, 27:10, 34:30, 40:73, 67:14
My Darling Clementine 31:27. *See also* Clementine
Shenandoah 22:125, 33:119, 40:96, 46:72
So Long, It's Been Good to Know You 40:103
Stewball 40:106, 63:68
Sweet Betsy from Pike 22:186, 33:128, 36:214, 40:108, 67:10
This Land Is Your Land 22:370, 40:116, 66:188
Whoa, Mule! Can't Get the Saddle On 63:64

FOOD AND EATING
Aiken Drum 25:20, 51:12, 75:16. *See also* Aikendrum; There Was a Man Lived in the Moon
Aikendrum 59:30. *See also* Aiken Drum; There Was a Man Lived in the Moon
Apples and Bananas 19:32, 55:19, 60:70
Because She Shines 6:12
Big Rock Candy Mountain 22:354, 36:37
Birds in the Wilderness 50:35
Biscuits in the Oven 60:9
Brite Bites 6:38
But I Still Don't Like Asparagus 56:170
Calling All Junk Foods 6:28
Chicken Lips and Lizard Hips 19:34, 32:39
Corner Grocery Store, The 59:76
Down by the River 65:66
Duchess at Tea 50:26

FOOD AND EATING (*cont.*)

Dunderbeck 36:76. *See also* Dunderbeck's Machine

Dunderbeck's Machine 49:21, 51:39. *See also* Dunderbeck

Early Sunday Morning 56:44

Fred 56:35

Fruit 21:30

Fruit Song 68:19

Going on a Picnic 59:64

Grease and Sweets 6:10

Hello There, Farmer 55:60

I Eat Kids 56:46

I Sneaked into the Kitchen in the Middle of the Night 56:32

I Want a Chocolate Malted 50:36

I Will Only Have a Sweet 6:44

I'm a 3-Toed, Triple-Eyed, Double-Jointed Dinosaur 56:20

I'm a Little Cookie 31:4, 55:32

Ice Cream 66:143

Junk Food Junkie 6:19

Keep Your Body Strong 6:26, 6:41

Landlord, Fill the Flowing Bowl 46:32

Let's Go Trick or Treatin' 73:26

Little Jack Horner 31:54, 36:157, 38:36, 44:18, 65:71, 66:225, 75:45

Little Miss Muffet 31:66, 38:40, 44:18, 66:227, 71:61

Little Tommy Tucker 31:75, 38:35, 44:17, 75:48. *See also* Little Tommy Tinker

Meat, Milk, and Grain 6:16

Mrs. Murphy's Chowder 20:46, 22:236, 49:82

Oh, My Goodness! 69:10

On Top of My Pizza 50:31, 51:98

On Top of Spaghetti 36:186, 37:38, 66:128. *See also* On Top of Old Smokey; On Top of Old Smoky

Peanut Butter 64:48

Peanut Butter and Jelly 55:57. *See also* Peanut Butter Song

Peanut Butter Sandwich 59:4

Peanut Butter Song 50:30. *See also* Peanut Butter and Jelly

Put Our Best Selves Forward 6:34

Quartermaster Corps 50:29, 51:43

Sandwiches 20:8

Shortnin' Bread 31:76

Sweet Potatoes 65:74

Swiss Cheese Song 50:32

They Said, "Eat the Broccoli" 56:90

Three Ways to Get Peanut Butter Off the Roof of Your Mouth 50:33

Vegetable Rap 6:14

Whoever Shall Have Peanuts 49:56

You Can't Build a Body on Junk 6:30

FORESTS

Hey Ho, to the Greenwood 46:83

In a Cabin 70:4

FORGIVENESS

God Knows Everything About Me 42:59

I Didn't Mean To 56:126

FOURTH OF JULY

In 1776 13:12

FOXES

Fox in a Box 15:44

Fox, The 19:40, 33:42, 36:88, 40:34, 66:88. *See also* Old Fox

Old Fox 63:32. *See also* Fox, The

FREEDOM

Always Remember You Were Born in America 29:56

America at Last! 29:30

Americans Are Singing About Lady Liberty 29:6

Blowin' in the Wind 22:360

Brown Eyes, Black Eyes 13:62

Down by the Riverside 33:33, 40:26

Fall Apart 13:35

Follow the Drinkin' Gourd 22:140. *See also* Follow the Drinking Gourd

Follow the Drinking Gourd 40:32. *See also* Follow the Drinkin' Gourd

Free Enterprise 13:49

Freedom 47:31

Go Down, Moses 22:128, 34:24, 36:98, 42:79, 43:8

God Bless the Statue of Liberty 29:70

Happy Birthday Miss Liberty 29:14

He Always Carried His Picture of Lady Liberty 29:48

Here in America 13:15

I Got Shoes 22:132

I Remember Ellis Island 29:20

I Wondered If I Were Dreaming 29:66

If You Believe in Me, I'll Never Die
29:44
It's Fun to Take the Ferry to the
Statue of Liberty 29:10
Long John 22:136
Lovely Lady of Liberty 29:40
Martin Luther King, Junior 47:30
Military Song 13:43
My Guiding Light Is Miss Liberty
29:60
Peace Is Flowing Like a River
34:34
Swing Low, Sweet Chariot 22:148,
59:66
We Shall Overcome 34:28, 40:128
We're the Children of America
29:24
World in Harmony 29:36

FRENCH LANGUAGE

A Cheval 62:77
A Paris 62:73
Ah Si Mon Moine 64:66
Alouette 66:194
Au Clair de la Lune 36:27
Bring a Torch, Jeannette, Isabella!
28:60
Chevaliers de la Table Ronde 46:62
En Passant par la Lorraine 46:64
Fais Do Do 64:64. See also Fais
Dodo
Fais Dodo 60:77. See also Fais Do
Do
French Cathedrals 1:24
Frere Jacques 1:114, 25:24, 31:7,
36:91, 38:134, 46:61, 59:79,
62:109, 66:234. See also Are
You Sleeping
Head and Shoulders 1:108, 20:40,
42:53, 65:12. See also Head and
Shoulders, Baby; Head, Shoul-
ders, Baby; Tete, Epaules
Jamais on na Vu 64:62
La Bastringue 64:67
Michaud 60:57, 64:63
Monte Sur un Elephant 64:58
One Elephant, Deux Elephants
37:58, 64:9
Petit Papa Noel 57:57
Petites Marionettes 59:49. See also
Petites Marionnettes
Petites Marionnettes 62:112. See
also Petites Marionettes

Savez-vous Planter des Choux?
58:20. See also Savez-vous
Planter les Choux?
Savez-vous Planter les Choux?
64:68. See also Savez-vous
Planter des Choux?
Sur le Pont d'Avignon 38:108,
59:80, 64:60
Tape Tape Petites Mains 62:59
Tete, Epaules 60:59. See also Head
and Shoulders; Head and Shoul-
ders, Baby; Head, Shoulders,
Baby
Tit Galop Pour Mamou 22:50
To Everyone in All the World 60:21
Une Poule Blanche 62:32
Y'a Un Rat 59:86
Zombis et les Loups-Garous, Les
59:81

FRIENDSHIP

All I Want Is You 56:61
Animals Are My Friends 71:19
Auld Lang Syne 36:28, 45:46
Be a Friend 9:26
Because I Love Him 11:62
Come Play with Me 5:39
Comin' Through the Rye 70:24. See
also Comin' Thru the Rye
Comin' Thru the Rye 66:203. See
also Comin' Through the Rye
Everybody Needs a Friend 12:42
Everybody Needs to Feel Love 8:22
Friend in Need 12:4
Give 71:22
God Can 42:108
Going on a Picnic 59:64
Hello, Hello! How Are You? 42:86
Hey, Won't Somebody Come and
Play 9:13
I Need You Like a Doughnut Needs
a Hole 56:24
I Want to Be Your Friend 47:32
I'm My Friend 12:53
I'm the Phone Girl 30:38
If Your Friend's in Trouble 8:2
Let's Be Friends 47:35
Little Drops of Water 38:63
Me and You 56:38
More We Get Together 31:28, 59:16
My Friend Jake 56:42
One Day My Best Friend Barbara
Turned Into a Frog 56:54
One Little Girl 4:10
Precious Friends 64:118

FRIENDSHIP (*cont.*)
  Sharing Song 59:18
  To a Distant Friend 67:12
  Togetherness Kids 7:14
  Two Sides to Forgiveness 10:34
  Valentine Friends 47:34
  Very Best Part of Christmas Time
    5:19
  We Volunteer 12:6
  We're Just Two Friends 11:37
  You Sing a Song and I'll Sing a
    Song 59:63

FROGS
  Clever Amphibian 3:21
  El Coquito 38:136
  Five Little Frogs 59:1
  Five Speckled Frogs 65:54
  Frog Went A-Courtin' 33:44, 36:94,
    66:182. *See also* Froggie Went
    A-Courting
  Froggie Went A-Courting 75:18.
    See also Frog Went A-Courtin'
  Glunk, Glunk, Glunk 50:14
  Green 66:10
  Keemo Kyemo 22:226
  Little Green Frog 55:59
  Little White Duck 36:158, 58:40,
    66:92
  One Day My Best Friend Barbara
    Turned Into a Frog 56:54
  Snake Baked a Hoecake 63:24
  There Was an Old Frog 63:48
  Three Green Speckled Frogs 50:21

FRONTIER LIFE
  Buffalo Gals 36:47, 40:9
  Covered Wagons 54:67
  Cowboy's Lament 40:22
  Cumberland Gap 22:82
  Desperado, The 20:14
  Get Along, Little Dogies 36:96. *See
    also* Git Along, Little Dogies
  Ghost Riders in the Sky 20:24
  Git Along, Little Dogies 22:290,
    40:40. *See also* Get Along,
    Little Dogies
  Home on the Range 33:56, 36:121,
    40:50, 67:7
  Hop Up, My Ladies 63:66
  I Ride an Old Paint 36:131, 40:52
  Little Pioneer Children 54:67
  My Home's in Montana 67:7
  O Pioneers 5:45

  Oh, Susanna! 31:68, 33:98, 36:179,
    38:126, 40:79
  Oh, Susannah 22:180
  Old Ground Hog 63:22
  On Top of Old Smokey 33:103. *See
    also* On Top of Old Smoky; On
    Top of Spaghetti
  On Top of Old Smoky 31:25, 40:83,
    67:6. *See also* On Top of Old
    Smokey; On Top of Spaghetti
  Ox Cart 54:65
  Pioneer Children 54:65
  Red River Valley 33:108, 40:85,
    67:13
  Sweet Betsy from Pike 22:186,
    33:128, 36:214, 40:108, 67:10
  Westward Ho over the Oregon Trail
    We Go 54:65
  When I First Came to This Land
    22:272
  White Covered Wagons 5:44

FROST
  Playful Little Jack Frost 5:18

FRUITS
  Apples and Bananas 19:32, 55:19,
    60:70
  Fruit 21:30
  Fruit Song 68:19
  Huckleberry, Gooseberry 69:11
  I'm Peeling My Banana 55:50
  Oranges and Lemons 44:31, 75:74
  Prune Song 50:27
  Vegetable Rap 6:14

**GARDENERS AND
  GARDENING**
  In My Garden 60:79
  Mary, Mary, Quite Contrary 44:21.
    See also Mistress Mary; Mis-
    tress Mary, Quite Contrary
  Mistress Mary 38:38. *See also*
    Mary, Mary, Quite Contrary;
    Mistress Mary, Quite Contrary
  Mistress Mary, Quite Contrary
    31:67. *See also* Mary, Mary,
    Quite Contrary; Mistress Mary

GARDENS
  I Have a Garden 54:51
  In My Garden 60:79
  Mary, Mary, Quite Contrary 44:21.
    See also Mistress Mary; Mis-
    tress Mary, Quite Contrary

Mistress Mary, Quite Contrary
    31:67. *See also* Mary, Mary,
    Quite Contrary; Mistress Mary
Oh, John the Rabbit 22:216, 49:55
Take Time 68:34

GEESE
Fox, The 19:40, 33:42, 36:88,
    40:34, 66:88. *See also* Old Fox
Go Tell Aunt Rhody 36:101,
    38:116, 40:42, 67:4
Goosey, Goosey, Gander 31:10,
    38:57, 75:25
Gray Goose 36:104, 63:38
Grey Goose 66:170
Mother Goose Summer 76:6
My Goose 46:86
Old Fox 63:32. *See also* Fox, The
Old Lady Goose 63:40
Three Geese in Straw 39:16
Where Is Your Goose? 50:15

GERMAN LANGUAGE
Ach! Du Lieber Augustin 36:16
Ah, Mama Mier 55:18
All That Has Life and Breath, Sing
    to the Lord 39:20
Bless This Meal 39:20
Bona Nox 39:30
C-O-F-F-E-E 39:29
Come Meet a Little Birdy Friend
    39:12
Cuckoo in the Forest 39:10
Die Musica 67:7
Du, Du Liegst Mir im Herzen 67:16
Fire! Fire! 39:6
Happy Birthday to You 31:7, 54:9,
    66:252
I'm a Very Happy Person 39:7
In the Ev'ning the Nightingale 39:9
Let's All Sing 39:7
Lo, How a Rose E'er Blooming
    28:38, 39:23
Lorelei, Die 46:34
Meow, Meow 39:17
Muss I Denn 46:36
Now Is the Close of Day 39:21
O Christmas Tree 2:9, 23:6, 28:66,
    45:18
Oh Hear the Bells Ringing 39:25
Ringel Rosen 1:124
Rooster's Dead 39:18
Schlaf, Kindlein, Schlaf 62:38. *See
    also* Cradle Song; Sleep, Baby,
    Sleep

Sleepers Wake 39:24
Thanks to God for His Love 39:22
Three Geese in Straw 39:16
Welcome April Sunshine 39:27
What Kind of Trees Are Found Out
    There? 39:13

GHANA
Che Che Koolay 64:105
Obwisana 64:111

GHOSTS
Casper the Friendly Ghost 66:80
Ghost of Tom, The 22:330
Ghost Riders in the Sky 20:24
Witches, Ghosts, and Goblins 47:6

GOATS
Old Hogan's Goat 51:117
Once I Saw Three Goats 64:77

GOOD BEHAVIOR
Don't Put Your Finger up Your
    Nose 56:84
Don't You Push Me Down 35:74
Give a Little Whistle 66:72
Gratitude Attitude 11:46
He Eats Asparagus, Why Can't You
    Be That Way? 56:18
Honor Your Parents 66:246
Honoring Mother and Father
    42:134
I Say Thank You 11:53
Kindness Begins with Me 54:49
Land of Obey 10:6
Lend a Helping Hand 12:8
Maybe You Laughed 9:28
Safety Don'ts 7:10
Shut Up in the Library 56:30
Thank You Dance 11:56
Think About a Thank You 11:50
We're Just Two Friends 11:37
Words You Speak 9:36

GOOSE. *See* **GEESE**

GOPHERS
Cross-Eyed Gopher 63:20

GOVERNMENT. *See* **CIVICS**

GRASS
Green Grass Grows All Around,
    The 24:4. *See also* Green
    Grass Grew All Around

GRASSHOPPERS
Grasshopper Song 50:10

GREETINGS

Good Morning to You 38:115
Happy Birthday 4:25
Happy Birthday to You 31:7, 54:9, 66:252
Hello 21:6
Hello, Hello! How Are You? 42:86
Hello There, Farmer 55:60
Hevenu Shalom Alechem 34:23
Valentines Are Special Greetings 47:33
We Have a Friend 55:54
We're Glad You're Here 42:55

GROOMING, PERSONAL

Bath, The 35:32
Bathtime 58:4
Brush Your Teeth 19:26, 59:8
Bubble Toes 12:29
Fingernails 12:24
Grandpa Gum 12:22
Here We Go Round the Mulberry Bush 15:41, 44:29, 74:45, 75:26. *See also* Mulberry Bush
I Brush My Teeth 72:29
I Don't Brush My Teeth and I Never Comb My Hair 56:22
Itchy Scritchy 53:7
Mulberry Bush 31:6, 33:84, 36:166, 38:80, 65:14, 66:216. *See also* Here We Go Round the Mulberry Bush
Old Family Toothbrush 25:6, 50:87, 51:34
Pressed and Dressed 12:35
Scrubit Land of Clean 12:40
Wash the Stickies down the Drain 12:32
Wash Your Hair 12:20

GROUNDHOG. *See* WOODCHUCKS

GROWING UP

Better Obey 10:12
But I Still Don't Like Asparagus 56:170
Did and Didn't 10:9
Do It Song 10:14
Growing Tall 42:46
He Eats Asparagus, Why Can't You Be That Way? 56:18
Honor Your Parents 66:246
I Didn't Mean To 56:126
I Like Me 10:39

I Never Did Like You, Anyhow 56:28
I Wonder If I'm Growing 59:9
I'm a Nut 50:67, 51:78
I'm Not Small 55:25
In a Minute 12:64
Indian Boy 11:6
It Takes Courage 11:9
Land of Obey 10:6
Leroy Is a Late Bloomer 56:102
Marching Shoulder to Shoulder 56:104
Mom and Dad Are Always Right 56:88
My Dog's Bigger Than Your Dog 66:84
One Inch Taller 42:102
Sharing Song 59:18
So Many Things 10:29
Standin' Tall 10:4
Take the Blame 42:48
To Mommy 56:29
Two Sides to Forgiveness 10:34
When We're Helping 54:15
When You Tell One Lie 10:25

GUESSING GAMES

Charades 14:13
Where Can Baby Be? 35:33

HAIR

Curly Locks 38:61, 65:38. *See also* Curly Locks, Curly Locks
Curly Locks, Curly Locks 44:50. *See also* Curly Locks
Dear Old Daddy's Whiskers 25:16, 51:36
Father's Old Grey Whiskers 19:16, 66:152
Itchy Scritchy 53:7
Wash Your Hair 12:20

HALLOWEEN

Beware 73:18
Black Cat, The 71:14
Halloween 71:15
Halloween Capers 47:8
Halloween Fun 47:9
Halloween Is Here! 47:11
Halloween Machine 73:22
Halloween Night 5:12
Heart Song 73:31
Holiday of Love 73:41
Jack-O'-Lantern 47:4
Let's Ban Halloween, Let's Save Halloween 73:11

Let's Go Trick or Treatin' 73:26
On Halloween 47:5
Pumpkin Picking 47:12
Pumpkins 47:10
Things Unseen 47:3
Think Positively 73:35
Three Little Witches 50:75
Waltz of the Witch 73:6
Witch, The 47:7
Witches, Ghosts, and Goblins 47:6

HAND PLAY. *See* **FINGER AND HAND PLAY**

HANDS
Don't Put Your Finger up Your
    Nose 56:84
Fingernails 12:24
Fingers 14:22
Five Little Fingers 72:51
Here Is the Church 35:53, 38:25
I Take My Little Hand 72:18
One Finger, One Thumb 35:64,
    49:30, 64:46, 74:41
Ten Fingers 35:60
Thumbkins 55:52
Where Is Thumbkin? 31:62, 35:66,
    36:247, 38:29, 42:57, 64:30,
    65:19, 72:49

HANUKKAH
Hanukah 71:20
Hanukkah 47:20
Hanukkah Is Happiness 47:18
Hanukkah Song 36:110, 38:144

HAPPINESS
Be Glad! 42:69
Do You Want to Feel Happy? 9:34
Happiness 42:144, 54:47
Happy, Happy! 42:70
I'm a Very Happy Person 39:7
If You're Happy 74:38. *See also* If
    You're Happy and You Know It
If You're Happy and You Know It
    49:28, 66:176, 70:20. *See also* If
    You're Happy
Joy 68:31
More We Get Together 31:28,
    59:16
Song of Happiness 22:25
When Is the Day? 42:56
When We're Helping 54:15

HARVEST
Bringing in the Sheaves 33:22

Come, Ye Thankful People, Come
    34:58, 36:57
Oats and Beans and Barley 60:13.
    See also Oats, Peas, and Beans;
    Oats, Peas, Beans; Oats, Peas,
    Beans and Barley Grow
Oats, Peas, and Beans 33:93. *See
    also* Oats and Beans and Bar-
    ley; Oats, Peas, Beans; Oats,
    Peas, Beans and Barley Grow
Oats, Peas, Beans 24:8, 36:171,
    38:89, 75:68. *See also* Oats and
    Beans and Barley; Oats, Peas,
    and Beans; Oats, Peas, Beans
    and Barley Grow
Oats, Peas, Beans and Barley
    Grow 66:228. *See also* Oats
    and Beans and Barley; Oats,
    Peas, and Beans; Oats, Peas,
    Beans
Pick a Bale o' Cotton 31:70, 59:57.
    See also Pick a Bale of Cotton
Pick a Bale of Cotton 36:190. *See
    also* Pick a Bale o' Cotton

HATS
My Tall Silk Hat 70:28
Tall Silk Hat 64:72

HAWAII
Aloha 71:9

HEALTH
All I Really Need 60:23
Baby Bear's Chicken Pox 71:52
Because She Shines 6:12
Dirty Bill 50:39, 51:35
Doctor, Doctor 35:88
GIGO 12:38
Grandpa Gum 12:22
Grease and Sweets 6:10
Helping God 42:49
I Brush My Teeth 72:29
I Don't Brush My Teeth and I
    Never Comb My Hair 56:22
I'm Popeye the Sailor Man 66:77.
    See also Popeye, the Sailor Man
I've Got a Cold in My Nose-Ker-
    choo! 49:86
If You Take Care of Your Body
    18:29
It's Bad, Bad Stuff 8:12
John Brown's Baby 16:30, 51:22,
    66:177
Junk Food Junkie 6:19
Keep Your Body Strong 6:26, 6:41

HEALTH (*cont.*)
Look Ma! No Cavities 71:36
Lowly Germ 12:18
Meat, Milk, and Grain 6:16
Miss Polly 55:41. *See also* Miss
　Polly Had a Dolly
Miss Polly Had a Dolly 49:39,
　65:77. *See also* Miss Polly
My Body Machine 6:6
My Dentist Is an Awfully Nice
　Man 56:24
Popeye, the Sailor Man 49:26,
　51:121. *See also* I'm Popeye the
　Sailor Man
Pretty White Teeth 72:14
Put Our Best Selves Forward 6:34
Vegetable Rap 6:14
You Can't Build a Body on Junk
　6:30

HEDGEHOGS
Animal Song 63:80

HOLIDAYS
Abe Lincoln 47:40
Alfie the Elf 2:56
Angel Band 2:26
Angels We Have Heard on High
　23:2, 28:22, 61:28
Auld Lang Syne 36:28, 45:46
Away in a Manger 2:19, 28:32,
　36:30, 45:24, 52:78, 61:10
Bells Are Ringing 2:36
Birthday of a King 2:22
Black Cat, The 71:14
Born This Night 2:31
Children, Go Where I Send Thee
　2:34
Christmas Bells 2:50, 54:27
Christmas Cradle Song 54:29
Christmas Day 2:53
Christmas Decorations 47:21
Christmas Eve 47:24
Christmas Is Coming 2:48, 36:54,
　45:14, 47:26
Christmas Time's a Coming 57:75
Christmastime Is Here 47:25
Come, Ye Thankful People, Come
　34:58, 36:57
Comin' Down the Chimney 59:34
December 54:27
Deck the Halls 2:7, 23:8, 28:58,
　36:62, 45:12, 61:12
Easter Bunny 38:141, 71:46
Easter Eggs 47:44

Every Little Wish 57:65
First Noel 2:14, 23:18, 28:10,
　36:86, 45:32, 57:62, 61:22
Friendly Beasts 2:41, 28:26, 36:92
Fum, Fum, Fum 2:23
George Washington 13:22, 47:39
Go Tell It on the Mountain 2:40,
　28:79, 40:43
God Rest You Merry, Gentlemen
　23:24, 28:54
Groundhog 22:92, 71:38
Halloween 71:15
Halloween Capers 47:8
Halloween Fun 47:9
Halloween Is Here! 47:11
Halloween Night 5:12
Hanukah 71:20
Hanukkah 47:20
Hanukkah Is Happiness 47:18
Happy New Year 5:20
Hear the Jingle Bells 2:51
Here Comes Santa Claus 2:44
Here We Come A-Caroling 2:6,
　23:26
Holiday of Love 73:41
Holidays 35:90
Holly and the Ivy 28:57, 45:22
Hooray for Mr. Lincoln 71:34
I Love America 13:9
I Love You 5:21
I Played a Joke on You 5:30
I Saw Three Ships 28:44, 38:139,
　44:43, 45:30
I Want to Be Your Friend 47:32
In 1776 13:12
Indian Brothers 47:13
It's Easter Time 5:29
Jack-O'-Lantern 47:4
Jingle Bells 2:10, 23:4, 31:78,
　36:142, 38:150, 45:26, 57:60,
　61:20
Jolly Old Saint Nicholas 23:12,
　45:16. *See also* Jolly Old St.
　Nicholas
Jolly Old St. Nicholas 2:60. *See
　also* Jolly Old Saint Nicholas
Joseph Dearest, Joseph Mine 2:30
Joy to the World 2:15, 23:16,
　28:53, 45:34, 61:6
Knock, Knock, Knock 5:22
Let's Ban Halloween, Let's Save
　Halloween 73:11
Let's Go Trick or Treatin' 73:26
Little Bells of Christmas 2:49

Little Boy Blue 31:15, 38:70, 44:15, 66:226, 75:44
Little Drummer Boy, The 2:32
March of the Kings 2:28
Martin Luther King, Junior 47:30
May Day 5:33
Merrily Caroling 2:48
Must Be Santa 2:54, 57:70, 59:26
Nine Little Reindeer 71:26
North Pole 47:29
O Christmas Tree 2:9, 23:6, 28:66, 45:18
O Come, All Ye Faithful 2:17, 28:41, 45:20, 52:64, 61:4. See also Oh Come, All Ye Faithful
O Come, Little Children 2:37, 45:40
O Little Town of Bethlehem 2:18, 28:46, 36:177, 61:14
Oh Come, All Ye Faithful 36:172. See also O Come, All Ye Faithful
Oh, Jolly Santa Claus 47:22
Old Toy Trains 57:74
On Christmas Morning 57:55
On Halloween 47:5
Once Within a Lowly Stable 54:29
Over the River and Through the Wood 38:142
Pat-a-Pan 2:38, 38:152
Peter Cottontail 66:243
Petit Papa Noel 57:57
Pilgrims and the Indians 5:14
Presidents Are Famous Men 47:38
Pumpkin Picking 47:12
Pumpkins 47:10
Reindeer Are Tapping 2:59
Ring, Ring, Ring the Bells 2:49
Ring Those Bells 2:58
Ring-a-Long Bells 47:27
Rocking 2:42
Rudolph the Red-Nosed Reindeer 57:68, 66:235
Santa Claus Is Comin' to Town 66:238
Santa Claus Is Coming 2:50
Santa's Chimney 38:146
Santa's Coming 47:28
Shamrocks and Leprechauns 47:41
Silent Night 2:20, 23:14, 28:18, 36:206, 45:42, 61:30
Sing Noel, Noel 23:10
Sleigh Bells Ring 47:23
St. Patrick's Day 47:42

Still, Still, Still 2:39
Take Your Hat Off 13:4
Tapping 2:61
Thanksgiving 47:15
Thanksgiving Day Is Coming 47:16
Thanksgiving Time 47:17
Things Unseen 47:3
Three Little Witches 50:75
Turkey Run 47:14
Twas in the Moon of Wintertime 2:24, 28:70
Twelve Days of Christmas 2:12, 23:20, 36:231
Up on the Housetop 2:46, 23:22, 57:53
Valentine 47:36
Valentine Friends 47:34
Valentine's Dance 47:37
Valentines Are Special Greetings 47:33
Very Best Part of Christmas Time 5:19
Veterans Day Salute 5:10
Wassail Song 28:76
We Three Kings 2:16, 36:242, 48:10, 52:28. See also We Three Kings of Orient Are
We Three Kings of Orient Are 28:48, 61:24. See also We Three Kings
We Wish You a Merry Christmas 2:8, 23:28, 28:80, 36:244, 38:153, 45:10, 48:11, 54:27, 57:82
Wearin' o' the Green 5:24
What Child Is This? 2:35, 28:29, 61:26
Where Is the Baby? 2:33
Wind Through the Olive Trees 2:30
Witch, The 47:7
Witches, Ghosts, and Goblins 47:6
Your Easter Basket 47:43

HOME
Daddy's Homecoming 54:17
Family 54:19
Family Night 54:19
Hey, Ho, Nobody Home 36:119
Home on the Range 33:56, 36:121, 40:50, 67:7
Home Sweet Home 33:60
My Happy Home 42:35
My Home 42:135
When Grandpa Comes 54:23

HORSES

A Paris 62:73
Alison's Camel 64:93
All the Pretty Little Horses
    22:268, 33:7, 35:72, 38:11,
    77:18. *See also* Go to Sleepy;
    Hush A Bye; Hush'n Bye; Hush-
    You-Bye; Rock-a-Bye Baby;
    Rockabye, Baby
Camptown Races 66:150
Dancing Horses 17:25
Go to Sleepy 36:102. *See also* All
    the Pretty Little Horses; Hush
    A Bye; Hush'n Bye; Hush-You-
    Bye; Rock-a-Bye Baby; Rock-
    abye, Baby
Hop Up, My Ladies 63:66
Horse Named Bill 49:18, 51:72
Horse Went Around, The 50:16
Hush'n Bye 62:36. *See also* All the
    Pretty Little Horses; Go to
    Sleepy; Hush A Bye; Hush-You-
    Bye; Rock-a-Bye Baby; Rock-
    abye, Baby
Hush-You-Bye 46:56. *See also* All
    the Pretty Little Horses; Go to
    Sleepy; Hush A Bye; Hush'n
    Bye; Rock-a-Bye Baby
I Ride an Old Paint 36:131, 40:52
Listen to the Horses 59:50
Mairzy Doats 66:138
Me and My Horse 15:47
Merry-Go-Round 30:18, 35:45
My Little Pony 3:9
My Pony Boy 65:32
Ride a Cock-Horse 38:52, 66:186.
    See also Ride a Cock-Horse to
    Banbury Cross; Ride a
    Cockhorse
Ride a Cock-Horse to Banbury
    Cross 44:26. *See also* Ride a
    Cock-Horse; Ride a Cockhorse
Ride a Cockhorse 31:9, 74:16. *See
    also* Ride a Cock-Horse; Ride a
    Cock-Horse to Banbury Cross
Ride Your Red Horse 69:22
See the Pony Galloping, Galloping
    38:98
Stewball 40:106, 63:68
This Is the Way the Ladies Ride
    74:12
Trot, Trot, Trot 62:71, 74:16

HOSPITALS

Nancy's Gone to the Hospital 21:34

HOUSES

Little Boxes 40:69
Where Do You Live? 21:32

HUMAN BODY

Ah, Mama Mier 55:18
All of Me 42:104
Baby's Face 72:50
Bathtime 58:4
Because She Shines 6:12
Brush Your Teeth 19:26, 59:8
Bubble Toes 12:29
Chester 64:53
Cocky Doodle Doodle Doo 72:21
Designer Genes 8:19
Do Your Ears Hang Low? 16:30,
    38:113, 50:66, 51:75, 70:6
Doctor, Doctor 35:88
Don't Put Your Finger up Your
    Nose 56:84
Dry Bones 22:326
Everything Grows 58:28
Fingernails 12:24
Fingers 14:22
Five Little Fingers 72:51
Get Your Fingers Off My Leg And
    Your Hand Off of My Shoe
    56:150
GIGO 12:38
God Made Me! 42:45
Gogo 38:93
Grease and Sweets 6:10
Head and Shoulders 1:108, 20:40,
    42:53, 65:12. *See also* Head and
    Shoulders, Baby; Head, Shoul-
    ders, Baby; Tete, Epaules
Head and Shoulders, Baby 64:54.
    See also Head and Shoulders;
    Head, Shoulders, Baby; Tete,
    Epaules
Head, Shoulders, Baby 49:33. *See
    also* Head and Shoulders; Head
    and Shoulders, Baby; Tete,
    Epaules
Hokey-Pokey 66:204
Huff and Puff 11:24
I Love Your Eyes 56:140
I Take My Little Hand 72:18
I Wonder If I'm Growing 59:9
I'm Being Eaten by a Boa Constric-
    tor 51:33
I've Got One Head 49:8
If You Take Care of Your Body
    18:29

If You're Happy 74:38. *See also* If You're Happy and You Know It
If You're Happy and You Know It 49:28, 66:176, 70:20. *See also* If You're Happy
It's Bad, Bad Stuff 8:12
Junk Food Junkie 6:19
Keep Your Body Strong 6:26, 6:41
Let's Watch 21:20
Look Ma! No Cavities 71:36
Meat, Milk, and Grain 6:16
My Body Machine 6:6
One Little Nose Like Mine 12:44
Open, Shut Them 55:58, 72:55
Pair of Feet 14:14
Put Our Best Selves Forward 6:34
Right Foot, Left Foot 21:19
Scrubit Land of Clean 12:40
See My Fingers 72:53
Senses Song 21:18
Skin and Bones 22:336, 59:43
Smiles 54:41
Something in My Shoe 60:55
Spider on the Floor 59:21
Ten Little Toesies 72:45
Tete, Epaules 60:59. *See also* Head and Shoulders; Head and Shoulders, Baby; Head, Shoulders, Baby
This Little Toe 72:44
Thumbkins 55:52
Ticklely 72:52
Vegetable Rap 6:14
Wash the Stickies down the Drain 12:32
Where Are Your Eyes? 35:14
Where Is Thumbkin? 31:62, 35:66, 36:247, 38:29, 42:57, 64:30, 65:19, 72:49
Who Stole My Chickens? 1:16
Wiggle Song 4:22, 42:54
You Can't Build a Body on Junk 6:30

HUMAN RELATIONS
Inequality Makes the World Go 'Round 56:152
Later 56:199
Lend a Helping Hand 12:8
Long, Long Ago 67:9
More We Get Together 31:28, 59:16
Your Power to Dream 18:9

HUNGARY
Boci Tarka 1:88

HUNTING
A-Hunting We Will Go 36:19, 38:88, 55:40
And We Hunted and We Hunted 63:36
Billy Barlow 36:40
Deer Song, The 63:34
Fox in a Box 15:44
Gray Goose 36:104, 63:38
Grey Goose 66:170
Groundhog 22:92, 71:38
Hey Ho, to the Greenwood 46:83
John Peel 38:69, 46:6
Keeper, The 36:148, 46:8
Lincolnshire Poacher 46:30
My Father Hunted a Kangaroo 51:32
Uncle Reuben 36:237

HYMNS
Alleluia 34:17
Amazing Grace 33:11, 34:39
Angels We Have Heard on High 23:2, 28:22, 61:28
Battle Hymn of the Republic 36:32
Bringing in the Sheaves 33:22
Come, Ye Thankful People, Come 34:58, 36:57
Fairest Lord Jesus 48:4
Glory to God in the Highest 42:110
Glory to Thee 46:92
Good Morning, Lord! 68:29
He Is Lord 42:67
Holy Bible, Book Divine 48:6
Holy, Holy, Holy 34:10
Hosanna! 42:64
I Sing a Song of the Saints of God 34:42
Joyful, Joyful, We Adore Thee 34:14
Lord Is My Shepherd, The 68:40
May Jesus Christ Be Praised 42:115
O Come, All Ye Faithful 2:17, 28:41, 45:20, 52:64, 61:4. *See also* Oh Come, All Ye Faithful
O Little Town of Bethlehem 2:18, 28:46, 36:177, 61:14
Oh Come, All Ye Faithful 36:172. *See also* O Come, All Ye Faithful
Old Rugged Cross 27:26
Praise God from Whom All Blessings Flow 34:20, 48:3

HYMNS (*cont.*)

Praise Him 42:81. *See also* Praise
Him, Praise Him

Praise Him, Praise Him 27:16. *See
also* Praise Him

Rejoice in the Lord Always 27:14

Sanctus 34:16

Shall We Gather at the River?
40:92

Shining Day 34:56

Simple Gifts 22:38, 33:120, 46:48.
See also Tis a Gift to Be Simple; Tis the Gift to Be Simple

Tis a Gift to Be Simple 40:122. *See
also* Simple Gifts; Tis the Gift
to Be Simple

Tis the Gift to Be Simple 34:62.
See also Simple Gifts; Tis a Gift
to Be Simple

We Gather Together 33:138, 34:60,
36:240. *See also* We Gather
Together to Ask the Lord's
Blessing

We Gather Together to Ask the
Lord's Blessing 66:251. *See
also* We Gather Together

Will the Circle Be Unbroken
40:133

IMAGINATION

Balloon, The 35:44

Choose the Animal 14:19

City Cowboy 30:14

Dark Brown Is the River 35:87

I Played a Joke on You 5:30

I Wanna Be a Dog 56:111

I Wish I Was 50:62

I Wonder How It Felt 42:120

If I Could Fly 35:40

If I Had a Dinosaur 59:36

Marvelous Toy 66:118

Octopus's Garden 60:75

Puff, the Magic Dragon 19:44,
66:161

Reuben, Reuben 50:68

Sandbox, The 35:42

Seahorse Merry-Go-Round 3:20

Smile, Dear Princess 11:23

Where Go the Boats? 35:87

Windmill 65:62

**INDIANS OF NORTH
  AMERICA.** *See* **NATIVE
  AMERICANS**

INSECTS

Anansi 59:72

Ants Go Marching 24:10, 50:6,
64:78

Arabella Miller 50:43, 64:37. *See
also* Little Arabella Miller

Battle of the Stags 53:29

Black Widow's Waltz, The 53:39

Busy Bee 53:33

Caterpillar 38:22, 56:186

Confession of a Praying Mantis
53:13

Creepy Crawly Caterpillar 53:41

Down by the Creek Bank 42:133

Fiddle-De-De 75:22. *See also*
Fiddle-dee-dee

Fiddle-dee-dee 31:29. *See also*
Fiddle-De-De

Flea Circus 53:26

Flea Fly Song 50:11

Fly Little Butterfly 3:23

Grasshopper Song 50:10

Hundred Feet Ahead 53:1

Itchy Flea 49:77, 51:120

Itchy Scritchy 53:7

Lady Bird, Lady Bird 75:31

Ladybug's Lullaby 53:53

Lament of the House Flies 53:49

Little Arabella Miller 74:23. *See
also* Arabella Miller

Little Bumble Bee 3:22

Little Peter Possum 24:2

Little Peter Rabbit 35:76, 50:19,
64:36

Little White Duck 36:158, 58:40,
66:92

Living a Day 53:37

Mama Mosquito's Midnight Whine
53:45

March of the Worker Ants 53:17

Return of the Baby Bumblebee 55:9

Shoo Fly 24:14, 35:54, 36:203

Spider on the Floor 59:21

Spin, Spider, Spin 68:20

There Was a Bee-Eye-Ee-Eye-Ee 50:12

Walking Sticks 53:11

IRELAND

Cockles and Mussels 66:196

Cucanandy 1:52

ISRAEL

Now, Now, Now 36:168

Salom Chaverim 67:9

Zum Gali Gali 34:22

JOY
I Am So Glad 48:1
Joy to the World 2:15, 23:16, 28:53, 45:34, 61:6
Joyful, Joyful, We Adore Thee 34:14
Sing Hosanna 34:12

JUDAISM
Hanukah 71:20
Hanukkah 47:20
Hanukkah Is Happiness 47:18
Hanukkah Song 36:110, 38:144

JUMP ROPE JINGLES
Lazy Susan 55:10
Miss Lucy 51:82. *See also* Miss Lucy Had a Baby
Miss Lucy Had a Baby 49:40. *See also* Miss Lucy
Miss Polly 55:41. *See also* Miss Polly Had a Dolly
Miss Polly Had a Dolly 49:39, 65:77. *See also* Miss Polly
Monkey in the Treetop 3:29
Teddy Bear, Teddy Bear 49:38

JUSTICE. *See* **PEACE AND JUSTICE**

KANGAROOS
Kangaroo, Kangaroo 3:35
My Father Hunted a Kangaroo 51:32

KINDNESS
Be a Friend 9:26
Be Ye Kind 42:39
Because I Love Him 11:62
Do You Want to Feel Happy? 9:34
Don't Forget the Family 12:14
Forgiveness 10:42
Friend in Need 12:4
Go the Second Mile 54:49
He's My Responsibility 11:58
How to Be a Good Citizen 71:10
I Know a Little Pussy 36:128, 65:50. *See also* I Love Little Kitty; I Love Little Pussy
I Love Little Kitty 31:65. *See also* I Know a Little Pussy; I Love Little Pussy
I Love Little Pussy 33:66, 36:130, 38:46, 44:6, 66:101, 75:30. *See also* I Know a Little Pussy; I Love Little Kitty

If Your Friend's in Trouble 8:2
Jesus Said Love Everyone 54:49
Kindness Begins with Me 54:49
Lend a Helping Hand 12:8
Little Purple Pansies 54:51
Maybe You Laughed 9:28
More We Serve 12:11
Mother Needs Me 5:36
My Responsibility 42:95
My Tongue 42:103
Never Cook Your Sister in a Frying Pan 56:92
Service with a Smile 12:16
Show a Little Love 9:4
Special Gift 54:49
We Volunteer 12:6

KING, MARTIN LUTHER, JR.
Martin Luther King, Junior 47:30

KINGS AND RULERS
En Passant par la Lorraine 46:64
I Had a Little Nut Tree 33:65, 36:127, 44:41
Lavender's Blue 20:18, 33:79, 36:151, 38:66, 44:54, 75:38
Let's Go Bowling in Bowling Green 50:64
Little Nut Tree 38:53, 75:64
March of the Kings 2:28
Noble Duke of York 16:31, 38:88
Old King Cole 31:30, 36:182, 38:74, 44:42, 65:40, 66:229, 75:70
Pussy Cat, Pussy Cat 31:35, 38:50, 44:6, 66:108, 75:49
Queen Caroline 1:6
Sing a Song of Sixpence 31:38, 36:208, 38:30, 44:45, 66:222, 75:55
We Three Kings 2:16, 36:242, 48:10, 52:28. *See also* We Three Kings of Orient Are
We Three Kings of Orient Are 28:48, 61:24. *See also* We Three Kings
When Good King Arthur Ruled This Land 44:39
Where Is the Baby? 2:33
Will Ye No Come Back Again? 46:22

KITES
Fly My Kite with Me 30:46

KOOKABURRA
Kookaburra 36:150, 46:75, 70:32

LADYBUGS
Ladybug's Lullaby 53:53

LAMBS. *See* **SHEEP**

LATIN AMERICA
Al Citron 64:110
Un Elephante 64:115

LIMERICKS
Mister Lister 69:24

LINCOLN, ABRAHAM
Abe Lincoln 47:40
Hooray for Mr. Lincoln 71:34

LIONS
Didn't My Lord Deliver Daniel?
43:16
King of the Jungle 71:44
Lions 17:29
Truth About Lions 3:30

LIZARDS
Mole in the Ground 63:25
Snake Baked a Hoecake 63:24

LOVE
As I Have Loved You 54:83
Give a Little Love 32:24
Happy Family 54:11
I Am So Glad 48:1
I Feel My Savior's Love 54:37
I've Got Peace Like a River 27:8
Jesus Loves the Little Children
48:5
Jesus Said Love Everyone 54:49
Long, Long Ago 67:9
More We Serve 12:11
Mother Dear 54:13
Mother Dear, I Love You 9:39
Mother, I Love You 54:11
My Dad 9:10, 54:17
Service with a Smile 12:16
Showing Love 42:38
Where Love Is 54:81

LULLABIES
All the Pretty Little Horses
22:268, 33:7, 35:72, 38:11,
77:18. *See also* Go to Sleepy;
Hush A Bye; Hush'n Bye; Hush-
You-Bye; Rock-a-Bye Baby;
Rockabye, Baby
All Through the Night 77:8

Baby Bunting 31:17
Baby Doll 35:24
Baiu-Baiushki-Baiu 62:42
Baloo Baleerie 77:20
Brahms' Lullaby 77:31. *See also*
Cradle Song; Cradlesong; Lulla-
by; Lullaby, and Good Night
By'm Bye 77:14. *See also* Bye 'n'
Bye; Bye'm Bye
Bye'm Bye 22:196, 72:58. *See also*
By'm Bye; Bye 'n' Bye
Bye 'n' Bye 49:66, 64:25. *See also*
By'm Bye; Bye'm Bye
Bye, Baby Bunting 35:68, 38:14,
41:67, 77:15
Bye, Bye, Baby 72:61
Bye-Low, My Baby 48:8
Coventry Carol 2:39, 28:35, 61:16
Cradle Is Warm 41:66
Cradle Song 35:70, 36:59. *See also*
Brahms' Lullaby; Cradlesong;
Lullaby; Lullaby, and Good
Night; Schlaf, Kindlein, Schlaf;
Sleep, Baby, Sleep
Cradlesong 31:11. *See also*
Brahms' Lullaby; Cradle Song;
Lullaby; Lullaby, and Good
Night
Cucanandy 1:52
Cum By Yah 77:22. *See also* Kum
Ba Yah; Kumbaya
Dona Nobis Pacem 34:33, 46:91
Down in the Valley 40:28, 67:5
El Coquito 38:136
Fais Do Do 64:64. *See also* Fais
Dodo
Fais Dodo 60:77. *See also* Fais Do
Do
Go Tell Aunt Rhody 36:101,
38:116, 40:42, 67:4
Go to Sleep 63:65
Go to Sleep Now, My Pumpkin
65:92
Go to Sleepy 36:102. *See also* All
the Pretty Little Horses; Hush
A Bye; Hush'n Bye; Hush-You-
Bye; Rock-a-Bye Baby; Rock-
abye, Baby
Golden Slumbers 25:28, 31:8,
38:16, 41:69, 74:6
Good Night 35:35
Good Night, Irene 59:88. *See also*
Goodnight, Irene
Hear the Wind Blow 4:30

LULLABIES (*cont.*)

Hush A Bye 72:59. *See also* All the Pretty Little Horses; Go to Sleepy; Hush'n Bye; Hush-You-Bye; Rock-a-Bye Baby; Rockabye, Baby

Hush-a-Bye Baby 41:67, 44:60

Hush, Little Baby 22:98, 25:18, 31:20, 33:62, 36:126, 38:12, 65:91, 66:181, 70:38, 72:57, 74:9, 77:10

Hush'n Bye 62:36. *See also* All the Pretty Little Horses; Go to Sleepy; Hush A Bye; Hush-You-Bye; Rock-a-Bye Baby; Rockabye, Baby

Hush-You-Bye 46:56. *See also* All the Pretty Little Horses; Go to Sleepy; Hush A Bye; Hush'n Bye; Rock-a-Bye Baby

Hushabye 69:18

I Ride an Old Paint 36:131, 40:52

I Rock My Doll 35:25

Kum Ba Yah 26:26. *See also* Cum By Yah; Kumbaya

Kumbaya 19:22, 60:31. *See also* Cum By Yah; Kum Ba Yah

Ladybug's Lullaby 53:53

Lavender's Blue 20:18, 33:79, 36:151, 38:66, 44:54, 75:38

Little Lap-Dog Lullaby 63:27

Lullaby 4:15, 38:17. *See also* Brahms' Lullaby; Cradle Song; Cradlesong

Lullaby, and Good Night 74:11. *See also* Brahms' Lullaby; Cradle Song; Cradlesong

Lullaby, My Jamie 46:60

Lullaby, My Pretty One 41:67

Lullabye 69:23, 72:60

Lulloo Lullay 77:12

Mockingbird Song 40:74

Morningtown Ride 19:46, 60:33

Nina Nana 1:74

No One Like You 66:14

Now the Day Is Over 33:91, 34:32, 38:21, 77:29

Numi Nim 62:45

Raisins and Almonds 77:16

Rock-a-Bye Baby 25:22, 31:34, 33:112, 36:198, 41:66, 65:93, 66:221, 74:8, 77:28. *See also* All the Pretty Little Horses; Go to Sleepy; Hush A Bye; Hush'n Bye; Hush-You-Bye; Rockabye, Baby

Rockabye, Baby 38:20. *See also* All the Pretty Little Horses; Go to Sleepy; Hush A Bye; Hush'n Bye; Hush-You-Bye; Rock-a-Bye Baby

Rocking 2:42

Ru-ruque 1:20

Russian Lullaby 55:24

Sandman Comes 25:26, 38:15, 74:7

Schlaf, Kindlein, Schlaf 62:38. *See also* Cradle Song; Sleep, Baby, Sleep

Shiny Lullaby 6:4

Shiny Silver Moon 35:36

Sleep, Baby, Sleep 38:18, 41:68, 74:8, 77:7. *See also* Cradle Song; Schlaf, Kindlein, Schlaf

Sleep My Baby 41:69

Sleeping Time 35:34

Suo Gan 77:24

Sweet and Low 62:40

Sweet Water Rolling 62:30

Une Poule Blanche 62:32

LUMBERJACKS AND LUMBERING

Frozen Logger 22:284, 40:38

MAKE-BELIEVE

Comin' Down the Chimney 59:34

Hooray, Professor Un 12:62

I Wish I Was 50:62

I'm a Little Teapot 16:32, 35:52, 38:95, 66:109, 74:28

I'm a Nut 50:67, 51:78

I'm Being Eaten by a Boa Constrictor 51:33

If All the Raindrops 65:57

If I Could Fly 35:40

If I Had a Dinosaur 59:36

Octopus's Garden 60:75

Sandbox, The 35:42

Thumbelina 60:41

MANNERS

Don't Put Your Finger up Your Nose 56:84

Don't You Push Me Down 35:74

Gratitude Attitude 11:46

He Eats Asparagus, Why Can't You Be That Way? 56:18

Honor Your Parents 66:246

Honoring Mother and Father 42:134

I Say Thank You 11:53

Kindness Begins with Me 54:49

Land of Obey 10:6
Lend a Helping Hand 12:8
Maybe You Laughed 9:28
Shut Up in the Library 56:30
Thank You Dance 11:56
Think About a Thank You 11:50
We're Just Two Friends 11:37
Words You Speak 9:36

MARCHING
Ants Go Marching 24:10, 50:6,
    64:78
Battle Hymn of the Republic 36:32
Caissons, The 36:51
Dixie 33:31, 36:68
First-Last 21:25
Grand Old Duke of York 65:29
Heigh-Ho 66:66
I'm in the Lord's Army 26:4
Left Right 4:24
March of the Worker Ants 53:17
Marching Shoulder to Shoulder
    56:104
Marching Song 42:51
Marines' Hymn 36:161
Noble Duke of York 16:31, 38:88
Onward, Christian Soldiers 27:4
Presidents Are Famous Men 47:38
Tiptoe March 21:15
Waltzing Matilda 66:200
We Are Soldiers 74:29
When Johnny Comes Marching
    Home 36:245
When the Saints Go Marching In
    27:6
Yankee Doodle 22:62, 31:57,
    33:140, 36:251, 38:122, 40:135,
    44:48, 66:250

MATHEMATICS
Inch Worm 66:40
Multiply 42:121

MAY
Living a Day 53:37
Today Is May 71:54

MAY DAY
May Day 5:33

MAYFLIES
Living a Day 53:37

MERRY-GO-ROUNDS
Merry-Go-Round 30:18, 35:45

MEXICO
Ol' Texas 20:22

MICE
Frog Went A-Courtin' 33:44, 36:94,
    66:182. See also Froggie Went
    A-Courting
Froggie Went A-Courting 75:18.
    See also Frog Went A-Courtin'
Hickory, Dickory, Dock 31:23,
    33:55, 35:61, 36:120, 38:51,
    44:2, 66:232, 72:43, 74:24
Long Time Ago 35:92
Six Little Mice Sat Down to Spin
    44:3
Tailor and the Mouse 49:72
Three Blind Mice 31:43, 36:224,
    44:2, 65:51, 66:233, 75:78

MILITARY LIFE
Gee, Mom, I Want to Go Home
    22:356
Marines' Hymn 36:161
Military Song 13:43
Quartermaster Corps 50:29, 51:43
Taps 36:216

MINERS AND MINING
Acres of Clams 22:192, 40:2
Clementine 33:26, 36:55, 40:20,
    50:40, 51:87, 66:164, 67:6. See
    also My Darling Clementine
My Darling Clementine 31:27. See
    also Clementine
Oh, Susannah 22:180

MISSISSIPPI
M-I-S-S-I-S-S-I-P-P-I 66:157

MOLES
Mole in the Ground 63:25

MONEY
Free Enterprise 13:49
Mommy, Mommy, I Gotta Get a Re-
    cord 56:120

MONKEYS
Five Little Monkeys 17:18, 50:52
Great Ape 3:38
Here Sits a Monkey 59:68
Monkey in the Treetop 3:29
Monkey See and Monkey Do 55:51
Pop! Goes the Weasel 31:46,
    33:106, 36:194, 38:32, 50:58,
    65:47, 66:187, 70:26, 75:50

MONTHS
December 54:27
Mother Goose Summer 76:6

MONTHS (*cont.*)

Remember September 5:7
Sing a Song of September 71:6
Today Is May 71:54

MOON

Aiken Drum 25:20, 51:12, 75:16.
    See also Aikendrum; There
    Was a Man Lived in the Moon
Aikendrum 59:30. *See also* Aiken
    Drum; There Was a Man Lived
    in the Moon
Au Clair de la Lune 36:27
Big Moon, Bright Moon 4:38
Hey, Diddle, Diddle 31:54, 38:67,
    44:35, 66:226, 71:63, 75:28
Mister Sun 19:14
Moonlight on the Ruined Castle
    67:15
Night with a Dim Moon 67:15
Shiny Silver Moon 35:36
There Was a Man Lived in the
    Moon 44:38. *See also* Aiken
    Drum; Aikendrum

MORMONS AND MORMONISM

Book of Mormon Stories 14:61
Golden Plates 14:61
Handcart Song 22:176
I Love to See the Temple 14:25

MORNING

Brush Your Teeth 19:26, 59:8
Canticle of the Sun, The 34:9
Day-O 19:10, 60:15
Early in the Morning 42:109
Early One Morning 46:10
Every Night and Every Morn 34:38
Frere Jacques 1:114, 25:24, 31:7,
    36:91, 38:134, 46:61, 59:79,
    62:109, 66:234. *See also* Are
    You Sleeping
Good Morning, Lord! 68:29
Good Morning to You 38:115
I'm Late 56:159
In the Leafy Tree Tops 54:45
Lazy Mary 33:80, 35:56, 36:153,
    38:62, 65:8, 72:24, 75:41. *See
    also* Lazy Mary, Will You Get
    Up?
Lazy Mary, Will You Get Up?
    31:64, 66:228. *See also* Lazy
    Mary
Lord of the Dance 34:18
Mister Sunshine 4:27
Morning Has Broken 34:8

On Christmas Morning 57:55
Rise and Shine 34:44, 50:91, 60:35
Sleepers Wake 39:24
Wake, Snake 22:248

MOSES

Dayenu 34:26
Go Down, Moses 22:128, 34:24,
    36:98, 42:79, 43:8

MOSQUITOES

Mama Mosquito's Midnight Whine
    53:45

MOUNTAINS

Bear Went over the Mountain
    36:34, 38:112, 70:22
Big Rock Candy Mountain 22:354,
    36:37
Climb, Climb Up Sunshine Moun-
    tain 27:24
Cumberland Gap 22:82
Douglas Mountain 57:72, 59:54
Happy Wanderer 36:112
On Top of Old Smokey 33:103. *See
    also* On Top of Old Smoky; On
    Top of Spaghetti
On Top of Old Smoky 31:25, 40:83,
    67:6. *See also* On Top of Old
    Smokey; On Top of Spaghetti

MOUSE. *See* MICE

MOVING PICTURES

Ding-Dong! The Witch Is Dead
    66:28
Do-Re-Mi 66:44
Give a Little Whistle 66:72
Heigh-Ho 66:66
Hi-Diddle-Dee-Dee 66:70
I Whistle a Happy Tune 66:48
I'm Popeye the Sailor Man 66:77.
    See also Popeye, the Sailor Man
If I Only Had a Brain 66:30
Inch Worm 66:40
Octopus's Garden 60:75
On the Good Ship Lollipop 66:42
One Song 66:64
Over the Rainbow 66:34
Popeye, the Sailor Man 49:26,
    51:121. *See also* I'm Popeye the
    Sailor Man
Rainbow Connection 66:22
Silly Song 66:68
Tomorrow 55:34, 56:60, 66:25
We're Off to See the Wizard 66:37
When I See an Elephant Fly 66:56

Whistle While You Work 66:62
Who's Afraid of the Big Bad Wolf?
    66:52
With a Smile and a Song 66:59
Yellow Submarine 66:74

MUD
Mud, Mud, Glorious Mud 50:79,
    51:31

MULES
Erie Canal 22:116, 36:81, 40:30
Kicking Mule 63:62
Whoa, Mule! Can't Get the Saddle
    On 63:64

MUSIC AND MUSICIANS
Arkansas Traveler 36:24, 40:4
Die Musica 67:7
Do-Re-Mi 66:44
Fiddlers 46:42
Five More Minutes 56:198
Mama Don't 'Low 49:59. See also
    Mama Don't Allow
Mama Don't Allow 40:71. See also
    Mama Don't 'Low
Old McDonald Had a Band 59:22
Very Best Band 64:20
You Sing a Song and I'll Sing a
    Song 59:63

MUSICAL INSTRUMENTS
Hey, Diddle, Diddle 31:54, 38:67,
    44:35, 66:226, 71:63, 75:28
I Love to Hear My Father Play the
    Piano 30:22
I've Been Working on the Railroad
    33:70, 36:135, 40:59, 66:158,
    67:12
Let's Do the Numbers Rumba 60:60
Let's Hear the Rhythm 21:16
Little David, Play on Your Harp
    43:12
Little Drummer Boy, The 2:32
Michaud 60:57, 64:63
Oh, Susanna! 31:68, 33:98, 36:179,
    38:126, 40:79
Oh, We Can Play 74:36
Old King Cole 31:30, 36:182,
    38:74, 44:42, 65:40, 66:229,
    75:70
Old McDonald Had a Band 59:22
Pat-a-Pan 2:38, 38:152
Play Your Horn Right Now 21:12
Very Best Band 64:20

Workin' on the Railroad 59:40. See
    also Working on the Railroad
Working on the Railroad 38:132.
    See also Workin' on the
    Railroad

MUSKRATS
Muskrat 63:21

NAMES
Cookie Jar 64:51
Dearest Names 54:23
First-Last 21:25
Hello 21:6
Little Girl/Boy Went Walking 55:55
Move Over 21:11
Riding on the New River Train
    55:31
Somebody Loves 4:8
Spell Some Names 21:8
We Have a Friend 55:54
What Is the Number? 21:28

NATIONAL SONGS. See
    PATRIOTIC SONGS

NATIVE AMERICANS
Dream Song 22:14
Indian Brothers 47:13
Pilgrims and the Indians 5:14
Song of Happiness 22:25
Twas in the Moon of Wintertime
    2:24, 28:70

NATURE
About Water 4:29
Afton Water 46:24
All I Really Need 60:23
All Things Bright and Beautiful
    42:91, 48:2
Autumn Day 54:55
Autumn Leaves Are Now Falling
    48:9
Baby Beluga 19:18, 60:7
Beautiful Autumn 5:8
Beauty Everywhere 54:45
Because It's Spring 54:43
Big Beautiful Planet 60:50
Blessing the Earth 68:48
Canticle of the Sun, The 34:9
Conversation with a Tree 71:55
Deer Song, The 63:34
Everything Grows 58:28
Everything That's Beautiful 68:26
For Us All 42:94
God Loves Each Child 42:28

NATURE (*cont.*)
God Made the World 42:88
God Who Made the Earth 42:139
God's Big World 42:29
God's Creation 42:89
Good Morning, Lord! 68:29
Good-Bye Winter, Hello Spring
    71:42
Green Grass Grew All Around
    49:22. *See also* Green Grass
    Grows All Around, The
Green Grass Grows All Around,
    The 24:4. *See also* Green
    Grass Grew All Around
Gust of Fall Wind, A 22:168
Happiness 42:144, 54:47
Hear the Wind Blow 4:30
Holy, Holy, Holy 34:10
I Had a Little Nut Tree 33:65,
    36:127, 44:41
I Like Spring 68:10
I Love the Flowers 4:28
I Often Go Walking 54:13
I Think the World Is Glorious 54:53
In the Beginning 42:90
In the Leafy Tree Tops 54:45
It Ain't Gonna Rain No More
    51:60, 66:148
It's Autumn Time 54:55
It's Easter Time 5:29
It's Spring Again 5:27
Just Like the Sun 58:45
Just Walkin' Along 42:131
Little Drops of Water 38:63
Little Nut Tree 38:53, 75:64
Little White Duck 36:158, 58:40,
    66:92
Living a Day 53:37
Mister Sun 19:14
Mister Sunshine 4:27
Mister Wind Is a Mischief 4:31
Morning Has Broken 34:8
Mr. Earth, I Love You 11:60
Mr. Sun 59:12
My Heavenly Father Loves Me
    54:53
My Way Home 59:58
Over in the Meadow 38:44, 49:16,
    60:27
Popcorn Popping 54:43
Rainbow 'Round Me 55:16
Riding in an Airplane 60:81
Robin in the Rain 59:28
Seasons 42:34, 42:93, 68:9

Seeds Are Planted Deep 55:12
Shining Day 34:56
Spring Inside 68:11
Take Time 68:34
Tell Me Why 32:6, 40:113
Thanking Song 68:30
Thanks a Lot 60:19
Tree in the Wood 33:134, 36:226
Uncle Reuben 36:237
Walk Outside 60:94
Water in the Rain Clouds 71:53
Wild Mountain Thyme 76:22
Worms 71:56

NEEDLEWORK
Sweet Rosie O'Grady 50:42

NEIGHBORS
He Eats Asparagus, Why Can't You
    Be That Way? 56:18
Hine Ma Tov 34:51
Town of Round 56:176

NEW YEAR
Auld Lang Syne 36:28, 45:46
Happy New Year 5:20

NEW YORK
Sidewalks of New York 36:204

NIGHT
Blanket for a Sail 32:36
Brahms' Lullaby 77:31. *See also*
    Cradle Song; Cradlesong; Lulla-
    by; Lullaby, and Good Night
By'm Bye 77:14. *See also* Bye 'n'
    Bye; Bye'm Bye
Bye'm Bye 22:196, 72:58. *See also*
    By'm Bye; Bye 'n' Bye
Bye 'n' Bye 49:66, 64:25. *See also*
    By'm Bye; Bye'm Bye
Cradle Song 35:70, 36:59. *See also*
    Brahms' Lullaby; Cradlesong;
    Lullaby; Lullaby, and Good
    Night; Schlaf, Kindlein, Schlaf;
    Sleep, Baby, Sleep
Cradlesong 31:11. *See also*
    Brahms' Lullaby; Cradle Song;
    Lullaby; Lullaby, and Good
    Night
Follow the Drinkin' Gourd 22:140.
    See also Follow the Drinking
    Gourd
Follow the Drinking Gourd 40:32.
    See also Follow the Drinkin'
    Gourd
Glory to Thee 46:92

Go Tell Aunt Rhody 36:101, 38:116, 40:42, 67:4
Go to Sleep Now, My Pumpkin 65:92
Golden Slumbers 25:28, 31:8, 38:16, 41:69, 74:6
Good Night 35:35
Good Night, Irene 59:88. *See also* Goodnight, Irene
Good Night, Ladies 31:73
Good Night Song 4:39
Goodnight, Irene 40:48. *See also* Good Night, Irene
Hush-You-Bye 46:56. *See also* All the Pretty Little Horses; Go to Sleepy; Hush A Bye; Hush'n Bye; Rock-a-Bye Baby
Hushabye 69:18
I Often Think of God 42:6
Little Red Bird 46:40
Lullaby 4:15, 38:17. *See also* Brahms' Lullaby; Cradle Song; Cradlesong
Lullaby, and Good Night 74:11. *See also* Brahms' Lullaby; Cradle Song; Cradlesong
Moonlight on the Ruined Castle 67:15
Night with a Dim Moon 67:15
Now the Day Is Over 33:91, 34:32, 38:21, 77:29
Sandman Comes 25:26, 38:15, 74:7
Schlaf, Kindlein, Schlaf 62:38. *See also* Cradle Song; Sleep, Baby, Sleep
Sleep, Baby, Sleep 38:18, 41:68, 74:8, 77:7. *See also* Cradle Song; Schlaf, Kindlein, Schlaf
Taps 36:216
Twinkle, Twinkle, Little Star 19:42, 25:2, 31:47, 33:137, 36:235, 38:64, 41:68, 44:32, 60:99, 65:85, 66:202, 67:4, 75:93
Wee Willie Winkie 38:19, 71:16

NIGHTINGALES
In the Ev'ning the Nightingale 39:9

NOAH
Didn't It Rain? 43:2
Rise and Shine 34:44, 50:91, 60:35
Who Built the Ark? 59:32

NONSENSE SONGS
A Cheval 62:77

Aiken Drum 25:20, 51:12, 75:16. *See also* Aikendrum; There Was a Man Lived in the Moon
Aikendrum 59:30. *See also* Aiken Drum; There Was a Man Lived in the Moon
Alfabet Song 56:119
Alison's Camel 64:93
All the Little Fishies Do a Hoochie Koochie Dance 55:23
Alouette 66:194
Anansi 59:72
Animal Fair 36:22, 66:87, 70:18
Apple of My Eye 56:74
Apples and Bananas 19:32, 55:19, 60:70
Arkansas Traveler 36:24, 40:4
Around the Corner 50:74, 51:8
Aunt Anna Came to Our House 56:130
Baby Bumble Bee 50:8, 51:112
Baby Cakewalk 69:16
Back of a Crocodile 64:49. *See also* Crocodile, The; Smile on the Crocodile
Barney Google 66:135
Be Kind to Your Web-Footed Friends 51:124, 66:190
Beans in My Ears 40:8
Bear Song 50:56
Bear Went over the Mountain 36:34, 38:112, 70:22
Belly and Tubs 69:19
Benjy Met a Bear 51:48
Bile Them Cabbage Down 49:81
Billboard Song 50:78
Bimbo Bombo 69:20
Black Socks 51:54
Boom Boom 51:68, 59:70. *See also* Boom, Boom Ain't It Great to Be Crazy
Boom, Boom Ain't It Great to Be Crazy 20:30. *See also* Boom Boom
Boom da li-da 1:84
Bring Back My Neighbors to Me 51:96
Bumblebee Song 56:112
But I'm Just Thirteen 56:70
Butterprint 69:7
Candy Man, Salty Dog 64:26
Cat Came Back 40:14, 49:52, 51:114
Catch a Wiffer Woffer 50:76

NONSENSE SONGS (*cont.*)

Cement Mixer 66:121

Chick, Chick, Chicken 65:69

Chicken Lips and Lizard Hips
19:34, 32:39

Chickery Chick 66:113

Chivalrous Shark 46:46

Cindy 46:44

Clock Without a "C" Is Still a Lock
56:116

Corner Grocery Store, The 59:76

Crocodile, The 16:31. *See also*
Back of a Crocodile; Smile on
the Crocodile

Crocodile Song 63:72

Cross-Eyed Gopher 63:20

Dear Old Daddy's Whiskers 25:16,
51:36

Desperado, The 20:14

Dilly Dilly 69:12

Dinga Dinga Doodle 36:66

Dinosaur Song 56:147

Dirty Bill 50:39, 51:35

Do This, Do That 56:106

Do Your Ears Hang Low? 16:30,
38:113, 50:66, 51:75, 70:6

Don't Put Your Finger up Your
Nose 56:84

Down by the Bay 19:28, 24:22,
49:71, 59:2

Down Derry Down 69:27

Drunken Sailor 46:68

Dunderbeck 36:76. *See also*
Dunderbeck's Machine

Dunderbeck's Machine 49:21,
51:39. *See also* Dunderbeck

Early Sunday Morning 56:44

Eenie Meenie and a Miney Moe
55:14

Eletelephony 38:124

Everybody Says Sit Down 55:49

Father's Old Grey Whiskers 19:16,
66:152

Fiddle-De-De 75:22. *See also* Fiddle-dee-dee

Fiddle-dee-dee 31:29. *See also* Fiddle-De-De

Five Little Monkeys 17:18, 50:52

Flat Foot Floogee 66:140

Flea Fly Song 50:11

Fooba-Wooba John 20:12

For My Sister, Wherever I May
Find Her 56:64

Fred 56:35

Fuzzy Wuzzy 50:60

Get Your Fingers Off My Leg And
Your Hand Off of My Shoe
56:150

Ghost Riders in the Sky 20:24

Giggle Tickle Fiddle Little Wiggle
Around 56:39

Go and Hush the Baby 56:165

Greasy, Grimy Gopher Guts 51:30

Gum Song 50:34

Had a Little Dog 55:39. *See also* I
Had a Little Dog

He Eats Asparagus, Why Can't You
Be That Way? 56:18

Here Sits a Monkey 59:68

Here's a Song 69:6

Hey Dum Diddeley Dum 64:12. *See
also* Hey Dum Diddley Dum

Hey Dum Diddley Dum 20:34. *See
also* Hey Dum Diddeley Dum

Hey Jack, What's in the Sack?
56:82

Higglety, Pigglety, Pop! 44:34,
65:48

Horse Named Bill 49:18, 51:72

Horse Went Around, The 50:16

How Would You Like? 55:53

Huckleberry, Gooseberry 69:11

Hut-Sut Song 66:146

I Am Slowly Going Crazy 50:69,
51:77, 64:79

I Can't Tie My Shoe 56:133

I Don't Brush My Teeth and I
Never Comb My Hair 56:22

I Don't Care for Underwear 51:53

I Don't Think My Teacher Likes
Me 56:160

I Eat Kids 56:46

I Got a Camel for Christmas 35:84

I Got a Teacher, She's So Mean
56:36

I Know an Old Lady 66:125

I Lost My Pants 56:144

I Love My Daddy 56:162

I Love Trash 66:19

I Played a Joke on You 5:30

I Sat Next to the Duchess at Tea
64:74

I Sneaked into the Kitchen in the
Middle of the Night 56:32

I Wanna Be a Dog 56:111

I Was Born About Ten Thousand
Years Ago 40:54

I Was Only Foolin' 25:8

I Went to the Movies Tomorrow
55:30
I Wish I Was 50:62
I With I Were 49:10, 51:18
I'm a 3-Toed, Triple-Eyed, Double-
Jointed Dinosaur 56:20
I'm a Nut 50:67, 51:78
I'm Late 56:159
I've Got a Dog and My Dog's Name
Is Cat 56:69
I've Got a Little Sister 56:72
Ice Cream 66:143
If All the Raindrops 65:57
If I Had a Dinosaur 59:36
If You've Got a Kid Who Complains
All the Time 56:136
It Ain't Gonna Rain No More
51:60, 66:148
It's Raining, It's Pouring 31:55,
33:69, 36:134
Itchy Flea 49:77, 51:120
Jack, Can I Ride? 63:76
Jack Was Every Inch a Sailor
64:116
Jamais on na Vu 64:62
Jennie Jenkins 33:76, 36:139. *See
also* Jenny Jenkins
Jenny Jenkins 22:74, 64:14. *See
also* Jennie Jenkins
Jeremiah 65:83
Jig Along Home 31:18, 59:60
Jim Along Josie 36:141. *See also*
Jim-a-long Josie
Jim-a-long Josie 1:66. *See also* Jim
Along Josie
John Jacob Jingleheimer Schmidt
50:90, 51:9, 64:75, 66:134
Keemo Kyemo 22:226
Kicking Mule 63:62
Lavender's Blue 20:18, 33:79,
36:151, 38:66, 44:54, 75:38
Lazy Fred 51:50
Let's Go Bowling in Bowling Green
50:64
Little Pig 63:50
Little Skunk Hole 50:53, 51:42
Little Tommy Tinker 64:74. *See
also* Little Tommy Tucker
Mairzy Doats 66:138
Michael Finnegan 22:244, 37:59,
51:79, 64:79. *See also* Michael
Finnigin
Michael Finnigin 75:62. *See also*
Michael Finnegan

Miss Lucy 51:82. *See also* Miss
Lucy Had a Baby
Miss Lucy Had a Baby 49:40. *See
also* Miss Lucy
Miss Mary Mack 1:78
Miss Quiss 69:26
Mister Lister 69:24
Mole in the Ground 63:25
Monkey's Wedding 31:44
Motorcycle Song 40:77
Mrs. Murphy's Chowder 20:46,
22:236, 49:82
My Brother Thinks He's a Banana
56:57
My Dame Hath a Lame, Tame
Crane 46:87, 75:73
My Father Hunted a Kangaroo
51:32
My Friend Jake 56:42
My Mommy Drives a Dump Truck
56:66
My Tall Silk Hat 70:28
Nanny Banny 69:21
Never Cook Your Sister in a Frying
Pan 56:92
New River Train 59:38
Nothing 56:158
Now You May Think 49:92, 51:123
Oh, Chester! 51:25
Oh Me, Oh My 59:44
Oh Mules We Find 51:52
Oh, My Goodness! 69:10
Oh, Pretty Polly 31:13
Ol' Dan Tucker 22:88
Old Dan Tucker 66:184
Old Family Toothbrush 25:6,
50:87, 51:34
Old Hen Cackled and the Rooster
Laid the Egg 63:42
Old Hogan's Goat 51:117
Old Joe Clark 40:81. *See also* Old
Joe Clarke
Old Joe Clarke 50:44. *See also* Old
Joe Clark
Old Lady Goose 63:40
Old MacTavish Is Dead 51:15
Old Mother Leary 50:38
Old Roger 64:88
On the Good Ship Lollipop 66:42
On Top of My Pizza 50:31, 51:98
On Top of Spaghetti 36:186, 37:38,
66:128. *See also* On Top of Old
Smokey; On Top of Old Smoky
Once I Saw Three Goats 64:77

NONSENSE SONGS (*cont.*)

One Day My Best Friend Barbara Turned Into a Frog 56:54

Ooey Gooey 55:15

Our Dog Bernard 56:58

Pizza Round 51:49

Possum on the Flying Trapeze 24:28. *See also* Man on the Trapeze

Puff, the Magic Dragon 19:44, 66:161

Rabbit Ain't Got No Tail at All 49:85

Reptile World 56:148

Sailor Went to Sea 51:63

Sailor Went to Sea Sea Sea 50:65

Sally Eats Shoelaces, Straw and String 56:156

Sandwiches 20:8

See Saw 69:25

She Went into the Water 24:20

Shiloh, Liza Jane 40:98

Shut Up in the Library 56:30

Silly Song 66:68

Skatter-Brak-Flath Who Lives in My Bath 56:53

Skin and Bones 22:336, 59:43

Skinnamarink 64:122, 65:95

Slithery D 50:94

Smile on the Crocodile 50:54. *See also* Back of a Crocodile; Crocodile, The

Snake Baked a Hoecake 63:24

Sniggle Song 71:25

Something in My Shoe 60:55

Spider on the Floor 59:21

Stanley Stole My Shoelace and Rubbed It in His Armpit 56:163

Sweet Rosie O'Grady 50:42

Swiss Cheese Song 50:32

Tall Silk Hat 64:72

Than I'll Ever Have with You! 49:90

There Was a Bee-Eye-Ee-Eye-Ee 50:12

There Was a Crooked Man 44:46, 75:57

There Was a Lady Loved a Swine 44:36

There Was a Man and He Was Mad 75:81

There Was a Man Lived in the Moon 44:38. *See also* Aiken Drum; Aikendrum

There Was an Old Lady 33:131, 36:221

There Was an Old Woman 38:42, 49:14, 75:82. *See also* There Was an Old Woman Tossed Up in a Basket

There Was an Old Woman Tossed Up in a Basket 44:47. *See also* There Was an Old Woman

There's a Cow in My Bedroom! 55:13

There's a Hole in My Bucket 36:218. *See also* There's a Hole in the Bucket

There's a Hole in the Bucket 40:114, 50:88, 70:8. *See also* There's a Hole in My Bucket

There's No Substitute for a Cat 56:141

They Said, "Eat the Broccoli" 56:90

Thirty Purple Birds 51:51

Three Crow 64:114

Three Little Fishies 66:154

Three Little Piggies 49:12

Three Ways to Get Peanut Butter Off the Roof of Your Mouth 50:33

Thumbkins 55:52

Ting-a-lay-o 19:12. *See also* Tinga Layo; Tingalayo

Tinga Layo 24:16. *See also* Ting-a-lay-o; Tingalayo

Tingalayo 37:39, 60:92, 64:106, 70:14. *See also* Ting-a-lay-o; Tinga Layo

Tit Galop Pour Mamou 22:50

Town of Round 56:176

Underwear 56:174

Up and Over and Down 4:32

Up in the Air 35:30

Uptown, Downtown 69:28

Vista 64:76

Waddaly Atcha 64:52

What Did Delaware, Boys? 49:48, 51:64

What If a Zebra Had Spots? 56:197

When I See an Elephant Fly 66:56

When Poppa Put the Paper on the Wall 49:76

When Suzie Sneezed 56:40

When the House Is Dark and Quiet 56:50

When You Come to the End of a Lollipop 49:89

Whoever Shall Have Peanuts 49:56

Willie the Whistling Giraffe 66:105

Willie the Worm 55:44

Willoughby Wallaby Woo 19:20, 59:7

Yellow Submarine 66:74

You Better Not Giggle, Now Don't You Laugh, But I'm in Love with a Giraffe 56:188

You Can't Get to Heaven 51:90. *See also* Oh, You Can't Get to Heaven

You Can't Say PSBPSBPSB on the Radio 56:81

Zoo, The 35:78

NORWAY

Happy Birthday to You 31:7, 54:9, 66:252

NUMBERS

Angel Band 2:26

Ants Go Marching 24:10, 50:6, 64:78

Children, Go Where I Send Thee 2:34

Devil's Questions, The 22:206

Eight Piggies in a Row 58:23

First-Last 21:25

Five Little Chickadees 38:77, 65:22

Five Little Ducks 60:47, 70:10

Five Little Fingers 72:51

Five Little Frogs 59:1

Five Little Monkeys 17:18, 50:52

Five Little Pumpkins 59:6

Five Little Pussycats 74:44

Five More Minutes 56:198

Five Speckled Frogs 65:54

Head and Shoulders 1:108, 20:40, 42:53, 65:12. *See also* Head and Shoulders, Baby; Head, Shoulders, Baby; Tete, Epaules

Inch Worm 66:40

Let's Do the Numbers Rumba 60:60

Mexican Counting Song 38:137

Ninety-nine Miles from Home 50:72

Roll Over 25:14, 38:121. *See also* Roll Over, Roll Over; Ten in the Bed

Roll Over, Roll Over 70:34. *See also* Roll Over; Ten in the Bed

Ten in the Bed 65:88. *See also* Roll Over; Roll Over, Roll Over

Ten Little Indians 36:217, 66:217

Ten Little Toesies 72:45

Twelve Days of Christmas 2:12, 23:20, 36:231

What Is the Number? 21:28

Who Built the Ark? 59:32

NURSERY RHYMES

A-Tisket, A-Tasket 15:41, 24:6, 31:63, 38:100, 66:110, 70:12. *See also* Itiskit, Itaskit

Baa, Baa, Black Sheep 31:3, 33:17, 33:32, 36:31, 38:47, 44:7, 59:14, 66:223, 75:32

Baby Bunting 31:17

Bobby Shafto 44:51, 65:39, 75:13. *See also* Bobby Shaftoe

Bobby Shaftoe 74:15. *See also* Bobby Shafto

Boys and Girls Come Out to Play 44:12

Bye, Baby Bunting 35:68, 38:14, 41:67, 77:15

Cock-a-Doodle-Doo! 38:68, 75:43

Curly Locks 38:61, 65:38. *See also* Curly Locks, Curly Locks

Curly Locks, Curly Locks 44:50. *See also* Curly Locks

Dance to Your Daddy 44:58, 65:80, 77:26

Diddle Diddle Dumpling 38:76, 71:48, 72:28

Ding, Dong, Bell 31:14

Doctor Foster 38:41

Eency Weency Spider 36:78. *See also* Eensy Weensy Spider; Eentsy Weentsy Spider; Incey Wincey Spider

Eensy Weensy Spider 31:60, 33:38, 65:61, 66:231, 72:19, 74:22. *See also* Eency Weency Spider; Eentsy Weentsy Spider; Incey Wincey Spider

Eentsy Weentsy Spider 35:58. *See also* Eency Weency Spider; Eensy Weensy Spider; Incey Wincey Spider

Farmer in the Dell 15:40, 31:26, 33:41, 36:84, 38:79, 66:232. *See also* Farmer's in the Dell

NURSERY RHYMES (*cont.*)

Farmer's in the Dell 74:40, 75:20. *See also* Farmer in the Dell

Georgie Porgie 31:67, 44:13. *See also* Georgy Porgy

Georgy Porgy 75:33. *See also* Georgie Porgie

Goosey, Goosey, Gander 31:10, 38:57, 75:25

Hail to Britannia 64:102

Hark, Hark! 38:54

Here Are My Lady's Knives and Forks 38:24

Here We Go Round the Mulberry Bush 15:41, 44:29, 74:45, 75:26. *See also* Mulberry Bush

Hickety, Pickety, My Black Hen 44:8

Hickory, Dickory, Dock 31:23, 33:55, 35:61, 36:120, 38:51, 44:2, 66:232, 72:43, 74:24

Higglety, Pigglety, Pop! 44:34, 65:48

Hippity Hop to the Barber Shop 38:55

Hot Cross Buns! 31:16, 36:124, 38:140, 44:40, 66:224

How Many Miles to Babylon? 44:27

Humpty Dumpty 31:41, 38:71, 44:35, 66:225, 75:29

Hush, Little Baby 22:98, 25:18, 31:20, 33:62, 36:126, 38:12, 65:91, 66:181, 70:38, 72:57, 74:9, 77:10

I Had a Little Nut Tree 33:65, 36:127, 44:41

I Know a Little Pussy 36:128, 65:50. *See also* I Love Little Kitty; I Love Little Pussy

I Love Little Kitty 31:65. *See also* I Know a Little Pussy; I Love Little Pussy

I Love Little Pussy 33:66, 36:130, 38:46, 44:6, 66:101, 75:30. *See also* I Know a Little Pussy; I Love Little Kitty

Incey Wincey Spider 38:28. *See also* Eency Weency Spider; Eensy Weensy Spider; Eentsy Weentsy Spider

Itiskit, Itaskit 36:133. *See also* A-Tisket, A-Tasket

Jack and Jill 31:41, 33:75, 36:138, 38:39, 44:14, 65:26, 66:223, 75:36

Jack, Be Nimble 38:104

Jazzy Three Bears 55:26

John Peel 38:69, 46:6

Knock at the Door 38:25

Lady Bird, Lady Bird 75:31

Lavender's Blue 20:18, 33:79, 36:151, 38:66, 44:54, 75:38

Lazy Mary 33:80, 35:56, 36:153, 38:62, 65:8, 72:24, 75:41. *See also* Lazy Mary, Will You Get Up?

Lazy Mary, Will You Get Up? 31:64, 66:228. *See also* Lazy Mary

Little Betty Blue 71:24

Little Bo-Peep 31:74, 36:156, 38:65, 44:16, 66:221, 75:34

Little Boy Blue 31:15, 38:70, 44:15, 66:226, 75:44

Little Jack Horner 31:54, 36:157, 38:36, 44:18, 65:71, 66:225, 75:45

Little Miss Muffet 31:66, 38:40, 44:18, 66:227, 71:61

Little Nut Tree 38:53, 75:64

Little Tommy Tucker 31:75, 38:35, 44:17, 75:48. *See also* Little Tommy Tinker

London Bridge 31:61, 33:83, 36:160, 38:105, 44:30, 65:24, 66:230, 75:58. *See also* London Bridge Is Falling Down

London Bridge Is Falling Down 15:43. *See also* London Bridge

Lucy Locket 31:51, 44:19

Mary Had a Little Lamb 31:58, 32:32, 36:163, 38:58, 44:20, 65:16, 75:60

Mary, Mary, Quite Contrary 44:21. *See also* Mistress Mary; Mistress Mary, Quite Contrary

Mistress Mary 38:38. *See also* Mary, Mary, Quite Contrary; Mistress Mary, Quite Contrary

Mistress Mary, Quite Contrary 31:67. *See also* Mary, Mary, Quite Contrary; Mistress Mary

Muffin Man 15:42, 36:165, 38:34, 64:98, 75:47

Mulberry Bush 31:6, 33:84, 36:166, 38:80, 65:14, 66:216. *See also* Here We Go Round the Mulberry Bush

Noble Duke of York 16:31, 38:88

North Wind Doth Blow 38:33, 44:10, 75:66

Oats and Beans and Barley 60:13. *See also* Oats, Peas, and Beans; Oats, Peas, Beans; Oats, Peas, Beans and Barley Grow

Oats, Peas, and Beans 33:93. *See also* Oats and Beans and Barley; Oats, Peas, Beans; Oats, Peas, Beans and Barley Grow

Oats, Peas, Beans 24:8, 36:171, 38:89, 75:68. *See also* Oats and Beans and Barley; Oats, Peas, and Beans; Oats, Peas, Beans and Barley Grow

Oats, Peas, Beans and Barley Grow 66:228. *See also* Oats and Beans and Barley; Oats, Peas, and Beans; Oats, Peas, Beans

Oh, Dear, What Can the Matter Be? 33:94, 36:174, 44:52, 65:34, 67:9, 70:30

Oh Where, Oh Where Has My Little Dog Gone? 44:9, 66:86. *See also* Where Has My Little Dog Gone?; Where, O Where; Where, Oh Where, Has My Little Dog Gone?

Old King Cole 31:30, 36:182, 38:74, 44:42, 65:40, 66:229, 75:70

Old Mother Hubbard 71:58

Oranges and Lemons 44:31, 75:74

Pat-a-Cake 31:32, 35:50, 38:27, 72:20. *See also* Pat-a-Cake, Pat-a-Cake

Pat-a-Cake, Pat-a-Cake 44:59. *See also* Pat-a-Cake

Pawpaw Patch 15:44, 64:96

Pease Porridge Hot 31:14, 38:104, 44:28, 65:11, 75:77

Peek-a-Boo 72:7, 74:20

Peter Piper 71:60

Phoebe in Her Petticoat 65:13

Polly 65:67. *See also* Polly, Put the Kettle On

Polly, Put the Kettle On 31:39, 33:105, 36:192, 38:60, 44:22, 75:14. *See also* Polly

Pop! Goes the Weasel 31:46, 33:106, 36:194, 38:32, 50:58, 65:47, 66:187, 70:26, 75:50

Pussy Cat, Pussy Cat 31:35, 38:50, 44:6, 66:108, 75:49

Rain, Rain 38:49. *See also* Rain, Rain, Go Away

Rain, Rain, Go Away 65:60. *See also* Rain, Rain

Ride a Cock-Horse 38:52, 66:186. *See also* Ride a Cock-Horse to Banbury Cross; Ride a Cockhorse

Ride a Cock-Horse to Banbury Cross 44:26. *See also* Ride a Cock-Horse; Ride a Cockhorse

Ride a Cockhorse 31:9, 74:16. *See also* Ride a Cock-Horse; Ride a Cock-Horse to Banbury Cross

Ring Around a Rosy 31:59, 38:107, 75:52. *See also* Ring Around the Rosy; Ring-a-Ring o' Roses

Ring Around the Rosy 72:13. *See also* Ring Around a Rosy; Ring-a-Ring o' Roses

Ring-a-Ring o' Roses 44:28, 65:21. *See also* Ring Around a Rosy; Ring Around the Rosy

Ringel Rosen 1:124

Rings on Her Fingers 65:33

Rock-a-Bye Baby 25:22, 31:34, 33:112, 36:198, 41:66, 65:93, 66:221, 74:8, 77:28. *See also* All the Pretty Little Horses; Go to Sleepy; Hush A Bye; Hush'n Bye; Hush-You-Bye; Rockabye, Baby

Rockabye, Baby 38:20. *See also* All the Pretty Little Horses; Go to Sleepy; Hush A Bye; Hush'n Bye; Hush-You-Bye; Rock-a-Bye Baby

Roses Are Red 71:8

Row, Row, Row 60:64. *See also* Row, Row, Row Your Boat

Row, Row, Row Your Boat 31:26, 36:199, 38:135, 65:83, 66:234, 74:25, 75:53. *See also* Row, Row, Row

Rub-a-Dub-Dub 38:45, 72:46

NURSERY RHYMES (*cont.*)

See-saw, Margery Daw 31:75, 44:27. *See also* See-Saw, Marjorie Daw; Seesaw, Marjorie Daw

See-Saw, Marjorie Daw 38:37. *See also* See-saw, Margery Daw; Seesaw, Marjorie Daw

Seesaw, Marjorie Daw 75:72. *See also* See-saw, Margery Daw; See-Saw, Marjorie Daw

Simple Simon 33:123, 38:48, 44:44, 65:31

Sing a Song of Sixpence 31:38, 36:208, 38:30, 44:45, 66:222, 75:55

Six Little Mice Sat Down to Spin 44:3

There Was a Crooked Man 44:46, 75:57

There Was a Lady Loved a Swine 44:36

There Was a Man Lived in the Moon 44:38. *See also* Aiken Drum; Aikendrum

There Was an Old Woman 38:42, 49:14, 75:82. *See also* There Was an Old Woman Tossed Up in a Basket

There Was an Old Woman Tossed Up in a Basket 44:47. *See also* There Was an Old Woman

There Was an Old Woman Who Lived in a Shoe 31:40, 66:227

This Is the Way the Ladies Ride 74:12

This Little Pig 35:62, 38:26, 74:19, 75:11. *See also* This Little Piggy

This Little Piggy 72:8. *See also* This Little Pig

Three Blind Mice 31:43, 36:224, 44:2, 65:51, 66:233, 75:78

Three Little Kittens 31:22, 38:72, 44:4, 75:90

To Market 65:44. *See also* To Market, to Market

To Market, to Market 31:33, 38:99, 74:16. *See also* To Market

Tom, He Was a Piper's Son 44:24. *See also* Tom, Tom, the Piper's Son

Tom, Tom, the Piper's Son 31:49, 38:56, 44:23, 65:44, 75:85. *See also* Tom, He Was a Piper's Son

Trot, Trot, Trot 62:71, 74:16

Twinkle, Twinkle, Little Star 19:42, 25:2, 31:47, 33:137, 36:235, 38:64, 41:68, 44:32, 60:99, 65:85, 66:202, 67:4, 75:93

Wee Willie Winkie 38:19, 71:16

When Good King Arthur Ruled This Land 44:39

Where Are You Going to, My Pretty Maid? 44:55

Where Has My Little Dog Gone? 31:42, 70:36. *See also* Oh Where, Oh Where Has My Little Dog Gone?; Where, O Where; Where, Oh Where, Has My Little Dog Gone?

Where, O Where 74:21. *See also* Oh Where, Oh Where Has My Little Dog Gone?; Where Has My Little Dog Gone?; Where, Oh Where, Has My Little Dog Gone?

Where, Oh Where, Has My Little Dog Gone? 36:248, 38:114. *See also* Oh Where, Oh Where Has My Little Dog Gone?; Where Has My Little Dog Gone?; Where, O Where

Who Killed Cock Robin? 75:88

OCCUPATIONS

Betty Wants to Be an Astronaut 30:42

Hi-Diddle-Dee-Dee 66:70

I Need You Like a Doughnut Needs a Hole 56:24

My Mommy Drives a Dump Truck 56:66

You Can Be Anything 9:26

OCEANS

Baby Beluga 19:18, 60:7

Octopus's Garden 60:75

OKLAHOMA

So Long, It's Been Good to Know You 40:103

OPOSSUMS

Little Peter Possum 24:2

Possum on the Flying Trapeze 24:28. *See also* Man on the Trapeze

Raccoon and Possum 63:15

OUTER SPACE

Ride Sally Ride 71:32

OUTLAWS
Botany Bay 46:78
Desperado, The 20:14
Jesse James 40:62
Lincolnshire Poacher 46:30
Streets of Forbes 46:76

OX CART
Ox Cart 54:65

PANTHERS
Of All the Beast-es 63:75

PATRIOTIC SONGS
Ach! Du Lieber Augustin 36:16
America 33:13
America at Last! 29:30
America, I Love You 5:43, 13:58
America the Beautiful 33:14, 36:20
Americans Are Singing About Lady
    Liberty 29:6
Brown Eyes, Black Eyes 13:62
Hands to the Sun 67:11
Happy Birthday Miss Liberty 29:14
Here in America 13:15
I Love America 13:9
I Remember Ellis Island 29:20
I'm the Statue of Liberty 30:28
If You Believe in Me, I'll Never Die
    29:44
In 1776 13:12
It's Fun to Take the Ferry to the
    Statue of Liberty 29:10
Lovely Lady of Liberty 29:40
Miracle in Philadelphia 13:24
My Guiding Light Is Miss Liberty
    29:60
This Land Is Your Land 22:370,
    40:116, 66:188
We Hold These Truths 13:18
We're the Children of America
    29:24
World in Harmony 29:36
Yankee Doodle 22:62, 31:57,
    33:140, 36:251, 38:122, 40:135,
    44:48, 66:250

PEACE. See PEACE AND
    JUSTICE

PEACE AND JUSTICE
Big Words 13:40
Blowin' in the Wind 22:360
Down by the Riverside 33:33, 40:26
Give a Little Love 32:24
I've Got Peace Like a River 27:8

Joe Hill 40:64
Peace Is Flowing Like a River
    34:34
Sing About Martin 71:30
Turn, Turn, Turn 40:126

PETS
He's a Dog 3:10
He's My Responsibility 11:58
I Had a Little Dog 49:9. See also
    Had a Little Dog
I Know a Little Pussy 36:128,
    65:50. See also I Love Little
    Kitty; I Love Little Pussy
I Love Little Kitty 31:65. See also I
    Know a Little Pussy; I Love
    Little Pussy
I Love Little Pussy 33:66, 36:130,
    38:46, 44:6, 66:101, 75:30. See
    also I Know a Little Pussy; I
    Love Little Kitty
I've Got a Dog and My Dog's Name
    Is Cat 56:69
Kitten in the Sun 3:8
Little Dog Named Right 63:26
My Dog Rags 20:38, 64:42
Oh, Blue 63:30
Oh Where, Oh Where Has My Little
    Dog Gone? 44:9, 66:86. See
    also Where Has My Little Dog
    Gone?; Where, O Where;
    Where, Oh Where, Has My Lit-
    tle Dog Gone?
Our Dog Bernard 56:58
Reptile World 56:148
That Doggie in the Window 66:82
Where Has My Little Dog Gone?
    31:42, 70:36. See also Oh
    Where, Oh Where Has My Lit-
    tle Dog Gone?; Where, O
    Where; Where, Oh Where, Has
    My Little Dog Gone?
Where, O Where 74:21. See also
    Oh Where, Oh Where Has My
    Little Dog Gone?; Where Has
    My Little Dog Gone?; Where,
    Oh Where, Has My Little Dog
    Gone?
Where, Oh Where, Has My Little
    Dog Gone? 36:248, 38:114. See
    also Oh Where, Oh Where Has
    My Little Dog Gone?; Where
    Has My Little Dog Gone?;
    Where, O Where

PICNICS

Going on a Picnic 59:64
Teddy Bears' Picnic 66:98

PIES

Huckleberry, Gooseberry 69:11
Simple Simon 33:123, 38:48, 44:44, 65:31
Sing a Song of Sixpence 31:38, 36:208, 38:30, 44:45, 66:222, 75:55

PIGS

Eight Piggies in a Row 58:23
Little Pig 63:50
Old Sow 63:52
Pig Song 69:8
There Was a Lady Loved a Swine 44:36
This Little Pig 35:62, 38:26, 74:19, 75:11. *See also* This Little Piggy
This Little Piggy 72:8. *See also* This Little Pig
Three Little Piggies 49:12
To Market 65:44. *See also* To Market, to Market
To Market, to Market 31:33, 38:99, 74:16. *See also* To Market
Who's Afraid of the Big Bad Wolf? 66:52
Whose Tail Is Curly? 3:16

PILGRIMS

Pilgrims and the Indians 5:14

PIONEER LIFE. *See* FRONTIER LIFE

PIONEERS

Buffalo Gals 36:47, 40:9
Covered Wagons 54:67
Cowboy's Lament 40:22
Cumberland Gap 22:82
Desperado, The 20:14
Get Along, Little Dogies 36:96. *See also* Git Along, Little Dogies
Git Along, Little Dogies 22:290, 40:40. *See also* Get Along, Little Dogies
Handcart Song 22:176
Home on the Range 33:56, 36:121, 40:50, 67:7
Hop Up, My Ladies 63:66
I Ride an Old Paint 36:131, 40:52
Little Pioneer Children 54:67
My Home's in Montana 67:7
O Pioneers 5:45
Oh, Susanna! 31:68, 33:98, 36:179, 38:126, 40:79
Oh, Susannah 22:180
Old Ground Hog 63:22
On Top of Old Smokey 33:103. *See also* On Top of Old Smoky; On Top of Spaghetti
On Top of Old Smoky 31:25, 40:83, 67:6. *See also* On Top of Old Smokey; On Top of Spaghetti
Ox Cart 54:65
Pioneer Children 54:65
Red River Valley 33:108, 40:85, 67:13
Sweet Betsy from Pike 22:186, 33:128, 36:214, 40:108, 67:10
Westward Ho over the Oregon Trail We Go 54:65
When I First Came to This Land 22:272
White Covered Wagons 5:44

PLANTS

Everything Grows 58:28
In My Garden 60:79
Oats and Beans and Barley 60:13. *See also* Oats, Peas, and Beans; Oats, Peas, Beans; Oats, Peas, Beans and Barley Grow
Oats, Peas, and Beans 33:93. *See also* Oats and Beans and Barley; Oats, Peas, Beans; Oats, Peas, Beans and Barley Grow
Oats, Peas, Beans 24:8, 36:171, 38:89, 75:68. *See also* Oats and Beans and Barley; Oats, Peas, and Beans; Oats, Peas, Beans and Barley Grow
Oats, Peas, Beans and Barley Grow 66:228. *See also* Oats and Beans and Barley; Oats, Peas, and Beans; Oats, Peas, Beans
Plant a Little Tree 5:32
Savez-vous Planter des Choux? 58:20. *See also* Savez-vous Planter les Choux?
Savez-vous Planter les Choux? 64:68. *See also* Savez-vous Planter des Choux?
Seeds Are Planted Deep 55:12

PLAY

Bike Song 68:15
Blocks 35:26
Boys and Girls Come Out to Play
    44:12
Charades 14:13
Come Play with Me 5:39
Don't You Push Me Down 35:74
Fly My Kite with Me 30:46
Following the Leader 14:9
Going Out to Play 71:28
Groundhog 22:92, 71:38
Hey, Won't Somebody Come and
    Play 9:13
Holidays 35:90
I Like to Play in the Snow 5:17
I Roll the Ball 35:27
Jungle Gym 35:43
Me and My Teddy Bear 66:94
Merry-Go-Round 30:18, 35:45
Mud, Mud, Glorious Mud 50:79,
    51:31
My Brother and I 4:16
My Jumping Song 14:6
My Way Home 59:58
Oh, What a Summer 76:8
Piggy Back Song 69:14
Play Your Horn Right Now 21:12
Puff, the Magic Dragon 19:44,
    66:161
Rig-A-Jig-Jig 20:10, 25:4, 38:94,
    65:30
Safety Don'ts 7:10
Sandbox, The 35:42
See-Saw 35:47
Slide, The 35:46
Spin, Spin, Spin 47:19
Swing, The 35:38, 68:16
Up in the Air 35:30
What Shall We Do When We All Go
    Out? 65:20
Where Can Baby Be? 35:33

POLICE

Remember Your Name and Ad-
    dress 66:213

POSTAL SERVICE

I Got a Letter 1:12
Mail Myself to You 20:44, 31:52,
    66:130

PRAYERS

Bless This Meal 39:20
Children All over the World 54:77

Did You Say Your Prayers Last
    Night? 9:22
Early in the Morning 42:109
Family Prayer 54:21
First Song of Isaiah, The 34:36
I Talk to God Wherever I May Be
    42:80
I Thank Thee, Dear Father 54:21
Let Us Break Bread Together 27:12
Lord's Prayer, The 34:37
Now I Lay Me Down to Sleep
    25:12, 31:80
Now unto the King 42:129
Open My Eyes That I May See
    34:40
Our Prayer 54:31
Pray, Pray, Pray 42:83
Show Me the Path, Lord 42:101
Sing Hosanna 34:12
Tell Me, Dear Lord 54:77
Thanks a Lot 60:19
We Praise Thy Name 42:125
We Thank Thee, Father, for Our
    Homes 42:138
Whisper a Prayer 27:18

PRAYING MANTIS

Confession of a Praying Mantis
    53:13

PRESIDENTS—
UNITED STATES

Abe Lincoln 47:40
George Washington 13:22, 47:39
Hooray for Mr. Lincoln 71:34
Presidents Are Famous Men 47:38

PRISONERS AND PRISONS

Catch a Wiffer Woffer 50:76

PUMPKINS

Five Little Pumpkins 59:6
Jack-O'-Lantern 47:4
Pumpkin Picking 47:12
Pumpkins 47:10

PUPPETS

Muppet Show Theme 66:4
Petites Marionettes 59:49. See also
    Petites Marionnettes
Petites Marionnettes 62:112. See
    also Petites Marionettes

QUESTION AND ANSWER
SONGS

Billy Boy 33:18, 36:42, 38:111,
    66:220

QUESTION AND ANSWER
SONGS (*cont.*)

Clever Amphibian 3:21
Cookie Jar 64:51
Devil's Questions, The 22:206
Did Jesus Really Live Again? 54:35
Did You Feed My Cow? 64:50
For Us All 42:94
Have You Ever Wondered 10:43
Hop Up, My Ladies 63:66
How Many People Do You Love?
    4:13
Is This What It Means to Have
    Courage 11:14
Lazy Mary 33:80, 35:56, 36:153,
    38:62, 65:8, 72:24, 75:41. *See
    also* Lazy Mary, Will You Get
    Up?
Lazy Mary, Will You Get Up?
    31:64, 66:228. *See also* Lazy
    Mary
Lulabel 50:50
Mistress Mary 38:38. *See also*
    Mary, Mary, Quite Contrary;
    Mistress Mary, Quite Contrary
Muffin Man 15:42, 36:165, 38:34,
    64:98, 75:47
Name the Days 21:31
Nothing 56:158
Old Cow Died 63:56
Old Sow 63:52
Riddle Song 33:110, 40:87
What Does Baby Hear 35:20
What Does Baby See 35:16
Where Are You Going to, My Pretty
    Maid? 44:55
Where Do You Live? 21:32
Where Is Your Goose? 50:15
You're a Hero at Last 11:16

RABBITS

Easter Bunny 38:141, 71:46
Hippity Hop 3:14
In a Cabin 70:4
Little Peter Rabbit 35:76, 50:19,
    64:36
Mister Rabbit 63:16
Oh, John the Rabbit 22:216, 49:55
Peter Cottontail 66:243
Rabbit Ain't Got No Tail at All
    49:85

RACCOONS

Raccoon and Possum 63:15

RAILROADS

Blocks 35:26
Casey Jones 40:11, 46:52
City of New Orleans 40:16
Down at the Station 74:37
Down by the Station 33:37, 36:73,
    38:129, 66:116
Drill, Ye Tarriers 22:158, 36:74
Freight Train 40:36
I've Been Working on the Railroad
    33:70, 36:135, 40:59, 66:158,
    67:12
John Henry 22:152, 36:144, 40:67
Morningtown Ride 19:46, 60:33
My Old Hen's a Good Old Hen
    63:44
New River Train 59:38
Old Hogan's Goat 51:117
Old Toy Trains 57:74
Pat Works on the Railway 36:188
Pufferbellies 64:47
Riding on the New River Train
    55:31
Rock Island Line 22:172, 40:89,
    66:172
She'll Be Comin' 'Round the Moun-
    tain 31:37, 33:116, 49:46,
    64:22, 66:178, 67:6. *See also*
    She'll Be Coming 'Round the
    Mountain; She'll Be Coming
    Around the Mountain; She'll Be
    Coming Round the Mountain
She'll Be Coming 'Round the Moun-
    tain 36:201. *See also* She'll Be
    Comin' 'Round the Mountain;
    She'll Be Coming Around the
    Mountain; She'll Be Coming
    Round the Mountain
She'll Be Coming Around the Moun-
    tain 15:46. *See also* She'll Be
    Comin' 'Round the Mountain;
    She'll Be Coming 'Round the
    Mountain; She'll Be Coming
    Round the Mountain
She'll Be Coming Round the Moun-
    tain 20:6, 38:128, 40:94. *See
    also* She'll Be Comin' 'Round
    the Mountain; She'll Be Com-
    ing 'Round the Mountain; She'll
    Be Coming Around the Moun-
    tain
Train Is A-Comin' 49:50
Wabash Cannonball 19:8

Workin' on the Railroad 59:40. *See also* Working on the Railroad
Working on the Railroad 38:132. *See also* Workin' on the Railroad

RAIN
Ain't Gonna Rain 31:77
Arkansas Traveler 36:24, 40:4
Didn't It Rain? 43:2
Ducks Like Rain 60:62
Eency Weency Spider 36:78. *See also* Eensy Weensy Spider; Eentsy Weentsy Spider; Incey Wincey Spider
Eensy Weensy Spider 31:60, 33:38, 65:61, 66:231, 72:19, 74:22. *See also* Eency Weency Spider; Eentsy Weentsy Spider; Incey Wincey Spider
Eentsy Weentsy Spider 35:58. *See also* Eency Weency Spider; Eensy Weensy Spider; Incey Wincey Spider
If All the Raindrops 65:57
It Ain't Gonna Rain No More 51:60, 66:148
It's Raining, It's Pouring 31:55, 33:69, 36:134
Little Raindrops 4:33
Old Tin Cup 69:15
One Misty, Moisty Morning 65:58
Rain 71:62
Rain Is Falling All Around 54:51
Rain, Rain 38:49. *See also* Rain, Rain, Go Away
Rain, Rain, Go Away 65:60. *See also* Rain, Rain
Rain Song 68:12
Robin in the Rain 59:28
Water in the Rain Clouds 71:53
Who Built the Ark? 59:32
Wise Man and the Foolish Man, The 26:12

RAINBOW
Over the Rainbow 66:34
Rainbow 'Round Me 55:16
Rainbow Connection 66:22
Up and Over and Down 4:32
Who Made the Rainbow? 42:33

RANCH LIFE. *See* **RURAL LIFE**

RELIGION
All of Me 42:104
All That Has Life and Breath, Sing to the Lord 39:20
All Things Bright and Beautiful 42:91, 48:2
Alleluia 34:17
Amazing Grace 33:11, 34:39
Amen 1:60
Angel Band 2:26
Angels We Have Heard on High 23:2, 28:22, 61:28
As I Have Loved You 54:83
Astronauts and Airplane Pilots 42:31
Away in a Manger 2:19, 28:32, 36:30, 45:24, 52:78, 61:10
Baby Moses 71:51
Baptism 54:69
Be Glad! 42:69
Be Thankful unto Him 42:21
Be Ye Kind 42:39
Beauty Everywhere 54:45
Bells Are Ringing 2:36
B-I-B-L-E, The 26:14
Bible Is a Special Book, The 42:13
Bible Is a Wonderful Book, The 42:76
Bible Thought Song 42:16
Big Brother 42:72
Birthday of a King 2:22
Bless This Meal 39:20
Book of Mormon Stories 14:61
Born This Night 2:31
Bring a Torch, Jeannette, Isabella! 28:60
Bringing in the Sheaves 33:22
Called to Serve 54:75
Canticle of the Sun, The 34:9
Chapel Doors 54:71
Cherry Tree Carol 28:69
Children All over the World 54:77
Children Who Love Jesus 42:37
Children, Go Where I Send Thee 2:34
Children, Obey Your Parents 42:97
Christian Families 42:98
Christmas Cradle Song 54:29
Christmas Joybells 68:42
Climb, Climb Up Sunshine Mountain 27:24
Come and Praise the Lord Our King 42:82
Come Dance and Sing 34:52

RELIGION (*cont.*)

Come, Let Me Tell 42:3

Come, Ye Thankful People, Come 34:58, 36:57

Coventry Carol 2:39, 28:35, 61:16

Cum By Yah 77:22. *See also* Kum Ba Yah; Kumbaya

Daniel 60:45

Dare to Do Right 54:63

Dayenu 34:26

Did Jesus Really Live Again? 54:35

Did You Say Your Prayers Last Night? 9:22

Didn't It Rain? 43:2

Didn't My Lord Deliver Daniel? 43:16

Do Lord 26:22

Do You Know That You're a Person? 42:105

Dona Nobis Pacem 34:33, 46:91

Douglas Mountain 57:72, 59:54

Down by the Creek Bank 42:133

Dry Bones 22:326

Early in the Morning 42:109

Eli, the Priest 42:18

Everybody Needs to Be Someone 42:106

Everybody Ought to Know 42:114

Everything That's Beautiful 68:26

Ezekiel Saw the Wheel 43:14

Fairest Lord Jesus 48:4

Families Can Be Together Forever 54:25

Family Love 42:136

Family Prayer 54:21

First Song of Isaiah, The 34:36

Fisherman Peter 26:6

Follow the Rules! 42:36

For Us All 42:94

Fum, Fum, Fum 2:23

Give Me a Heart of Love 42:141

Give Me That Old-Time Religion 27:2

Give, Said the Little Stream 54:39

Glory to God in the Highest 42:110

Glory to Thee 46:92

Go Down, Moses 22:128, 34:24, 36:98, 42:79, 43:8

Go Tell It on the Mountain 2:40, 28:79, 40:43

God Can 42:108

God Gave Us the Bible 42:17

God Is Like My Daddy 42:58

God Is Love 11:70

God Is Our Wonderful God 42:92

God Is So Good 42:62, 48:12

God Is Stronger Than the Devil 42:78

God Knows Everything 42:60

God Knows Everything About Me 42:59

God Knows Where You Are 42:4

God Loves Each Child 42:28

God Made Me! 42:45

God Made the World 42:88

God of Wisdom 42:112

God Watches Over Me 42:111

God Who Made the Earth 42:139

God's Big World 42:29

God's Creation 42:89

God's Own People 42:117

God's Plan for Families 42:96

Golden Plates 14:61

Good King Wenceslas 28:62

Good Morning, Lord! 68:29

Great Big Family 42:99

Green Grow the Rushes-O 33:48, 36:106

Growing Tall 42:46

Handcart Song 22:176

Hanukah 71:20

Hanukkah 47:20

Hanukkah Is Happiness 47:18

Hanukkah Song 36:110, 38:144

Happiness 42:144, 54:47

Happy, Happy! 42:70

Hark! The Herald Angels Sing 28:30, 36:114, 45:36, 52:96, 61:18

He Is Lord 42:67

He Owns the Cattle on a Thousand Hills 42:132

He Plants Me Like a Seed 42:142

He's Got the Whole World 20:48, 26:24, 36:118, 60:48

Heavenly Sunshine 27:22

Hello, Hello! How Are You? 42:86

Helping God 42:49

Helping Mother 42:42

Here Is the Church 35:53, 38:25

Hine Ma Tov 34:51

Holly and the Ivy 28:57, 45:22

Holy Bible, Book Divine 48:6

Holy, Holy, Holy 34:10

Honoring Mother and Father 42:134

Hop Up and Jump Up 34:53

Hosanna! 42:64

How Do You Obey God's Word?
42:73
Human Spirit 18:25
Hush! 42:19
I Am a Child of God 14:7, 54:7
I Am Quiet 42:25
I Am So Glad 48:1
I Am with Thee and Will Keep
Thee 42:122
I Feel My Savior's Love 54:37
I Got Shoes 22:132
I Have a Friend 42:5
I Have a Garden 54:51
I Have Two Little Hands 54:73
I Heard the Bells on Christmas
Day 28:37
I Just Keep Trusting My Lord
42:61
I Know My Father Lives 14:7, 54:7
I Love God 42:63
I Love Jesus 42:71
I Love My Family 54:25
I Love to See the Temple 14:25
I Often Think of God 42:6
I Open My Bible Book and Read
42:10
I Sing a New Song 42:119
I Sing a Song of the Saints of God
34:42
I Talk to God Wherever I May Be
42:80
I Thank God 42:41
I Thank Thee, Dear Father 54:21
I Thank You, God 42:9. *See also*
Thank You, God
I Think the World Is Glorious 54:53
I Think When I Read That Sweet
Story 54:33
I Want to Go Teach the Gospel
54:75
I Will Listen 42:11
I Will Sing 42:27
I Will Sing of the Mercies of the
Lord 42:127
I Will Sing Praise 42:84
I Wonder How It Felt 42:120
I'll Be a Sunbeam 27:28
I'm a Special Person 42:100
I'm Going Up, Up, Up 42:124
I'm Gonna Sing 26:28
I'm in the Lord's Army 26:4
I'm Not One of the Crowd 42:143
I'm Trying to Be Like Jesus 54:61
I've Got Peace Like a River 27:8

In the Beginning 42:90
It Came upon a Midnight Clear
61:8. *See also* It Came upon the
Midnight Clear
It Came upon the Midnight Clear
28:15, 45:44. *See also* It Came
upon a Midnight Clear
Jesus 26:16
Jesus and the Children 42:123
Jesus Has Risen 54:35
Jesus Is Living in Heaven Today
42:1
Jesus, Jesus 42:65
Jesus Loves Me 26:20
Jesus Loves Me, Jesus Loves Me
42:66
Jesus Loves the Little Children
48:5
Jesus Once Was a Little Child
54:31
Jesus Said Love Everyone 54:49
Jesus Wants Me for a Sunbeam
54:39
Jesus Went About Doing Good 42:8
Jesus Worked 42:7
John 3:16 42:74
Joseph Dearest, Joseph Mine 2:30
Joshua Fit the Battle of Jericho
43:10. *See also* Joshua Fought
the Battle of Jericho
Joshua Fought the Battle of
Jericho 36:146. *See also*
Joshua Fit the Battle of Jericho
Joy to the World 2:15, 23:16,
28:53, 45:34, 61:6
Joyful, Joyful, We Adore Thee
34:14
Just Walkin' Along 42:131
Keep the Commandments 54:63
Kum Ba Yah 26:26. *See also* Cum
By Yah; Kumbaya
Kumbaya 19:22, 60:31. *See also*
Cum By Yah; Kum Ba Yah
Last Supper 42:14
Let Us Break Bread Together 27:12
Listen to the Plink, Plink, Plink
42:24
Little Bitty Baby 36:154
Little Brown Church, The 26:2
Little David, Play on Your Harp
43:12
Little Drummer Boy, The 2:32
Lo, How a Rose E'er Blooming
28:38, 39:23

RELIGION (*cont.*)

Lone Wild Bird 34:48
Lord, I Want to Be a Christian
  42:140
Lord Is a Great God, The 42:107
Lord Is My Shepherd, The 68:40
Lord of the Dance 34:18
Lord's Prayer, The 34:37
Make Channels 34:50
March of the Kings 2:28
May Jesus Christ Be Praised
  42:115
Maybe You Laughed 9:28
Morning Has Broken 34:8
Multiply 42:121
My Bible 42:12
My Happy Home 42:35
My Heavenly Father Loves Me
  54:53
My Responsibility 42:95
My Song of Praise 42:128
Nobody Knows the Trouble I've
  Seen 33:89
Nothing but Sing 42:30
Now I Lay Me Down to Sleep
  25:12, 31:80
Now Is the Close of Day 39:21
Now unto the King 42:129
Now, Now, Now 36:168
O Come, All Ye Faithful 2:17,
  28:41, 45:20, 52:64, 61:4. *See
  also* Oh Come, All Ye Faithful
O Come, Little Children 2:37, 45:40
O Come, O Come Emmanuel 28:9
O Little Town of Bethlehem 2:18,
  28:46, 36:177, 61:14
Oh Come, All Ye Faithful 36:172.
  See also O Come, All Ye
  Faithful
Oh, Come, Let Us Worship 42:23
Oh, How I Love Jesus 42:2
Oh, You Can't Get to Heaven 26:8.
  See also You Can't Get to
  Heaven
Old Rugged Cross 27:26
Once in Royal David's City 28:16
Once Within a Lowly Stable 54:29
Only a Boy Named David 27:20
Onward, Christian Soldiers 27:4
Open My Eyes That I May See
  34:40
Our Prayer 54:31
Praise and Thanksgiving 42:126

Praise God from Whom All Bless-
  ings Flow 34:20, 48:3
Praise God with Songs of Joy 42:26
Praise Him 42:81. *See also* Praise
  Him, Praise Him
Praise Him, Praise Him 27:16. *See
  also* Praise Him
Pray, Pray, Pray 42:83
Prayer Song 42:77
Psalm 8 26:18
Quickly I'll Obey 54:15
Rejoice in the Lord Always 27:14
Rejoice, Give Thanks! 42:130
Repentance 54:61
Reverently, Quietly 54:73
Rise and Shine 34:44, 50:91, 60:35
Rise Up, Shepherd, and Follow
  28:24
Rock-a My Soul 43:4
Sanctus 34:16
Seasons 42:34, 42:93, 68:9
Shall We Gather at the River?
  40:92
Shepherd's Song 42:116
Shine On 54:79
Shining Day 34:56
Show Me the Path, Lord 42:101
Showing Love 42:38
Silent Night 2:20, 23:14, 28:18,
  36:206, 45:42, 61:30
Simple Gifts 22:38, 33:120, 46:48.
  See also Tis a Gift to Be Sim-
  ple; Tis the Gift to Be Simple
Sing Hosanna 34:12
Sing Noel, Noel 23:10
Sometimes I Get a Feeling Inside
  9:32
Still Small Voice 54:69
Still, Still, Still 2:39
Stop . . . and Go! 42:118
Swing Low, Sweet Chariot 22:148,
  59:66
Teach Me to Walk in the Light
  54:79
Tell Me, Dear Lord 54:77
Tell Me the Stories of Jesus 54:33
Tell Me Why 32:6, 40:113
Thank You, God 42:22. *See also* I
  Thank You, God
Thank You, Lord 68:39
Thanking Song 68:30
Thanks to God for His Love 39:22
There Was a Little Baby 57:80

There's No One Exactly Like Me 42:50

This Is My Commandment 42:75

This Is the Day We Come to Church 42:20

This Little Light 34:46. *See also* This Little Light of Mine

This Little Light of Mine 19:48, 26:10, 40:119, 60:65. *See also* This Little Light

This Makes a Happier Home 42:40

Tis a Gift to Be Simple 40:122. *See also* Simple Gifts; Tis the Gift to Be Simple

Tis the Gift to Be Simple 34:62. *See also* Simple Gifts; Tis a Gift to Be Simple

Turn, Turn, Turn 40:126

Twas in the Moon of Wintertime 2:24, 28:70

Wake Up! Jonah 43:18

We Are Climbing Jacob's Ladder 34:31, 43:6

We Gather Together 33:138, 34:60, 36:240. *See also* We Gather Together to Ask the Lord's Blessing

We Gather Together to Ask the Lord's Blessing 66:251. *See also* We Gather Together

We Praise Thy Name 42:125

We Shall Overcome 34:28, 40:128

We Thank Thee, Father, for Our Homes 42:138

We Three Kings 2:16, 36:242, 48:10, 52:28. *See also* We Three Kings of Orient Are

We Three Kings of Orient Are 28:48, 61:24. *See also* We Three Kings

What Child Is This? 2:35, 28:29, 61:26

What Do I Have? 42:113

What Is the Answer? 68:41

When He Comes Again 54:37

When I Go to Church 54:71

When I'm Happy 42:85

When the Saints Go Marching In 27:6

Where Is the Baby? 2:33

Where Love Is 54:81

While Shepherds Watched Their Flocks by Night 28:12

Whisper a Prayer 27:18

Who Made the Animals? 42:32

Who Made the Rainbow? 42:33

Will the Circle Be Unbroken 40:133

Wind Through the Olive Trees 2:30

Wise Man and the Foolish Man, The 26:12

Wonderful Things to Know 42:68

Word of God 42:15

You Are Special 42:44

You Can't Get to Heaven 51:90. *See also* Oh, You Can't Get to Heaven

You're Something Special 42:137

Young Folks, Old Folks 51:56

REVOLUTIONARY WAR IN AMERICA (1776-1781)

Bennington Rifles 36:35

Fall Apart 13:35

In 1776 13:12

Johnny Has Gone for a Soldier 22:66

Revolutionary Tea 22:54

Yankee Doodle 22:62, 31:57, 33:140, 36:251, 38:122, 40:135, 44:48, 66:250

RHYTHMS

Cement Mixer 66:121

Let's Hear the Rhythm 21:16

RIDDLES

Riddle 3:42

Riddle Song 33:110, 40:87

RIVERS

Afton Water 46:24

Dark Brown Is the River 35:87

Peace Is Flowing Like a River 34:34

Red River Valley 33:108, 40:85, 67:13

Rio Grande 46:70

Shenandoah 22:125, 33:119, 40:96, 46:72

Sur le Pont d'Avignon 38:108, 59:80, 64:60

Where Go the Boats? 35:87

ROBINS

North Wind Doth Blow 38:33, 44:10, 75:66

Robin in the Rain 59:28

Rockin' Robin 20:42

Who Killed Cock Robin? 75:88

ROUNDS

All That Has Life and Breath, Sing to the Lord 39:20
Amen 1:60
Are You Sleeping 39:26, 72:25. *See also* Frere Jacques
Benjy Met a Bear 51:48
Bless This Meal 39:20
Bona Nox 39:30
Canoe Round 76:12
C-O-F-F-E-E 39:29
Come Here and Sing! 46:90
Come Meet a Little Birdy Friend 39:12
Cuckoo in the Forest 39:10
Die Musica 67:7
Dona Nobis Pacem 34:33, 46:91
Epigram on Singers 46:89
Family Love 42:136
Fire! Fire! 39:6
Fish and Chips 64:24
French Cathedrals 1:24
Frere Jacques 1:114, 25:24, 31:7, 36:91, 38:134, 46:61, 59:79, 62:109, 66:234. *See also* Are You Sleeping
Great Tom Is Cast 46:84
Here We Are 68:38
Hey, Ho, Nobody Home 36:119
Hey Ho, to the Greenwood 46:83
Hine Ma Tov 34:51
I Am Slowly Going Crazy 50:69, 51:77, 64:79
I Don't Care for Underwear 51:53
I Sat Next to the Duchess at Tea 64:74
I Want a Chocolate Malted 50:36
I'm a Very Happy Person 39:7
In the Ev'ning the Nightingale 39:9
Jamais on na Vu 64:62
Jesus and the Children 42:123
Kookaburra 36:150, 46:75, 70:32
Koom Bachur Atsel 1:118
Lazy Fred 51:50
Let's All Sing 39:7
Little Bells of Christmas 2:49
Little Tommy Tinker 64:74. *See also* Little Tommy Tucker
Lo, How a Rose E'er Blooming 28:38, 39:23
Matthew, Mark, Luke and John 64:18
Meow, Meow 39:17
Merrily Caroling 2:48

My Bonnie Lies over the Ocean 33:87
My Dame Hath a Lame, Tame Crane 46:87, 75:73
My Goose 46:86
Now Is the Close of Day 39:21
O How Lovely Is the Evening 48:7
Oh Hear the Bells Ringing 39:25
Oh, How Lovely Is the Evening 33:96, 36:176, 38:134
Pizza Round 51:49
Praise and Thanksgiving 42:126
Ring, Ring, Ring the Bells 2:49
Rooster's Dead 39:18
Row, Row, Row 60:64. *See also* Row, Row, Row Your Boat
Row, Row, Row Your Boat 31:26, 36:199, 38:135, 65:83, 66:234, 74:25, 75:53. *See also* Row, Row, Row
Salom Chaverim 67:9
Santa Claus Is Coming 2:50
Sleepers Wake 39:24
Swan, The 1:102
Sweetly Sings the Donkey 46:88
Thanks to God for His Love 39:22
There Was an Old Woman 38:42, 49:14, 75:82. *See also* There Was an Old Woman Tossed Up in a Basket
Things Unseen 47:3
Thirty Purple Birds 51:51
Three Blind Mice 31:43, 36:224, 44:2, 65:51, 66:233, 75:78
Three Geese in Straw 39:16
To Portsmouth 46:74
Turn Again Whittington 46:85
Uurgh, Eeegh, Ugh, 53:44
We Praise Thy Name 42:125
Welcome April Sunshine 39:27
What Kind of Trees Are Found Out There? 39:13

RURAL LIFE

Chickens in the Barnyard 3:12
Did You Feed My Cow? 64:50
Down on Grandpa's Farm 60:87
Farmer in the Dell 15:40, 31:26, 33:41, 36:84, 38:79, 66:232. *See also* Farmer's in the Dell
Farmer's in the Dell 74:40, 75:20. *See also* Farmer in the Dell
Gobble Strut, Strut 3:13

Old MacDonald 31:48, 33:100, 36:184, 74:48. *See also* Old Mac-Donald Had a Farm

Old MacDonald Had a Farm 38:118, 66:96. *See also* Old Mac-Donald

Pick a Bale o' Cotton 31:70, 59:57. *See also* Pick a Bale of Cotton

Pick a Bale of Cotton 36:190. *See also* Pick a Bale o' Cotton

Whoa, Mule! Can't Get the Saddle On 63:64

RUSSIA
Baiu-Baiushki-Baiu 62:42
Russian Lullaby 55:24

SAFETY. *See* **SAFETY AWARENESS**

SAFETY AWARENESS
Beware 73:18
Designer Genes 8:19
Fire Drill 21:35
Go for a Natural High 8:8
Halloween Machine 73:22
I'm in Charge 7:21
If Your Friend's in Trouble 8:2
Look For a Grandma 7:28
Remember Your Name and Address 66:213
Safety Don'ts 7:10
Safety Kid Smart 8:6
Stay Outside of My Line 7:24
Telephone Song 7:18
Togetherness Kids 7:14
We're the Safety Kids 7:6
Yell and Scream 7:27
You're Not Gonna Get Rich on Me 8:26

SAILING
Allee, Allee-O 65:65
Blanket for a Sail 32:36
Blow, Boys, Blow 22:110
Blow, Ye Winds, in the Morning 22:103
Christopher Columbus 47:1
Columbus 5:9, 47:2
Jamaica Farewell 19:30
Lorelei, Die 46:34
Merrily We Roll Along 38:59
My Bonnie Lies over the Ocean 33:87
Skye Boat Song 33:127
Sloop John B. 40:100

Wake Up! Jonah 43:18
Walloping Windowblind 50:83

SAILORS
Blow the Man Down 46:66
Blow, Boys, Blow 22:110
Blow, Ye Winds, in the Morning 22:103
Bobby Shafto 44:51, 65:39, 75:13. *See also* Bobby Shaftoe
Bobby Shaftoe 74:15. *See also* Bobby Shafto
Donkey Riding 36:71
Drunken Sailor 46:68
I'm Popeye the Sailor Man 66:77. *See also* Popeye, the Sailor Man
Jack Was Every Inch a Sailor 64:116
Lorelei, Die 46:34
Popeye, the Sailor Man 49:26, 51:121. *See also* I'm Popeye the Sailor Man
Sailor Went to Sea 51:63
Sailor Went to Sea Sea Sea 50:65
Skye Boat Song 33:127
Walloping Windowblind 50:83

SAINT NICHOLAS. *See* **SANTA CLAUS**

SAINT PATRICK'S DAY
Shamrocks and Leprechauns 47:41
St. Patrick's Day 47:42
Wearin' o' the Green 5:24

SAINTS
I Sing a Song of the Saints of God 34:42

SANTA CLAUS
Alfie the Elf 2:56
Christmas Day 2:53
Comin' Down the Chimney 59:34
Here Comes Santa Claus 2:44
Jolly Old Saint Nicholas 23:12, 45:16. *See also* Jolly Old St. Nicholas
Jolly Old St. Nicholas 2:60. *See also* Jolly Old Saint Nicholas
Must Be Santa 2:54, 57:70, 59:26
North Pole 47:29
Oh, Jolly Santa Claus 47:22
Reindeer Are Tapping 2:59
Santa Claus Is Comin' to Town 66:238
Santa Claus Is Coming 2:50

SANTA CLAUS (*cont.*)
Santa's Coming 47:28
Up on the Housetop 2:46, 23:22,
57:53

SCHOOL LIFE
I Don't Think My Teacher Likes
Me 56:160
I Don't Wanna Go to School 56:128
I Got a Teacher, She's So Mean
56:36
I'm Late 56:159
Mary Had a Little Lamb 31:58,
32:32, 36:163, 38:58, 44:20,
65:16, 75:60
Nothing 56:158
Shut Up in the Library 56:30
Stanley Stole My Shoelace and
Rubbed It in His Armpit
56:163

SCOTLAND
Aiken Drum 25:20, 51:12, 75:16.
See also Aikendrum; There
Was a Man Lived in the Moon
Aikendrum 59:30. *See also* Aiken
Drum; There Was a Man Lived
in the Moon
Charlie Is My Darling 46:20
Comin' Through the Rye 70:24. *See
also* Comin' Thru the Rye
Comin' Thru the Rye 66:203. *See
also* Comin' Through the Rye
Lock Lomond 67:14
Road to the Isles 76:13
Three Crow 64:114

SEA HORSE
Seahorse Merry-Go-Round 3:20

SEA LIFE. *See* **FISH AND SEA
LIFE**

SEA SONGS
Blow, Ye Winds, in the Morning
22:103
Bobby Shafto 44:51, 65:39, 75:13.
See also Bobby Shaftoe
Bobby Shaftoe 74:15. *See also*
Bobby Shafto
My Bonnie Lies over the Ocean
33:87
Skye Boat Song 33:127
Sloop John B. 40:100

SEALS
Seal and a Walrus 3:26

SEAMEN. *See* **SAILORS**

SEAS. *See* **OCEANS**

SEASHORE
Oh, What a Summer 76:8

SEASONS
Autumn Leaves Are Now Falling
48:9
Summer's End 76:30

SEESAWS
See-Saw 35:47

SELF CONCEPT. *See*
SELF-IMAGE

SELF-IMAGE
All You Gotta Say Is No 8:15
Better Obey 10:12
Betty Wants to Be an Astronaut
30:42
Captain Dependable 12:60
Communication 18:39
Dad Says That I Look Like Him
56:100
Dare to Do Right 54:63
Designer Genes 8:19
Did and Didn't 10:9
Do It Song 10:14
Do You Know That You're a
Person? 42:105
Don't Forget the Family 12:14
Everybody Needs a Friend 12:42
Everybody Needs to Be Someone
42:106
GIGO 12:38
God Made Me! 42:45
Gratitude Attitude 11:46
Green 66:10
Honor Your Parents 66:246
Hooray, Professor Un 12:62
How Do You Obey God's Word?
42:73
How to Be a Good Citizen 71:10
Human Spirit 18:25
I Get a Hundred 12:68
I Get Angry at Myself 10:36
I Have a Garden 54:51
I Have a Little Shadow 68:12
I Like Me 10:39
I Looked into the Mirror-What Did
the Mirror Say? 56:182
I Say Thank You 11:53
I Think I'm Happy Now 11:30
I Told the Truth 10:22

I Wonder If I'm Growing 59:9
I Would Be True 34:54
I'd Be Me 56:180
I'm a Special Person 42:100
I'm a V.I.P. 4:7
I'm in Charge 7:21
I'm My Friend 12:53
I'm Not One of the Crowd 42:143
I'm Not Small 55:25
If I Only Had a Brain 66:30
If I Were the Hero 11:4
If You Take Care of Your Body
    18:29
In a Minute 12:64
Indian Boy 11:6
Inequality Makes the World Go
    'Round 56:152
Ingrate Song 11:41
Is This What It Means to Have
    Courage 11:14
It Pays to Advertise! 49:68
It Takes Courage 11:9
It's Bad, Bad Stuff 8:12
Kindness Begins with Me 54:49
Land of Obey 10:6
Little Seed 9:16
Make People Laugh 18:20
My Dad 9:10, 54:17
Never Tell a Lie 9:42
No One Else Can Smile My Smile
    4:9
No One Like You 66:14
Oh, I'm So Embarrassed 12:46
One Little Nose Like Mine 12:44
Opposites 9:19
Power Is You, The 18:44
Power of Thinking 18:16
Power to Love 18:34
Secret of Happiness 11:32
Senses Song 21:18
Sing! 66:7
Small Recorder 9:44
So Many Things 10:29
Somebody Loves 4:8
Sometimes I Get a Feeling Inside
    9:32
Standin' Tall 10:4
Stay Outside of My Line 7:24
Straight Home, Straight Aim,
    Straight Arrow 12:70
That's Dependability 12:58
There's Always Room for Change
    18:13

There's No One Exactly Like Me
    42:50
Think About a Thank You 11:50
Think Positively 73:35
Three Steps Forward 11:12
We Are One 68:37
We're Different 12:50
We've Got to Get Back to Basics
    18:4
What Do You Like? 21:7
When You Tell One Lie 10:25
Where's the Justice 13:38
Who Broke My Window 10:19
Words You Speak 9:36
Work Work Work 10:46
You Are Special 42:44
You Can Be Anything 9:26
You're a Hero at Last 11:16
You're Not Gonna Get Rich on Me
    8:26
You're Something Special 42:137

SEPTEMBER
Sing a Song of September 71:6

SHADOWS
Groundhog 22:92, 71:38
I Have a Little Shadow 68:12

SHARING
Don't Forget the Family 12:14
Give 71:22
Give, Said the Little Stream 54:39
Giving Song 21:10
More We Serve 12:11
Sharing 4:12
Sharing Song 59:18
We Don't Have to Share 56:122
Whoever Shall Have Peanuts 49:56

SHARKS
Chivalrous Shark 46:46
Jaws 55:46

SHEEP
Baa, Baa, Black Sheep 31:3, 33:17,
    33:32, 36:31, 38:47, 44:7, 59:14,
    66:223, 75:32
Big Sheep, The 63:58
Black Sheep, Black Sheep 63:57
Cluck, Cluck, Red Hen 20:32, 59:84
It's a Rosebud in June 76:25
Little Bo-Peep 31:74, 36:156,
    38:65, 44:16, 66:221, 75:34
Little Boy Blue 31:15, 38:70,
    44:15, 66:226, 75:44

SHEEP (*cont.*)
Mairzy Doats 66:138
Mary Had a Little Lamb 31:58,
32:32, 36:163, 38:58, 44:20,
65:16, 75:60
Old Bell'd Yoe 63:60
Shearer's Dream 46:80

SHELLS (MOLLUSKS)
Cockles and Mussels 66:196

SHIPS
Allee, Allee-O 65:65
Blow, Boys, Blow 22:110
Blow, Ye Winds, in the Morning
22:103
Christopher Columbus 47:1
Gallant Ship 38:84
I Saw Three Ships 28:44, 38:139,
44:43, 45:30
Nina, the Pinta, the Santa Maria,
The 66:248
Sweet and Low 62:40
To Portsmouth 46:74
Walloping Windowblind 50:83

SHOES
Cock-a-Doodle-Doo! 38:68, 75:43
I Can't Tie My Shoe 56:133
I Got Shoes 22:132
Something in My Shoe 60:55

SICKNESS
John Brown's Baby 16:30, 51:22,
66:177

SINGING
Americans Are Singing About Lady
Liberty 29:6
Chickery Chick 66:113
Come Dance and Sing 34:52
Come Here and Sing! 46:90
Epigram on Singers 46:89
Freedom 47:31
Happiness 42:144, 54:47
Heigh-Ho 66:66
Here We Come A-Caroling 2:6,
23:26
Hey Dum Diddeley Dum 64:12. *See
also* Hey Dum Diddley Dum
Hey Dum Diddley Dum 20:34. *See
also* Hey Dum Diddeley Dum
I Think the World Is Glorious 54:53
I Will Sing 42:27
I Will Sing of the Mercies of the
Lord 42:127

I'm Gonna Sing 26:28
I'm in the Mood 60:52
Keemo Kyemo 22:226
Let's All Sing 39:7
Lift Up Your Voice and Sing 54:41
Lightly Row 38:138, 67:4, 76:10
Little Tommy Tucker 31:75, 38:35,
44:17, 75:48. *See also* Little
Tommy Tinker
Louder 56:47
Me and You 56:38
Nothing but Sing 42:30
Now, Now, Now 36:168
One Song 66:64
Psalm 8 26:18
Silly Song 66:68
Sing a Song of September 71:6
Sing Along with Me 30:6
Sing! 66:7
Song of Happiness 22:25
There's Always a Song to Sing
30:50
Time to Sing 60:67
United 71:40
With a Smile and a Song 66:59
You Gotta Sing 19:6, 59:56
You Sing a Song and I'll Sing a
Song 59:63
Zum Gali Gali 34:22

SINGING GAMES
A-Hunting We Will Go 36:19,
38:88, 55:40
A-Tisket, A-Tasket 15:41, 24:6,
31:63, 38:100, 66:110, 70:12.
See also Itiskit, Itaskit
Al Citron 64:110
Alison's Camel 64:93
All I Really Need 60:23
Barnyard Stomp 56:68
Bear Went over the Mountain
36:34, 38:112, 70:22
Billy Boy 33:18, 36:42, 38:111,
66:220
Bluebird 38:83, 65:9
Charlie over the Ocean 64:95
Che Che Koolay 64:105
Do As I'm Doing 54:57
Farmer in the Dell 15:40, 31:26,
33:41, 36:84, 38:79, 66:232. *See
also* Farmer's in the Dell
Farmer's in the Dell 74:40, 75:20.
See also Farmer in the Dell
Fun to Do 54:57
Gallant Ship 38:84

Go In and Out the Window 31:45, 33:47, 36:100

Go Round and Round the Village 38:85

Gogo 38:93

Here We Go Looby Loo 31:12, 36:116. *See also* Looby Loo

If You're Happy 74:38. *See also* If You're Happy and You Know It

If You're Happy and You Know It 49:28, 66:176, 70:20. *See also* If You're Happy

Itiskit, Itaskit 36:133. *See also* A-Tisket, A-Tasket

John Brown's Baby 16:30, 51:22, 66:177

Let's Ban Halloween, Let's Save Halloween 73:11

Little Echo Voice 14:4

London Bridge 31:61, 33:83, 36:160, 38:105, 44:30, 65:24, 66:230, 75:58. *See also* London Bridge Is Falling Down

London Bridge Is Falling Down 15:43. *See also* London Bridge

Looby Loo 24:26, 38:92, 64:83. *See also* Here We Go Looby Loo

Lucy Locket 31:51, 44:19

Me Stone 64:111

M-I-S-S-I-S-S-I-P-P-I 66:157

Muffin Man 15:42, 36:165, 38:34, 64:98, 75:47

Ninety-nine Miles from Home 50:72

Nuts in May 38:81

Obwisana 64:111

Old MacDonald 31:48, 33:100, 36:184, 74:48. *See also* Old Mac-Donald Had a Farm

Old MacDonald Had a Car 72:34

Old MacDonald Had a Farm 38:118, 66:96. *See also* Old Mac-Donald

Pawpaw Patch 15:44, 64:96

Peek-a-Boo 72:7, 74:20

Punchinello 47 64:94

Rig-A-Jig-Jig 20:10, 25:4, 38:94, 65:30

Sally, Go Round 38:87. *See also* Sally Go Round the Sun

Sally Go Round the Sun 65:23. *See also* Sally, Go Round

Somebody Loves 4:8

Street Song 38:117

There's a Hole in My Bucket 36:218. *See also* There's a Hole in the Bucket

There's a Hole in the Bucket 40:114, 50:88, 70:8. *See also* There's a Hole in My Bucket

This Old Man 19:38, 31:56, 36:223, 54:13, 60:29, 65:59, 66:218, 70:16, 72:17, 75:86

Three White Gulls 38:97

SIZE AND SHAPE
Big Moon, Bright Moon 4:38

Dad Says That I Look Like Him 56:100

How Would You Like? 55:53

Listen to the Noises 35:28

My Dog's Bigger Than Your Dog 66:84

Opposites 9:19

Town of Round 56:176

SKIN
Wash the Stickies down the Drain 12:32

SKIPPING ROPE SONGS. *See* **JUMP ROPE JINGLES**

SKUNKS
I Thought It Was a Kitten 3:36

Little Skunk Hole 50:53, 51:42

SLAVERY
Down by the Riverside 33:33, 40:26

Follow the Drinkin' Gourd 22:140. *See also* Follow the Drinking Gourd

Follow the Drinking Gourd 40:32. *See also* Follow the Drinkin' Gourd

Go Down, Moses 22:128, 34:24, 36:98, 42:79, 43:8

I Got Shoes 22:132

Long John 22:136

Nobody Knows the Trouble I've Seen 33:89

Swing Low, Sweet Chariot 22:148, 59:66

SLEEP
All the Pretty Little Horses 22:268, 33:7, 35:72, 38:11, 77:18. *See also* Go to Sleepy; Hush A Bye; Hush'n Bye; Hush-You-Bye; Rock-a-Bye Baby; Rockabye, Baby

Sleep My Baby 41:69
Sleeping Princess 25:10
Sleeping Time 35:34
Still, Still, Still 2:39
Suo Gan 77:24
Sweet Potatoes 65:74
Taps 36:216
Wee Willie Winkie 38:19, 71:16

SMILES
It Isn't Any Trouble Just to Smile
49:65
Make People Laugh 18:20
No One Else Can Smile My Smile
4:9
Smile, Dear Princess 11:23
Smiles 54:41
What Do You Do When You're
Happy 11:34
With a Smile and a Song 66:59

SNAILS
Slow, Slow Snail 53:4
Snail 15:47

SNAKES
Baby Bumble Bee 50:8, 51:112
I'm Being Eaten by a Boa Constric-
tor 51:33
Return of the Baby Bumblebee 55:9
Snake Baked a Hoecake 63:24
Snakes 68:23
Wake, Snake 22:248

SNOW
Christmas Time's a Coming 57:75
Dainty Little Snowflakes 4:35
Douglas Mountain 57:72, 59:54
Falling Snow 54:59
Frosty the Snow Man 66:240. *See
also* Frosty the Snowman
Frosty the Snowman 57:50. *See
also* Frosty the Snow Man
I Like to Play in the Snow 5:17
Jingle Bells 2:10, 23:4, 31:78,
36:142, 38:150, 45:26, 57:60,
61:20
North Wind Doth Blow 38:33,
44:10, 75:66
Once There Was a Snowman 54:59
Sleigh Bells Ring 47:23

SOLDIERS
Gee, Mom, I Want to Go Home
22:356
Johnny Has Gone for a Soldier
22:66

Marines' Hymn 36:161
Onward, Christian Soldiers 27:4
Soldier and the Maid 65:36
Taps 36:216
Veterans Day Salute 5:10
When Johnny Comes Marching
Home 36:245

SOUNDS
A-Driving We Will Go 72:36
Glunk, Glunk, Glunk 50:14
Hey Jack, What's in the Sack?
56:82
Hush! 42:19
I'm a Nut 50:67, 51:78
Let's Hear the Rhythm 21:16
Let's Make Some Noise 58:26
Listen to the Horses 59:50
Listen to the Noises 35:28
Mary Had a Little Car 72:35
Once an Austrian Went Yodeling
55:33
Please Be Quiet 42:87
Snakes 68:23
Something in My Shoe 60:55
Thump, Thump, Thump 56:79
Time to Sing 60:67
Tippy-Tippy Toes 14:16
Tiptoe March 21:15
Uurgh, Eeegh, Ugh, 53:44
What Does Baby Hear 35:20
You Can't Say PSBPSBPSB on the
Radio 56:81
You Gotta Sing 19:6, 59:56

SPACE. *See* **OUTER SPACE**

SPANISH LANGUAGE
Aserrin, Aserran 62:75
Colores, De 60:96
Cuanto Le Gusta 37:28
El Coquito 38:136
Happy Birthday to You 31:7, 54:9,
66:252
La Bamba 20:28
Mexican Counting Song 38:137
Sereno, El 64:108
Un Elephante 64:115

SPIDERS
Anansi 59:72
Black Widow's Waltz, The 53:39
Eency Weency Spider 36:78. *See
also* Eensy Weensy Spider;
Eentsy Weentsy Spider; Incey
Wincey Spider

SPIDERS (*cont.*)

Eensy Weensy Spider 31:60, 33:38, 65:61, 66:231, 72:19, 74:22. *See also* Eency Weency Spider; Eentsy Weentsy Spider; Incey Wincey Spider

Eentsy Weentsy Spider 35:58. *See also* Eency Weency Spider; Eensy Weensy Spider; Eentsy Weentsy Spider; Incey Wincey Spider

Incey Wincey Spider 38:28. *See also* Eency Weency Spider; Eensy Weensy Spider; Eentsy Weentsy Spider

Little Miss Muffet 31:66, 38:40, 44:18, 66:227, 71:61

Spider on the Floor 59:21

Spin, Spider, Spin 68:20

SPINNING

Sarasponda 1:30, 22:40, 67:10

Spin, Spider, Spin 68:20

SPIRITUALS

Autumn Day 54:55

Cum By Yah 77:22. *See also* Kum Ba Yah; Kumbaya

Didn't It Rain? 43:2

Didn't My Lord Deliver Daniel? 43:16

Down by the Riverside 33:33, 40:26

Ezekiel Saw the Wheel 43:14

Fisherman Peter 26:6

Go Down, Moses 22:128, 34:24, 36:98, 42:79, 43:8

Go Tell It on the Mountain 2:40, 28:79, 40:43

God Is Love 11:70

He's Got the Whole World 20:48, 26:24, 36:118, 60:48

I Got Shoes 22:132

I Think the World Is Glorious 54:53

Joshua Fit the Battle of Jericho 43:10. *See also* Joshua Fought the Battle of Jericho

Joshua Fought the Battle of Jericho 36:146. *See also* Joshua Fit the Battle of Jericho

Kum Ba Yah 26:26. *See also* Cum By Yah; Kumbaya

Kumbaya 19:22, 60:31. *See also* Cum By Yah; Kum Ba Yah

Little David, Play on Your Harp 43:12

Michael, Row the Boat Ashore 20:26, 27:10, 34:30, 40:73, 67:14

Nobody Knows the Trouble I've Seen 33:89

Rock-a My Soul 43:4

Swing Low, Sweet Chariot 22:148, 59:66

There's a Little Wheel A-Turnin' in My Heart 55:38. *See also* There's a Little Wheel A-Turning; There's a Little Wheel A-Turning in My Heart

There's a Little Wheel A-Turning 38:120. *See also* There's a Little Wheel A-Turnin' in My Heart; There's a Little Wheel A-Turning in My Heart

There's a Little Wheel A-Turning in My Heart 20:20. *See also* There's a Little Wheel A-Turnin' in My Heart; There's a Little Wheel A-Turning

This Little Light 34:46. *See also* This Little Light of Mine

This Little Light of Mine 19:48, 26:10, 40:119, 60:65. *See also* This Little Light

Wake Up! Jonah 43:18

We Are Climbing Jacob's Ladder 34:31, 43:6

We Shall Overcome 34:28, 40:128

SPRING

Because It's Spring 54:43

Bike Song 68:15

Good-Bye Winter, Hello Spring 71:42

Haru Ga Kita 58:42

I Like Spring 68:10

It's Easter Time 5:29

It's Spring Again 5:27

Oh Hear the Bells Ringing 39:25

Popcorn Popping 54:43

Seasons 42:34, 42:93, 68:9

Spring Inside 68:11

SQUARE DANCING

Old Joe Clark 40:81. *See also* Old Joe Clarke

Old Joe Clarke 50:44. *See also* Old Joe Clark

Skip to My Lou 15:45, 31:21, 33:124, 36:210, 38:90

Sourwood Mountain 36:212

Turkey in the Straw 36:228,
40:124, 51:84

SQUIRRELS
Furry Squirrel 71:12
Peep Squirrel 63:18
Squirrel, The 35:39
Squirrel Is a Pretty Thing 63:19

ST. NICK. *See* SANTA CLAUS

STAGECOACHES
She'll Be Comin' 'Round the Moun-
tain 31:37, 33:116, 49:46,
64:22, 66:178, 67:6. *See also*
She'll Be Coming 'Round the
Mountain; She'll Be Coming
Around the Mountain; She'll Be
Coming Round the Mountain
She'll Be Coming 'Round the Moun-
tain 36:201. *See also* She'll Be
Comin' 'Round the Mountain;
She'll Be Coming Around the
Mountain; She'll Be Coming
Round the Mountain
She'll Be Coming Around the Moun-
tain 15:46. *See also* She'll Be
Comin' 'Round the Mountain;
She'll Be Coming 'Round the
Mountain; She'll Be Coming
Round the Mountain
She'll Be Coming Round the Moun-
tain 20:6, 38:128, 40:94. *See
also* She'll Be Comin' 'Round
the Mountain; She'll Be Com-
ing 'Round the Mountain;
She'll Be Coming Around the
Mountain

STAIRWAYS
Little Man 1:46

STARS
By'm Bye 77:14. *See also* Bye 'n'
Bye; Bye'm Bye
Bye'm Bye 22:196, 72:58. *See also*
By'm Bye; Bye 'n' Bye
Bye 'n' Bye 49:66, 64:25. *See also*
By'm Bye; Bye'm Bye
Follow the Drinkin' Gourd 22:140.
See also Follow the Drinking
Gourd
Follow the Drinking Gourd 40:32.
See also Follow the Drinkin'
Gourd
Ha, Ha, This-a-Way 66:168. *See
also* Ha, Ha, Thisaway

Ha, Ha, Thisaway 58:33. *See also*
Ha, Ha, This-a-Way
I Often Think of God 42:6
One Sparkling Star 4:37
Tell Me Why 32:6, 40:113
Twinkle, Twinkle, Little Star
19:42, 25:2, 31:47, 33:137,
36:235, 38:64, 41:68, 44:32,
60:99, 65:85, 66:202, 67:4, 75:93

STATES. *See* UNITED STATES

STATUE OF LIBERTY
God Bless the Statue of Liberty
29:70
Happy Birthday Miss Liberty 29:14
He Always Carried His Picture of
Lady Liberty 29:48
I Wondered If I Were Dreaming
29:66
I'm the Statue of Liberty 30:28
It's Fun to Take the Ferry to the
Statue of Liberty 29:10
Lovely Lady of Liberty 29:40

STORIES
Fox, The 19:40, 33:42, 36:88,
40:34, 66:88. *See also* Old Fox
Frog Went A-Courtin' 33:44, 36:94,
66:182. *See also* Froggie Went
A-Courting
Froggie Went A-Courting 75:18.
See also Frog Went A-Courtin'
I Think When I Read That Sweet
Story 54:33
Long, Long Ago 67:9
Lord of the Dance 34:18
Old Chisholm Trail 20:36
Old Fox 63:32. *See also* Fox, The
Only a Boy Named David 27:20
Sleeping Princess 25:10
So Long, It's Been Good to Know
You 40:103
Tell Me the Stories of Jesus 54:33
When I First Came to This Land
22:272
Wise Man and the Foolish Man,
The 26:12
Young Folks, Old Folks 51:56

STRANGERS
I'm in Charge 7:21
Safety Don'ts 7:10

STREET CRIES
Cockles and Mussels 66:196
Jamaica Farewell 19:30

SUMMER

All the Little Fishies Do a Hoochie
    Koochie Dance 55:23
Come Play with Me 5:39
It's a Rosebud in June 76:25
Lazy Days 5:40
Oh, What a Summer 76:8
Oh, What Do You Do in the
    Summertime? 54:47
Seasons 42:34, 42:93, 68:9
Summer Breeze 76:21
Summer Is A-Coming In 46:26
Unite and Unite 76:4
Wild Mountain Thyme 76:22

SUN

Mister Sun 19:14
Mister Sunshine 4:27
Mr. Sun 59:12
One Light, One Sun 60:100
Welcome April Sunshine 39:27

SUNRISE

Canticle of the Sun, The 34:9
Morning Has Broken 34:8

SWANS

Epigram on Singers 46:89
Swan, The 1:102

SWINGS AND SWINGING

Swing, The 35:38, 68:16

TANZANIA

Haiye Kirumbe 1:70

TEA

Down by the River 65:66
Duchess at Tea 50:26
I Sat Next to the Duchess at Tea
    64:74
I'm a Little Teapot 16:32, 35:52,
    38:95, 66:109, 74:28
Polly 65:67. See also Polly, Put the
    Kettle On
Polly, Put the Kettle On 31:39,
    33:105, 36:192, 38:60, 44:22,
    75:14. See also Polly
Revolutionary Tea 22:54

TEETH

Brush Your Teeth 19:26, 59:8
Grandpa Gum 12:22
Look Ma! No Cavities 71:36
My Dentist Is an Awfully Nice
    Man 56:24

Old Family Toothbrush 25:6,
    50:87, 51:34

TELEPHONES

I'm the Phone Girl 30:38
Telephone Song 7:18
Ticka-Tacka 64:75

TELEVISION

Casper the Friendly Ghost 66:80
I'm Popeye the Sailor Man 66:77.
    See also Popeye, the Sailor Man
Muppet Show Theme 66:4
Popeye, the Sailor Man 49:26,
    51:121. See also I'm Popeye the
    Sailor Man

TELLING TIME

Five More Minutes 56:198

TEXAS

Ol' Texas 20:22

THANKSGIVING DAY

Come, Ye Thankful People, Come
    34:58, 36:57
Indian Brothers 47:13
Over the River and Through the
    Wood 38:142
Pilgrims and the Indians 5:14
Thanksgiving 47:15
Thanksgiving Day Is Coming 47:16
Thanksgiving Time 47:17
Turkey Run 47:14
We Gather Together 33:138, 34:60,
    36:240. See also We Gather
    Together to Ask the Lord's
    Blessing
We Gather Together to Ask the
    Lord's Blessing 66:251. See
    also We Gather Together

THUNDERSTORMS

Clap, Clap, Clap 4:34
I Hear Thunder 65:56

TIME

Five More Minutes 56:198
Later 56:199
Living a Day 53:37
Spin, Spider, Spin 68:20

TOADS

El Coquito 38:136

TONGUE TWISTERS

Benjy Met a Bear 51:48
Flea Fly Song 50:11
Fuzzy Wuzzy 50:60

I With I Were 49:10, 51:18
Itchy Flea 49:77, 51:120
John Jacob Jingleheimer Schmidt
    50:90, 51:9, 64:75, 66:134
Little Sally Saucer 64:86, 65:23.
    See also Little Sally Waters
Little Sally Waters 38:101. *See*
    also Little Sally Saucer
Mairzy Doats 66:138
My Dame Hath a Lame, Tame
    Crane 46:87, 75:73
Peter Piper 71:60
Sailor Went to Sea 51:63
Sailor Went to Sea Sea Sea 50:65
Sally Eats Shoelaces, Straw and
    String 56:156
See-Saw 35:47
There Was an Old Frog 63:48

TOPS
Oh, Dreidel I Will Play 55:22

TOWNS. *See* **URBAN LIFE**

TOYS
Alfie the Elf 2:56
Blocks 35:26
Bumping Up and Down 59:5
Good Night 35:35
Ha, Ha, This-a-Way 66:168. *See*
    also Ha, Ha, Thisaway
Ha, Ha, Thisaway 58:33. *See also*
    Ha, Ha, This-a-Way
Holidays 35:90
Marvelous Toy 66:118
Me and My Teddy Bear 66:94
Miss Polly 55:41. *See also* Miss
    Polly Had a Dolly
Miss Polly Had a Dolly 49:39,
    65:77. *See also* Miss Polly
Mommy, Mommy, I Gotta Get a
    Record 56:120
My Brother Threw Up on My
    Stuffed Toy Bunny 56:62
North Pole 47:29
Oh, Dreidel I Will Play 55:22
Old Toy Trains 57:74
Petites Marionettes 59:49. *See also*
    Petites Marionnettes
Petites Marionnettes 62:112. *See*
    also Petites Marionettes
Rig-A-Jig-Jig 20:10, 25:4, 38:94,
    65:30
Rubber Duckie 66:16
Slide, The 35:46
Spin, Spin, Spin 47:19

Tapping 2:61
Teddy Bear Hug 58:35
Teddy Bear, Teddy Bear 49:38
Teddy Bears' Picnic 66:98

TRANSPORTATION
Big Wheels 10:50
Erie Canal 22:116, 36:81, 40:30
New River Train 59:38
Rock Island Line 22:172, 40:89,
    66:172
Wabash Cannonball 19:8

TRAVEL
Many Ways to Travel 14:24

TREES
Ash Grove 67:13
Autumn Leaves Are Now Falling
    48:9
Cherry Blossoms 67:8
Conversation with a Tree 71:55
Green Grass Grows All Around,
    The 24:4. *See also* Green
    Grass Grew All Around
Hush-a-Bye Baby 41:67, 44:60
I Had a Little Nut Tree 33:65,
    36:127, 44:41
In the Leafy Tree Tops 54:45
Japanese Maple 67:8
Little House, The 58:13
Little Nut Tree 38:53, 75:64
O Christmas Tree 2:9, 23:6, 28:66,
    45:18
Plant a Little Tree 5:32
Tree in the Wood 33:134, 36:226
Under the Spreading Chestnut
    Tree 36:239
What Kind of Trees Are Found Out
    There? 39:13

TRINIDAD
Me Stone 64:111

TRUTH
I Would Be True 34:54

TURKEY
Tamzara 1:128

TURKEYS
Gobble Strut, Strut 3:13
Turkey in the Straw 36:228,
    40:124, 51:84
Turkey Run 47:14
Turkey Song 63:46
Turkey Talk 71:21

TURTLES
Baby Bumble Bee 50:8, 51:112
Mr. Tickles 68:21
Turtles 21:29
You Can't Make a Turtle Come
    Out 49:63

UNITED STATES
Acres of Clams 22:192, 40:2
Aloha 71:9
Always Remember You Were Born
    in America 29:56
America 33:13
America at Last! 29:30
America, I Love You 5:43, 13:58
America the Beautiful 33:14, 36:20
Americans Are Singing About Lady
    Liberty 29:6
Arkansas Traveler 36:24, 40:4
Big Words 13:40
Brown Eyes, Black Eyes 13:62
Checks and Balances 13:27
City of New Orleans 40:16
Clementine 33:26, 36:55, 40:20,
    50:40, 51:87, 66:164, 67:6. See
    also My Darling Clementine
Cowboy's Lament 40:22
Dixie 33:31, 36:68
Free Enterprise 13:49
Freight Train 40:36
God Bless the Statue of Liberty
    29:70
Happy Birthday Miss Liberty 29:14
He Always Carried His Picture of
    Lady Liberty 29:48
Here in America 13:15
I Love America 13:9
I Remember Ellis Island 29:20
I Wondered If I Were Dreaming
    29:66
I'm the Statue of Liberty 30:28
If You Believe in Me, I'll Never Die
    29:44
It's Fun to Take the Ferry to the
    Statue of Liberty 29:10
Joe Hill 40:64
Lovely Lady of Liberty 29:40
Military Song 13:43
My Darling Clementine 31:27. See
    also Clementine
My Guiding Light Is Miss Liberty
    29:60
Ol' Texas 20:22
Polly-Wolly-Doodle 19:36, 31:50,
    66:174

So Long, It's Been Good to Know
    You 40:103
Stewball 40:106, 63:68
Take Your Hat Off 13:4
That's My Flag 5:42
This Land Is Your Land 22:370,
    40:116, 66:188
Wabash Cannonball 19:8
We Hold These Truths 13:18
We the People 13:32
We're the Children of America
    29:24
What Did Delaware, Boys? 49:48,
    51:64

UNITED STATES HISTORY
Fall Apart 13:35
Miracle in Philadelphia 13:24

URBAN LIFE
Cockles and Mussels 66:196
Sidewalks of New York 36:204

VALENTINE'S DAY
I Love You 5:21
I Want to Be Your Friend 47:32
Knock, Knock, Knock 5:22
Let's Be Friends 47:35
Valentine 47:36
Valentine Friends 47:34
Valentine's Dance 47:37
Valentines Are Special Greetings
    47:33

VEGETABLES
I'm Popeye the Sailor Man 66:77.
    See also Popeye, the Sailor Man
Keep Your Body Strong 6:26, 6:41
Oh, John the Rabbit 22:216, 49:55
Popeye, the Sailor Man 49:26,
    51:121. See also I'm Popeye the
    Sailor Man
Savez-vous Planter des Choux?
    58:20. See also Savez-vous
    Planter les Choux?
Savez-vous Planter les Choux?
    64:68. See also Savez-vous
    Planter des Choux?
Vegetable Rap 6:14

VIOLINS
Fiddlers 46:42

VOLUNTEERS
We Volunteer 12:6

WAGONS
Bumping Up and Down 59:5

WAKE-UP SONGS
Are You Sleeping 39:26, 72:25. *See also* Frere Jacques
Frere Jacques 1:114, 25:24, 31:7, 36:91, 38:134, 46:61, 59:79, 62:109, 66:234. *See also* Are You Sleeping
Good Morning to You 38:115
Koom Bachur Atsel 1:118
Lazy Mary 33:80, 35:56, 36:153, 38:62, 65:8, 72:24, 75:41. *See also* Lazy Mary, Will You Get Up?
Lazy Mary, Will You Get Up? 31:64, 66:228. *See also* Lazy Mary
Rise and Shine 34:44, 50:91, 60:35
Sleepers Wake 39:24
Wake, Snake 22:248
Wake Up, Little Baby 72:26
What Do We Do? 35:12

WALES
Ash Grove 67:13

WALKING
Foot Traveler 76:18
Happy Wanderer 36:112
I Often Go Walking 54:13
Little Girl/Boy Went Walking 55:55
Road to the Isles 76:13
Walk Forward and Backward 21:22
Walk Outside 60:94
Walk, Walk, Walk 60:37
Walking Song 14:26, 76:16

WALKING STICKS
Walking Sticks 53:11

WALLABIES
Willoughby Wallaby Woo 19:20, 59:7

WAR SONGS AND CRIES
Battle Hymn of the Republic 36:32
Bennington Rifles 36:35
Caissons, The 36:51
Gee, Mom, I Want to Go Home 22:356
Marines' Hymn 36:161
Revolutionary Tea 22:54
When Johnny Comes Marching Home 36:245
Yankee Doodle 22:62, 31:57, 33:140, 36:251, 38:122, 40:135, 44:48, 66:250

WASHINGTON, GEORGE
George Washington 13:22, 47:39

WATER
About Water 4:29
Bath, The 35:32
Chivalrous Shark 46:46
Clementine 33:26, 36:55, 40:20, 50:40, 51:87, 66:164, 67:6. *See also* My Darling Clementine
I Wish I Were a Fish 3:19
I've Got Peace Like a River 27:8
Lock Lomond 67:14
Make Channels 34:50
My Darling Clementine 31:27. *See also* Clementine
She Went into the Water 24:20
Sweet Water Rolling 62:30
Water 56:190
Water in the Rain Clouds 71:53

WEATHER
Ain't Gonna Rain 31:77
Clap, Clap, Clap 4:34
I Hear Thunder 65:56
It's Raining, It's Pouring 31:55, 33:69, 36:134
Little Raindrops 4:33
Mister Wind Is a Mischief 4:31
North Wind Doth Blow 38:33, 44:10, 75:66
One Misty, Moisty Morning 65:58
Rain Is Falling All Around 54:51
Rain, Rain 38:49. *See also* Rain, Rain, Go Away
Rain, Rain, Go Away 65:60. *See also* Rain, Rain
Rain Song 68:12
Summer Breeze 76:21

WEAVING
Sarasponda 1:30, 22:40, 67:10

WHALES
Baby Beluga 19:18, 60:7
Wake Up! Jonah 43:18

WHEELS
Bus Song 20:16, 36:49, 38:130. *See also* Wheels on the Bus
Wheels on the Bus 16:32, 49:44, 60:43. *See also* Bus Song

WHISTLES AND WHISTLING
Give a Little Whistle 66:72
I Whistle a Happy Tune 66:48

WHISTLES AND WHISTLING
(*cont.*)
I've Been Working on the Railroad
33:70, 36:135, 40:59, 66:158,
67:12
Rock Island Line 22:172, 40:89,
66:172
Whistle While You Work 66:62
Whistler and His Dog 66:102
Willie the Whistling Giraffe 66:105
Workin' on the Railroad 59:40. *See
also* Working on the Railroad
Working on the Railroad 38:132.
See also Workin' on the
Railroad

WIND
Blowin' in the Wind 22:360
Down in the Valley 40:28, 67:5
Gust of Fall Wind, A 22:168
Hear the Wind Blow 4:30
Mister Wind Is a Mischief 4:31
North Wind Doth Blow 38:33,
44:10, 75:66
Old Tin Cup 69:15
Summer Breeze 76:21
Sweet and Low 62:40
What Shall We Do with the Baby-
O? 55:43. *See also* What Will
We Do with the Baby-O?
What Will We Do with the Baby-
O? 35:51. *See also* What Shall
We Do with the Baby-O?
Wind Through the Olive Trees 2:30

WINTER
Douglas Mountain 57:72, 59:54
Falling Snow 54:59
Going Out to Play 71:28
Gust of Fall Wind, A 22:168
I Like to Play in the Snow 5:17
Jingle Bells 2:10, 23:4, 31:78,
36:142, 38:150, 45:26, 57:60,
61:20
North Wind Doth Blow 38:33,
44:10, 75:66
Once There Was a Snowman 54:59
Over the River and Through the
Wood 38:142
Playful Little Jack Frost 5:18
Seasons 42:34, 42:93, 68:9
Soft Falls the Snow 69:30
Twas in the Moon of Wintertime
2:24, 28:70

WITCHES
Ding-Dong! The Witch Is Dead
66:28
Five Little Pumpkins 59:6
Three Little Witches 50:75
Waltz of the Witch 73:6
Witch, The 47:7
Witches, Ghosts, and Goblins 47:6

WOLF. *See* **WOLVES**

WOLVES
Who's Afraid of the Big Bad Wolf?
66:52
Wolves A-Howling 63:79

WOODCHUCKS
Groundhog 22:92, 71:38
Old Ground Hog 63:22

WOODS. *See* **FORESTS**

WOOL
Baa, Baa, Black Sheep 31:3, 33:17,
33:32, 36:31, 38:47, 44:7, 59:14,
66:223, 75:32
Big Sheep, The 63:58
Shearer's Dream 46:80

WORK. *See* **WORK AND LABOR**

WORK AND LABOR
He's My Responsibility 11:58
I Am Learning How to Work 10:52
I've Been Working on the Railroad
33:70, 36:135, 40:59, 66:158,
67:12
Joe Hill 40:64
March of the Worker Ants 53:17
My Mommy Drives a Dump Truck
56:66
Ride Sally Ride 71:32
Sarasponda 1:30, 22:40, 67:10
United 71:40
Whistle While You Work 66:62
Work Work Work 10:46
Workin' on the Railroad 59:40. *See
also* Working on the Railroad
Working on the Railroad 38:132.
See also Workin' on the
Railroad
Zum Gali Gali 34:22

WORK SONGS
Acres of Clams 22:192, 40:2
Blow the Man Down 46:66
Blow, Boys, Blow 22:110
Day-O 19:10, 60:15

Donkey Riding 36:71
Drill, Ye Tarriers 22:158, 36:74
Drunken Sailor 46:68
Erie Canal 22:116, 36:81, 40:30
Frozen Logger 22:284, 40:38
Git Along, Little Dogies 22:290,
 40:40. *See also* Get Along,
 Little Dogies
Go On, Old 'gator 63:74
Here We Go Round the Mulberry
 Bush 15:41, 44:29, 74:45,
 75:26. *See also* Mulberry Bush
I Am Learning How to Work 10:52
I've Been Working on the Railroad
 33:70, 36:135, 40:59, 66:158,
 67:12
If I Had a Hammer 40:56
Mulberry Bush 31:6, 33:84, 36:166,
 38:80, 65:14, 66:216. *See also*
 Here We Go Round the Mul-
 berry Bush
Oh, Susannah 22:180
Pat Works on the Railway 36:188
Riding Along 64:16
Rio Grande 46:70
Rock Island Line 22:172, 40:89,
 66:172
Sarasponda 1:30, 22:40, 67:10
She'll Be Comin' 'Round the Moun-
 tain 31:37, 33:116, 49:46,
 64:22, 66:178, 67:6. *See also*
 She'll Be Coming 'Round the
 Mountain; She'll Be Coming
 Around the Mountain; She'll Be
 Coming Round the Mountain
She'll Be Coming 'Round the Moun-
 tain 36:201. *See also* She'll Be
 Comin' 'Round the Mountain;
 She'll Be Coming Around the
 Mountain; She'll Be Coming
 Round the Mountain
She'll Be Coming Around the Moun-
 tain 15:46. *See also* She'll Be
 Comin' 'Round the Mountain;
 She'll Be Coming 'Round the
 Mountain; She'll Be Coming
 Round the Mountain

She'll Be Coming Round the Moun-
 tain 20:6, 38:128, 40:94. *See
 also* She'll Be Comin' 'Round
 the Mountain; She'll Be Com-
 ing 'Round the Mountain;
 She'll Be Coming Around the
 Mountain
Shuckin' of the Corn 76:28
Whistle While You Work 66:62
Work Work Work 10:46
Workin' on the Railroad 59:40. *See
 also* Working on the Railroad
Working on the Railroad 38:132.
 See also Workin' on the
 Railroad

WORMS
Can of Worms 53:21
Inch Worm 66:40
Ooey Gooey 55:15
Return of the Baby Bumblebee 55:9
Willie the Worm 55:44
Worms 71:56

YIDDISH LANGUAGE
Bim Bom 1:56
Dayenu 34:26
Hevenu Shalom Alechem 34:23
Hine Ma Tov 34:51
Koom Bachur Atsel 1:118
Numi Nim 62:45
Salom Chaverim 67:9
Zum Gali Gali 34:22

YODELS
Once an Austrian Went Yodeling
 55:33
Walking Song 14:26, 76:16

ZEBRAS
Zebra, The 3:33

ZOOS
Bronx Zoo Is for Me and You 30:10
Going to the Zoo 40:45, 59:24, 66:90
Great Ape 3:38
Mister Stand-On-One-Leg 3:25
Zoo, The 35:78